11/13/90

For Cedric Frieke

My good friend from
Eldorado to the Big
Bonanza.

Larry Barbone

THE FIGHTING HORSE
OF THE STANISLAUS

EDITED BY LAWRENCE I. BERKOVE

THE FIGHTING HORSE

OF THE STANISLAUS

STORIES & ESSAYS BY DAN DE QUILLE

University of Iowa Press　Ꮗ　Iowa City

University of Iowa Press, Iowa City 52242
Copyright © 1990 by the University of Iowa
All rights reserved
Printed in the United States of America
First edition, 1990

Design by Richard Hendel

Printed on acid-free paper

Library of Congress Cataloging-in-Publication Data

De Quille, Dan, 1829–1898.
[Selections. 1990]
The fighting horse of the Stanislaus: Stories and essays / by Dan De Quille;
edited by Lawrence I. Berkove.—1st ed.
p.   cm.
Includes bibliographical references.
ISBN 0-87745-283-0 cloth, ISBN 0-87745-299-7 paper
1. Western stories.   2. West (U.S.)—Social life and customs.
I. Berkove, Lawrence I.   II. Title.
PS1525.D35A6   1990   90-10751
813'.4—dc20   CIP

To
Ethan, Naomi, and Daniel
My children and my
builders

CONTENTS

ACKNOWLEDGMENTS

Like a traveler on a lonely road, a scholar of a neglected author is particularly aware of, and grateful for, each bit of help and every instance of friendly cooperation. I wish to express my gratitude for the financial support and release time made available to me by the University of Michigan—Dearborn Campus Grants Committee and the Academic Affairs Advisory Council Sub-Committee on Research and by the Rackham Graduate School of the University of Michigan. I also wish to thank the interlibrary loan staff of the University of Michigan—Dearborn Library for their patience and diligence in helping me obtain obscure articles and microfilms of unusual periodicals from the dim and dusty past.

I wish to thank the Bancroft Library of the University of California—Berkeley for giving me access to the treasure trove of the William Wright Papers and granting me permission to copy material found therein. I am also grateful to the University of Nevada—Reno Library for its impressive collection of microfilms of nineteenth-century periodicals and to the Special Collections Division for introducing me to its holdings and giving me permission to publish one of its manuscripts.

I owe sincere thanks to the Nevada Historical Society at Reno for many favors, not the least of which was its pioneering work in locating many of De Quille's publications. I am awed by Eric Moody's deep familiarity with the Society's holdings and by his remarkable ability to instantly recall unusual bits of information which I found crucial. Both he and Phillip I. Earl are scholar-curators who represent the best of their profession.

It has been a pure pleasure to work with the State Historical Society of Iowa, at Iowa City. Ginalie Swaim and Mary Bennett are answers to a scholar's prayer. May they live long and prosper!

Major assistance and outstanding friendliness have been extended to me by Dr. Robert Hirst and the staff of the Mark Twain Project. It has been inspiring to observe them at work and I am truly grateful to have been a beneficiary of their wide-ranging expertise and kindnesses.

A pleasant new experience was opened up for me by the opportunity to meet and work with Dan De Quille's great-grandchildren: Evans Morris of West Liberty, Iowa; Mrs. Harlan L. Anderson of Des Moines; and Mrs. Rosemary Morris of Blandinsville, Illinois. I am more in debt than I can say to them for their generosity and cooperation, first in granting me access to De Quille material in their possession, and then in sharing it with all scholars through their establishment of the Morris Family Collection of Dan De Quille in the State Historical Society of Iowa library at Iowa City. Mrs. Eloise Richardson of Greeley, Colorado, related by marriage to another De Quille descendant, has been most gracious and helpful in granting me permission to use other memorabilia in her possession.

I also wish to thank the following people for their help and encouragement: Professor Kenneth Robb of Bowling Green State University, Bowling Green, Ohio; Tom Tenney of the *Mark Twain Journal* and the Citadel, Charleston, South Carolina; Dave Basso, of Sparks, Nevada; and Marc Frank of Capitola, California.

My family has long been accustomed to being drafted, dragooned, browbeaten, hijacked, and shanghaied into helping me with various projects, but this time they gave more, and more willingly, than I had a right to expect. I wish to express my loving gratitude to my sons, Ethan and Daniel, for accompanying me on separate research trips to Iowa and sharing the driving and work and to my daughter, Naomi, for her assistance in typing. And, once again, my unqualified love to my wife, Gail, for her critical judgment, her ever-ready willingness to proofread, and for her unflagging encouragement.

DAN AND HIS QUILLS

BY C. C. GOODWIN

Across the table from us Dan De Quille is writing one of his abominable locals, and we have been studying his face. Of late he has thrown away his pencils and procured old-fashioned quill pens. He never passes a produce store now without casting furtive glances around to see if there is not a goose or turkey or some other bird convenient, from which he can surreptitiously extract a quill. He writes ordinary locals with a turkey quill; for important affairs, like runaways, and dog fights, he takes a goose quill; for obituary notices he keeps the plume of a raven; for mining reviews nothing will do but a swan's quill. His scientific articles are fashioned by the quill of an owl; while for the dreadful legends he strings together for Sunday's *Enterprise* nothing will answer but a feather from the pinion of an eagle or an albatross. It is unnecessary to ask him any more what the nature of his theme for the moment may be. A glance at the pen in his hand reveals the whole thing, for his pens are graded. The dry statement, the magnified trifle, the thrilling occurrence, the advertiser's puff, the moderate falsehood embellished, the outrageous astonisher, etc. all have their respective pens. We quizzed Dan at first to find out why he had thrown off upon his old friend, the pencil, and accused him of having acquired metropolitan ideas during his visit East; told him it was a vain desire, notwithstanding his new book, to try to wrap himself up in the drapery of literature; that all the ink, dressing gowns and quill pens in the universe would not conceal him or stop the children of Virginia City from calling out to him: "How are you, Dan?" as he met them in the street. He blushed in attempting to deny that any motive of egotism or vanity had actuated him, and quoted for our benefit the line which begins: "O why should the spirit of mortal be proud?" He overwhelmed us with a dissertation on the degeneration of modern graphite, declaring that it was always too hard or too soft, and was never found now without grit in it. We permitted him to think he had convinced us, but he did not, and we know all about his reasons for the change. There are times when we all have spells of looking back; times when hope fails us or seems to paint pictures less bright than those of memory. Dan is having one of those spells now. His array of pens have to him a significance which he thinks exultingly that we cannot fathom. But we know all about it. Every one represents a lovely girl who Dan used to sharpen pencils for years ago in some primitive western schoolhouse. One means a rosy face, dark eyes and a smile which was wont to make all the boys in school crazy. And while Dan holds that pen he thinks that sunny face was hid beneath a coffin lid years ago, and while he writes his heart is crying for the beautiful girl who is dead. Another means a blonde whose golden curls have touched Dan's cheek in dreams for years, and whose low voice has rung in his ears a thousand times when the world believed he had no thought in his mind except to describe correctly the overturning of a load of hay or to relate the minutiae of a bar-room fight. The pen with which he writes his outrageous falsehoods is the big girl that put snow down his back in school and told him with grave face that it was his sweetheart who did it. And there he sits and writes, and smiles sometimes, and then grows sober and changes his pen and thinks we do not penetrate his secret. Who would have dreamed of any deception in quaint, candid, honest old Dan?

Territorial Enterprise, February 3, 1876

INTRODUCTION

Normally, an author who was as well known in his day as Dan De Quille would have left more of a legacy of published works to future generations. In his lifetime he did publish one outstanding book, *The Big Bonanza* (1876), which is still in print and is regarded as the classic contemporary account of the Comstock lode. But that book, until recently almost the only printed text of De Quille's available, represents but a fraction of his extensive literary range and output. In order to write *The Big Bonanza*, De Quille had to put aside a project that was dear to his heart: an anthology of his best short works. For some reason—diffidence, ill health, the press of work, or fate—he never got around to completing this anthology. After he died in 1898, his daughter tried for several years to arrange for the publication of an anthology while his readers' memory of him was still fresh, but she was not successful. Thus, the whimsy, erudition, and literary skill which had delighted American audiences from coast to coast for close to four decades faded from memory, and the scattered texts that comprised the record of his literary career lay uncollected, unused, and forgotten. As a further consequence, later generations of readers and scholars lost contact with an important part of their literary heritage, for Dan De Quille was a noted and beloved author in his own time, and his literary achievements and influence have yet to be properly assessed.

William Wright was the true name of the man the American reading public knew as Dan De Quille. He was born to Paxton and Lucy (née Markley) Wright on a farm three miles outside of Fredericktown, Knox County, Ohio, on May 9, 1829. The extent of his formal education is unknown, but in one of his letters to a sister he recollected that theirs was a reading family and that the appreciation of good literature was part of his home life. De Quille had a sharp eye for detail and a retentive memory. He cultivated these qualities during his lifetime, and they served him well.

Few records remain to tell us of De Quille's early life. Knox County records reveal that while William was a child his father sold the farm but remained on the land as a renter. Ohio still had much wild country, but the appeal of better land to the west convinced Paxton in 1847 to pull up stakes and follow other local families who had already begun to settle the fertile eastern Iowa soil of Muscatine County, near what has become West Liberty. Paxton died shortly after the move, however, and as William was the eldest of nine children, the main responsibility for supporting the family fell on his shoulders.

William married Carolyn Coleman in 1853, leaving the family farm to start their own nearby. Five children, two of whom died in infancy, were born to the couple in the next four years. In 1857 William left his family to seek his fortune in the California gold fields and remained in the West for most of the next forty years. He returned to Iowa once, for several months in 1862, and he visited Mark Twain in Hartford, Connecticut, for several months in 1875. His wife and daughters occasionally stayed with him in Nevada for periods of time thereafter, but he inexplicably lived the majority of his productive years as a single man. He returned to Iowa in 1897 to spend the last few months of his life as an invalid with his daughter and her family. He died in 1898 at the age of sixty-eight.

Occasional references in various of his writings reveal that Wright made his way to the Comstock by way of the isthmus of Panama and spent several years gold prospecting in California. By the time he arrived in California, most of the choice gold-mining locations on the western slope of the Sierras had been taken or cleaned out, and a backward wave of fortune hunters had begun prospecting the eastern slope. Wright tried his luck for the next three years with indifferent success in southeastern California, between Death Valley and Lake Tahoe. Then he heard of the silver discoveries on the Comstock lode in western Nevada and went to Virginia City, Nevada, in 1860. From then on, that was his home.

William Wright did not strike it rich as a prospector during the four years he searched for gold and silver. But during those same four years he did become successful as a writer. The travel letters, newsletters, fiction, and humorous pieces he sent to periodicals in California, Nevada, Iowa, and New York found favor with the editors, and by 1860 he was publishing on a regular basis in the *Cedar Falls* (Iowa) *Gazette* and in the prestigious San Francisco literary magazine, the *Golden Era*. From the beginning, his contributions displayed ambition and literary talent. Many of his highly readable letters were two or more newspaper columns in length. In addition to describing the country and the adventures of the miners and settlers, they captured the stir and spirit of the time and often were graced with humorous or picturesque anecdotes. Mark Twain very likely knew De Quille's travel letters and used them as models for *Roughing It* (1872).

The point at which De Quille's putative mining activities ceased being his main goal in life and became instead the means for him to pursue writing must have occurred early, if the level of literary activity suggested by his April 12, 1861, newsletter in the *Cedar Falls Gazette* was at all typical. Written in Silver City, Utah Territory, on the evening of February

20 while "the boys in next cabin below me are roaring themselves hoarse on that good old tune of 'Auld lang syne,' " it begins: "Dear Gazette: I have just finished and sent off a letter to the [Golden] 'Era,' and one to the [San Francisco] 'Bulletin,' and now comes your turn. . . ." These long epistolary reports were also occasionally replaced or supplemented by short stories. By 1862 some of his short stories were long enough to be serialized and one ran for six successive issues in the Golden Era.

From the first, he wrote under pseudonyms. M. S. (Milton Shakespeare) Dobbs, Picaroon Pax, and Ebenezer Queerkutt were his earliest noms de plume. By 1860 he hit upon Dan De Quille. He stuck with that name and made it famous. For the rest of his life he was known by his friends and readers as Dan De Quille and that is how posterity will know him.

In 1861 De Quille joined the Virginia City Territorial Enterprise, the most famous paper on the Comstock and one of the most famous newspapers of the West. Eminent and highly talented men worked on that paper: Joseph Goodman, Denis McCarthy, Rollin Daggett, C. C. Goodwin, Alf Doten, Steve Gillis, and a young Missourian with a pronounced drawl and a droll sense of humor who soon chose the pen name of Mark Twain.

De Quille and Twain appeared to be kindred spirits and were roommates for a year. Twain took his first step to literary fame on the Enterprise. In 1864 he left the paper and Nevada but De Quille stayed on and continued to make his living at journalism. Everyone knows what became of Twain, but few today have heard of De Quille. It was not so in his lifetime, however. His present obscurity (except for The Big Bonanza) stems largely from his failure to collect and republish the best of his writings. In the absence of a literary corpus in book form, subsequent generations of readers and literary scholars had no way of knowing what and how much he wrote. He was extraordinarily prolific and very versatile, and by means of both the periodicals which paid for his work and those many more—perhaps hundreds—which treated him as a favorite author by frequently republishing his work in unpaid exchanges, his reputation extended well beyond the Comstock and also beyond the West.

It has generally been assumed that De Quille was primarily a journalist. That is partially correct, but it is also somewhat misleading. Nineteenth-century newspapers were much more varied in content than are modern papers. A good deal, if not most, of De Quille's journalism was what today would be called feature writing: signed columns of commentary, local history, and humor. In place of, or in addition to his regular columns he also published a considerable amount of fiction. In fact, De Quille's "second career" as a free-lance writer of fiction and feature articles actually preceded his formal career as a journalist and continued to parallel it. If we include as literary productions all of his essays and works of humor and fiction, long and short, there are many hundreds of them.

It is difficult to be certain how much of what De Quille wrote differed from conventional, reportorial journalism because he did not write for just one periodical, or even several, but for no less than twenty or thirty, and much of his writing is still uncollected and even unidentified. Although De Quille is permanently associated with the *Territorial Enterprise*, it is now known that his tenure on that paper was broken and his work there of uneven quality. De Quille became an alcoholic at an early stage of his writing career. He occasionally suffered from delirium tremens and sometimes had to be institutionalized for months. He was fired a number of times from the *Territorial Enterprise* because he was too drunk to work, and at least one of those discharges lasted from 1885 to 1887. When he recovered enough to be rehired, his salary was such that he did not have an incentive to give the *Enterprise* his best fiction and feature writing.

When De Quille was cut off from his regular income by the *Enterprise*, he did not become despondent but instead, paradoxically, grew more resourceful and productive. To earn money, he fell back on free-lancing. He took occasional jobs on other Virginia City newspapers and in nearby Gold Hill. He maintained a regular signed column in the *Carson Free Lance* from 1885 to 1886. About the same time, he began to write weekly signed columns for the *Salt Lake Daily Tribune*, an association he kept up until 1896. He placed signed stories and articles in the San Francisco *Call*, *Post*, *Chronicle*, *Alta*, and *Examiner*, the most important newspaper in the West and the flagship of the Hearst empire. He became an associate editor of the *Montana Mining Review* and a frequent contributor to such professional mining journals as *Mining Industry and Tradesman*, *Mining and Scientific Press*, and the *Engineering and Mining Journal*. Stories and feature articles by De Quille appeared on a regular basis for periods of several years in the *Cedar Falls Gazette* and the *Carson City Appeal* and sporadically in a variety of local newspapers in Nevada and California. He placed signed stories and articles in the *New York Sun*, *New York Times*, and *New York Weekly*, the *Cincinnati Enquirer*, the *Chicago Tribune* and *Chicago Current*, the *Louisville Weekly Courier-Journal*, and local papers in Ohio and Iowa. He wrote invited articles for the *Encylopedia Britannica* and for Johnson's *Cyclopedia*. He placed stories in such western magazines as the *Wasp*, the *Argonaut*, the *Californian*, the *California Illustrated Magazine*, the *California Maverick*, the *San Franciscan*, and the *Nevada Monthly* and in such national magazines as *Worthington's Magazine, Cosmopolitan*, and the *Overland Monthly*. He signed up with three national syndicates, S. S. McClure, the American Press Association (which published his novelettes in a magazine), and the Lorborn Company. These syndicates placed his stories in numerous newspapers all over the country. Even in 1896, when De Quille was sick and decrepit, James Gordon Bennett of the New York *Herald Tribune* authorized him by telegraph to send copy.

Not all of his contributions to these different journals were original work. De Quille was in the habit of recycling his stories. At a time when Virginia City miners might earn four dollars for a ten-hour day, he usually received from ten to twenty dollars apiece for his stories, far short of what Mark Twain commanded, but more than many authors earned, including the early Jack London. The S. S. McClure Syndicate paid him ten dollars per thousand words in 1886. In order to improve his earnings, De Quille would send a piece he had originally published in a western newspaper, for example, to eastern or midwestern journals and be paid twice or even more often for it. Or he would wait a few years and simply republish favorite stories. Sometimes he would change the title and names in a story and publish it as a new story. "Tongue-Oil Timothy," for example, was previously published more than once as "Butter-mouth Bill." To give him his due, De Quille often made significant editorial changes in the different versions of these stories, so that one cannot automatically assume that because a story with the same name was published in several places, all the versions are identical. On occasion, De Quille would also considerably expand some brief sketch—"Rev. Olympus Jump" is a case in point—or develop an episode or element from one piece into a full and independent story.

One aspect of De Quille's resourcefulness that probably contributed to the marketability of his work was his mode of casting fiction as autobiography or history. This kind of writing is much closer to the technique of verisimilitude that Daniel Defoe practiced before him than it is to the realism of his own day, and he became extremely good at it. At times he did write some validly autobiographical or historical sketches; both "Trailing a Lost Child" and "Lorenzo Dow's Miracle," though undoubtedly embellished, appear to be substantially based on fact. De Quille wrote so plausibly that it is often impossible to be sure whether a given work is autobiographical or fictional. The normally demanding task of dating his clippings and checking his works for accuracy is made even more difficult by the absence of a full biography. As can be seen in the introductory comments for "Elam Storm," intriguing hints about De Quille's life and connections to stories sometimes occur in his journalism, but these, too, cannot always be taken at face value. What might have had its origins as a tactic for marketability has become a major complication in ascertaining the exact character of individual works.

The editorial difficulties behind this anthology, therefore, have been considerable, and although I have assiduously identified, tracked down, and studied a great deal of his oeuvre I cannot claim to have read everything he wrote and to be familiar with all the variants and modifications even of the material I have collected. Even so, a fairly wide range of sources has been checked, and this anthology includes not only works from different stages of his career, but also works from a representative variety of sources, such as the *Cedar Falls Gazette*, *Golden Era*, and *Territorial Enterprise* from his early period; the San Francisco *Examiner*, *Californian*, *Overland Monthly*, New York *Sun*, and *Cosmopolitan* from his late period; and also some manuscript material.

The diversity of De Quille's writing has made the selection process for this anthology fascinating but very challenging. De Quille, like most other authors, wrote many potboilers which were never very good to begin with and have not improved with age. These were excluded. Some of his work is also dated or otherwise out of taste. The humor of his time was not that of ours. Pointed sketches about farmers, contemporary slang, mothers-in-law, or ethnic stereotypes that might have been considered funny at one time are no longer perceived as amusing. To include much of this material would serve no good purpose, yet to omit all of it would distort the fact that De Quille naturally reflects his era.

De Quille also wrote a number of popularly sentimental stories and exotic tales set in locations with which he had no firsthand familiarity, medieval France, for example, or the England and India of his own day. I have not included these stories in this anthology partly because some of them are being reprinted elsewhere.

De Quille would not have been such a popular and respected author in his own time had his works lacked entertainment value. The issue for us, therefore, is not whether or not his works are entertaining—there can be no disputing De Quille's mastery of the art of storytelling—but whether or not they are *only* entertaining. Some of what is included in this anthology may be only entertaining, but the majority of it will justify close and thoughtful reading. A generation such as ours, trained in sophisticated techniques of literary analysis, should find much in De Quille's deceptively simple stories and sketches to note and consider. He will be found to be subtle and deliberate with words and psychologically astute—a true artist sure of what he describes and very much in control of what he says.

One unexpected example of what might be found beneath the surface of his works is the religious dimension of his values. We know that De Quille's family was of Quaker origin, but he has left us very little explicit information about either his early religious training or his subsequent practice. What we do know is that he had a reputation for integrity, and that his professional articles about mines and mining were regarded as dependable and authoritative. It is clear, also, that like many of his contemporaries, he was familiar with the Bible and comfortably made numerous allusions to characters, episodes, and passages in both testaments. For him, such allusions were not merely ornamental. Even if De Quille did not attend church often, he seems to have had a mystical streak in his nature—this is particularly apparent in two early letters to his sister—and he gave considerable thought to religion.

Ultimately, De Quille was a believer, and the older he grew the more religion and religious values played a part in his writing. His posthumously published novella, *Dives and Lazarus* (1988), is the outstanding example of an overtly religious presence in his art, and his posthumously published story, "Pahnenit, Prince of the Land of Lakes" (1988), may also function in part as a sacred fable or religious allegory. But in a story like "Rev. Olympus Jump," it is not difficult to discern his attitudes toward preachers, and the reasons for his attitudes. De Quille was usually not so obvious, however; more typically his values have to be inferred. In "The Seven Nimrods of the Sierras," for example, considerable irony is built into the choices of Biblical names by the young men who thought it a lark to steal, especially the one called "Acts of the Apostles," who also lied.

Running like a leitmotif through many of his works, furthermore, is an aversion to materialism. This is surprising to find in one whose business it was to promote as well as report mining, and who was a sincere and wholehearted advocate of the generation of prospectors who went west specifically to become rich. Wealth, to De Quille, was the means to a better life but not an end in itself. He regarded prospecting and mining as legitimate occupations, like farming or keeping a shop. It was not the seeking of gold that he objected to but the position quietly stated in "The Eagles' Nest" that "for gold men will venture all things,—even life."

Another unexpected dimension in De Quille's works is his criticism of society and eminent personalities. Not being as brash or as fiery as either Mark Twain or the famous *Territorial Enterprise* editor Joe Goodman, De Quille usually left the stinging satire or open denunciations to others. Compared to such outspoken journalists De Quille seemed mild-mannered and gentle to most Comstockers. This was not because he did not have strong convictions, however, but because he had learned to govern his feelings and preferred to express his criticisms of Comstock life understatedly.

Only twice in his career did De Quille get so ungovernedly passionate as to become vituperative. The first time occurred briefly in the early 1860s when his loathing for the Confederacy spilled over into both the newsletters and stories he sent to the *Cedar Falls Gazette*. Perhaps he learned a lesson from this incident, for he subsequently kept himself under control until the end of his long career, when his profound outrage at the opponents of free silver burst through his restraint one last time and overrode his judgment and habitual circumspection. This occurred from the late 1880s until the mid 1890s, when De Quille had become a champion of free silver and a populist fellow traveler. In their service he wrote long and bitter attacks on their real and imagined enemies that can only be called diatribes. He was not at his best in these shrill and heavy-handed outpourings of passion and bias.

De Quille had to learn to be circumspect. He could not always afford to speak his mind when he daily reported drunkenness, brawling, stock manipulations, and political machinations, because some influential people, including friends and patrons, were occasionally involved. Further, although he might not have lied when it came to actual mining reports, there is some evidence that he bent under pressure. It was common practice, for example, for mine owners to give "feet" of their mining properties to reporters in exchange for favorable comments that might influence investors. De Quille received many such gifts—as did most other reporters—and his mining reports accordingly tended to accentuate the positive. It also may not have been accidental that De Quille did not make a name for himself as an investigative reporter, one who exposed swindles or politically hot issues. If he had wanted to do this, no reporter on the Comstock would have been better prepared.

Forced by Comstock mine owners into a corner where he had to take a stand, De Quille confided to his sister in an 1875 letter that he was "being pushed and crowded . . . every day" to promote the entire Comstock in the book that became *The Big Bonanza*. One gesture of appeasement to some of that pressure was "Millionaire Proprietors," chapter 69 of the book, which is entirely devoted to public relations sketches of five of the Silver Kings: Mackay, Fair, Sharon, Curtis, and Jones. But De Quille did not like them all equally and may not have liked Sharon at all. According to Francis P. Weisenburger, Sharon was a manipulator who became wealthy in the Comstock without investing a penny of his own. Joe Goodman had fought Sharon bitterly until 1874, when Sharon bought the *Enterprise* from him. De Quille surely knew all this, but he was an employee of Sharon's when he wrote his book. It is obvious, therefore, that he did not tell everything he knew about the Silver Kings, and that what he told about some of them did not come very close to the truth.

Occasions such as these, when he was unable to mediate between his strong feelings and the contrary pressures on him, probably contributed to his alcoholism. But some of his best writing conversely represents constructive channelings of those same passions and pressures. He learned to be understated and to camouflage his purposes. He adroitly vented a criticism of Fair, for example, in his mildly biting sketch of the "fatherly" mine superintendent. But his left-handed compliment of John P. Jones and his exposure of western brutishness in "The Fighting Horse of the Stanislaus" are certainly outstanding examples of his deftness at indirection.

De Quille's attitudes toward minorities constitute another aspect of his social criticism that is worth exploring. He was not a late twentieth-century liberal in the nineteenth century; he occasionally indulged in ethnic jokes and stereotypical figures. More characteristically, however, he accurately depicted the people of his time and place, such as the "Old California Prospector," with all their conscious and unconscious prejudices. For most of his career, De Quille was ahead of his time in understanding and sympathizing with downtrodden minorities, especially Indians and blacks. If he occasionally made light of them in passing, more typically he redeemed himself with kindliness when he focused on them and dealt with them seriously. What makes this a complicated subject is that toward the end of his life he did become more prejudiced and attacked some of the minorities he had earlier supported.

One additional aspect of De Quille's importance must be addressed: his relationship to other authors of his time, particularly Mark Twain. It may be said flatly that De Quille was the darling of the Comstock. He was universally beloved and respected not just by the unsophisticated readers of the eastern slope of the Sierras but also by editors and fellow writers. As long as De Quille lived, they generally regarded him as the best writer of the Comstock, even better than Mark Twain.

To us, this seems most strange. Twain's artistic powers have been so well established that an extended comparison of the two authors makes it clear that Twain is by far the greater. Yet there were a number of reasons why Comstockers and many other westerners preferred De Quille to Twain. For one, they judged Twain as a western writer, and the fact that Twain had lived in the Comstock less than three years and in the West less than six gave him less credibility than De Quille, who had made the West his home for forty years and knew it much more thoroughly. For another, Twain was simply not well liked on the Comstock, and De Quille was. Twain's limited popularity is a matter of fact that has been long accepted by his biographers. This attitude was reinforced by a widely held belief on the Comstock that Twain had taken many ideas from De Quille without giving him credit. This was at least partially true, and De Quille was not the only writer from whom Twain appropriated ideas and techniques without acknowledgment and then used them more successfully than did his source.

Twain did not exist and develop in a vacuum. He cannot be adequately studied or understood apart from his contemporaries and colleagues. Inevitably, some comparisons will have to be made between Twain and the circle of writers who touched him, and it will surely be seen that, although Twain will remain the greatest writer of them all, nevertheless in some specific ways, in certain points of style or in particular works, the lesser authors may locally outshine him.

De Quille was an important writer in Twain's circle. He influenced Twain considerably more than has been generally recognized, and Twain in turn influenced him even more extensively. "The Silver Man" hoax is a clear instance where Twain's influence on De Quille is direct; "Elam Storm" may be another. But if "The Silver Man" is compared to its predecessor, Twain's "Petrified Man," a good case may be made for preferring De Quille's piece to Twain's. Of course, it is neither desirable, appropriate, nor necessary to compare everything De Quille wrote to something that Twain or some other author wrote. De Quille was an original literary talent in his own right and one whose rediscovery now makes his narrative, history, and humor of enduring quality available once more. His works stand on their own and can be read and appreciated for their intrinsic and considerable merits.

The goal of this anthology has been to recover De Quille's works from the neglected archives and microfilm files of extinct periodicals where they have been lost for a century and reintroduce him as a talented writer worthy of renewed attention and respect. Accordingly, from the best I have been able to find in each of the categories represented, this anthology demonstrates the range of the writings that made De Quille so widely read and respected in his time. He has been not a rejected author but an almost lost one. Even still, some of his works, particularly humorous ones, are considered American classics. Among his fiction, either unknown or less well known, are excellent stories that can hold their own, in my opinion, with fiction that regularly appears in anthologies of American literature.

De Quille also deserves to be more widely known again because so much of what he wrote is a precious record of American attitudes, legend, folklore, and humor—the stuff of our national character and perhaps the stock of future works of art. To appreciate this point fully, it is useful to recollect that De Quille was an important member of the first generation of western authors. He lived in a truly epic era, the settlement of the West. As a boy he knew the pioneer generation of Ohio, and as a young man he was part of the pioneer generation that settled Iowa and the Far West. In other words, he had firsthand knowledge of frontier life and participated in that extraordinary half-century which explored, settled, tamed, and exploited half a continent. Most of what we read about the frontier and the Old West is derivative. De Quille is a primary source about his era. He is probably the best literary source about prospectors and miners and his writings embody a wealth of information. We are fortunate indeed that De Quille wrote so much and so well.

C. C. Goodwin was ahead of his time in recognizing that De Quille used several styles of writing and sometimes had hidden motivations driving his pens. Some of those motivations are now better understood. They reveal a complex personality with knowledgeable and thoughtful perspectives on his age and the skill to put them to work in his art. This anthology is long overdue, and it is offered in the hope that the present and future generations will find interest and enjoyment in the products of De Quille's "respective pens."

A NOTE ON THE TEXT

Significant textual variations occur between many De Quille items in print and the originals, and between different published versions of the same work. I have chosen for this anthology what have seemed to me to be the most literary and optimally developed versions. Every item in it, however, closely follows the wording, paragraphing, and headlining of an original newspaper, magazine, or manuscript text. I have attempted to preserve De Quille's style by refraining from polishing his writing to remove every possible blemish. De Quille was normally a careful and correct writer. With few exceptions, such as his consistent misspellings of "hight" for "height" and "metalic" for "metallic," his spelling was usually excellent. Where occasional and nonsubstantive errors of spelling or punctuation have occurred in passages of conventional writing, I have emended the text without noting the changes. There were not many such errors, and the majority appeared to be typographical. I have left unaltered passages whose punctuation—usually the use of commas—is different from modern usage but was acceptable in his time. In the rare cases where the text itself was faulty or doubtful I have used brackets to mark my interventions.

Where De Quille wrote in vernacular, I have usually been conservative and simply reproduced the text I had, even when inconsistencies were apparent. Like his contemporaries, Twain and Joel Chandler Harris, De Quille endeavored to capture differences of dialect and also of individual usages. Accordingly, not all of De Quille's prospectors sound the same, and his use of irregular orthography is not always consistent. In "Old Johnny Ranchero," for example, "thar" is usually used for "there," and "ther" for "their," but sometimes they are used interchangeably; and some words have the normal -ing ending in one location but the abbreviated -in' form in another. I trust De Quille's ear; he was there.

Dan De Quille was forty-nine when this portrait
was painted. Signed "Petrovits 1878," it is reproduced
here through the courtesy of his great-grandson
Evans Morris.

I
HOAXES, HUMOR, AND PRACTICAL JOKES

De Quille did not have to work hard at being funny. He was naturally witty, had a sophisticated imagina-tion, and was readily able to create gentle but ingenious works of hu-mor on short notice. Among the earliest of his publications are humor-ous ones, and some of his best pieces derive from the early stage of his literary career. When he and Twain worked together on the Territorial Enterprise, *they engaged in constant joshing of each other, in real life as well as in print. The two men honed their skills against each other, and their skills were the better for it.*

"The Silver Man" is a direct outcome of De Quille's interaction with Twain, as it was inspired by Twain's "The Petrified Man" (1862). A comparison of the two reveals how De Quille managed to be original even when following Twain's model and even when addressing an au-dience that was familiar with the earlier piece. The technique that De Quille developed into a fine art was to so embellish an absurdity or an impossibility with plausible detail that it became believable, and credulous or unwary readers would buy the hoax. Today we call this technique "putting on." "The Traveling Stones of Pahranagat" and the "Solar Armor" pieces are two more choice examples of De Quille's polish and daring in building delightful but convincing hoaxes out of mere fancy. The "Eyeless Fish" article is a newly rediscovered hoax that created a stir when it was first published. A small number of literal-minded readers bought the hoax. They objected to De Quille's divulging that hot water flooded the deep levels of the mines and to the specu-lation that some enormous underground reservoir had been tapped; they were afraid investors would be put off. Most Comstock readers and neighboring journalists understood the humor, however, and ex-pressed their appreciation and admiration of De Quille's talent.

De Quille's humor was seldom cutting. Except for his hoaxes, he usu-ally signaled his humorous intentions to his audience by being obvious in his exaggerations. The next three pieces are light-hearted and range in tone from tongue-in-cheek to gently ironic.

De Quille's inclination to gentleness was at odds with the tendency of western humor, especially practical joking, to be a bit rough and sometimes verge on cruelty. De Quille certainly learned from rooming with Mark Twain that although practical jokers enjoy tricking others, few accept reciprocity gracefully. "Tom Collette's Bath" may therefore be viewed as a mild example of De Quille's occasional sallies into social criticism—one of those interesting exceptions that prove the rule of De Quille's typical good-naturedness. The tale's pose as an amusing account of a humorous episode enables the reality of spite to masquerade as fun. From the story's subtle but definite mockery of three "jolly" prospectors who disabled each other, we may infer De Quille's discreet scorn for this kind of immature horseplay and the popular mores which tolerated it.

A Silver Man

THE WONDER OF THE AGE

Dear Era:—Everybody, no doubt, has heard of the discovery of the wonderful "Silver Man," found in a mine between Esmeralda and Owen's River.

Everybody, however, has not heard the full particulars of the discovery, and many will hoot the idea of any such discovery ever having been made.

They will at once say that it is impossible for a human body to be changed to silver ore.—Let them have their say!

Although the story is almost too much for belief, yet I hope to be able to show, before finishing this account, that, startling as the assertion may appear, such a change in the substance of the human body is not only possible, but that there is on record one well authenticated instance of a similar changing of a human body into a mass of ore.

We have had all kinds of astonishing discoveries. Many things formerly classed among the impossibilities, are now familiar, every-day possibilities. We are now to acknowledge that it is not impossible for a human body to be changed—through contact in a mineral vein with solutions of certain salts, carbonic and hydrosulphuric gases, and the electrical currents induced by the reaction of said solutions upon each other—into a mass of sulphuret of silver.

As no particular account of the discovery of the Silver Man has ever been published, and as all who have heard of the wonder will be pleased to know something in regard to the finding of the body thus curiously mineralized, I will venture to give a full history.

Mr. Peter Kuhlman, a gentleman who has for some months past been engaged prospecting in a range of mountains lying to the southeast of Mono Lake, between Esmeralda and Owen's River, has kindly furnished me with the particulars given below:

The body is that of a full grown man, and was found in what is known as the Hot Springs Lead.

The body, when first found, was almost perfect, even to the fingers and toes. The features are distinctly traceable, but not wholly perfect. They present a blurred appearance.

In removing the body from its resting place, an arm was broken off. It

3

was from observing the peculiar appearance of the fractured arm that Mr. Kuhlman—who is not only a good practical miner, but an excellent chemist and mineralogist—was induced to make a careful assay of pieces taken from the severed limb.

When it was announced to the miners that what they had looked upon as merely a most remarkable petrifaction, was a mass of sulphuret of silver, slightly mixed with copper and iron (in the shape of pyrites) they were at first incredulous. But repeated and careful tests, made before their own eyes, at length convinced them that such was the indisputable fact. The iron and copper pyrites are found lining the cavities of the bones and filling the spaces occurring between the body and the robe in which it was found partially enveloped, as these minerals often occur in holes and crevices in petrified wood. Pieces taken from the arm were tested with acids, with the blow-pipe, and in other ways; always with the same result. A small button of pure silver, extracted by means of the blow-pipe, was shown me by Mr. Kuhlman. He started for this city with part of the hand from the severed arm, with the thumb and two fingers attached and entire, but was induced to leave it with a scientific friend at Aurora, Esmeralda.

The body is supposed to be, and doubtless is, that of an Indian; but in its present changed state it is impossible to be certain on that point. The robe found about the body, part of which crumbled away on being exposed to the air, appears to have been of some kind of coarse cloth. Nothing but a few sticks of charred wood, also mineralized, was found with the body.

The lead in which the "Silver Man," as he is popularly termed, was found, was discovered last year, about the first of May, by three prospectors—Wm. R. Prescott, Oscar E. Hartman, and Patrick O'Haloran. On account of there being several hot springs on the cañon, some twenty rods above the vein, they called it the "Hot Springs Lead." The lead was discovered at a point where it was laid bare by the action of the water of the cañon in passing over it. Here the cañon is very deep, the mountains rising in rugged walls on either side. Getting the course of the vein, the miners opened a cut on the side of the mountain about sixty feet above the bed of the cañon. On striking the lead, a tunnel was driven in upon it to the distance of seventy-five feet. The lead being found of rather a loose structure, it was thought best to start a shaft at the end of the tunnel and follow the lead down to where it became more solid, in the hope that the metal it contained would there be found more concentrated. While sinking this shaft, and after it had reached the depth of forty-five feet, a blow with a pick, by the man working below, was followed by a tremendous rush of air, and the terrified miner shouted lustily to his partners above to haul him up. The upward rush of air continued for some minutes after he had reached the surface, coming out with a noise like that made in blowing off a steam boiler, much to the astonishment and consternation of the three honest miners, who stood quaking in the tunnel above. Upon consultation, after the startling noise had ceased, the true cause of the singular phenomenon was conjectured. Having made up their minds that the noise was caused by the escape of a large body of air compressed in a cavern in the lead, they at once determined to cut through into it and see what it might contain. Tying the windlass rope securely about his waist, one of the men descended and with a heavy drill succeeded, after a few minutes' labor, in staving out a hole nearly the full size of the bottom of the shaft; the shell left being little more than a mass of metallic concretions of a pyritous nature. On sounding the cavern with a rope, it was found to be no more than twelve to fifteen feet deep. As a candle burned clearly at the bottom, which looked safe and solid, two of the men were let down to explore the opening. It was found to be nothing more than a huge crevice in the rock, four or five feet in width at the point where cut into by the shaft, but back in the direction of the mountain closing in till not more than ten inches in width.

The body I have been talking about was found stretched upon the ground, a few feet from where the men landed, lying face upwards.

Had the finders been any other than California or Washoe miners, there would have been a jolly stampede and some frantic climbing of the windlass rope. Although startled and greatly astonished, they stood their ground and soon sufficiently regained their composure to make a critical examination of the singular object before them.

The news of the wonderful strike soon spread through the neighborhood, and the "Petrified Man," as he was then called, was visited by all living near—that is to say, within twenty or thirty miles.

When Mr. Kuhlman first visited the "Silver Man," which was three days after the discovery—he living twenty-three miles southwest of Hot Springs—that argentiferous *homo* was still reposing, as found, in the cavern.

At his suggestion the body was loosened from the floor, where it was held by an accumulation of pyritous concretions, and hoisted out to the light of day. During this operation, one of the arms—the right one—was broken off, as has been stated. The left arm, being pressed across the body, as though in the act of clutching the robe, was saved.

Mr. Kuhlman describes the walls of the cavern as presenting the most magnificent appearance imaginable, being a complete mass of pyrites of the most perfect and brilliant description,—all as fresh as the crystals in the heart of an unbroken geode. The cavern, or crevice, widens in the direction of the cañon and is blocked up by a mass of rocks; all, however, covered, as well as the walls, with a thick and bristling incrustation of pyrites.

The opinion of Mr. Kuhlman—which is very reasonable—is that the body so singularly discovered is that of an Indian who ages ago sought shelter in this cleft in the rocks during a rain storm, and that the face of the mountain, worn perpendicularly by the water of the cañon and softened by the rain, slid down, confining the lone red man in the cavity, and leaving him to die of starvation and become mineralized—to become, in short, a "Silver Man," for us in this age to wonder about.

The miners who have this great curiosity intend taking it to San Francisco, thence to New York, and expect to make fortunes by its exhibition; but Mr. Kuhlman says it is certain soon to fall to pieces and be destroyed by the action of the atmosphere,—in fact that it is already crumbling.

As I said at the outset, his story of a human body turning to silver ore will doubtless strike the majority of my readers as a thing wholly impossible and absurd in the extreme, but I will try to show that it is neither one nor the other.

In Sweden is an old mining town called Falun, situated on Lake Runn, and about fifty-four miles south-west of Gefle. This town is the capital of the Swedish laen, or province, of the same name, though sometimes called Kopparburg's-Laen, on account of its extensive copper mines. The mines, which are west of the town, are worked for copper, though the ore contains a small per cent. of gold, silver and lead. These mines have been worked hundreds of years, and are still quite productive. By the falling in of ancient galleries, a vast chasm has been formed on the surface, the opening being no less than 300 feet deep, 1,200 long, and 600 wide. Stairs now lead down the sides of this chasm to its bottom, whence, by means of ladders, the workmen descend to the pits and galleries below. The works extend for miles under ground, and far below are many vast galleries. In one of these immense chambers, magnificently illuminated for the occasion, Bernadotte and his queen once banqueted.

But with all this we have nothing to do, further than to understand that the mines are of very ancient date and that they contain many great galleries, a portion of which were once broken in and filled up, and doubtless great loss of life occasioned by the accident. In re-opening these old galleries, bodies of miners are often found, more or less preserved by the action of the copper and gases of the mine.

The particular case which I wish to quote is one mentioned by Breithaupt, who says:

"In one instance, the body of a miner was recovered from a very deep part of the mine, where it had remained no longer than sixty years, yet it was found converted into iron pyrites which had slowly and completely replaced the organic materials, retaining their forms."

Here is positive proof, on indisputable authority, that this supposed great absurdity of a "Silver Man" is not so absurd after all.

All who have the least knowledge of palæontology know that all those wonderful remains of fishes, animals, etc., found in limestone and other rocks, and about which so much is said and written, are not the creatures themselves, but merely their shapes replaced by mineral substances.

There are many instances of veins once worked out being filled afresh with mineral deposited by gases ascending from the depths of the mine, in connection, perhaps, with water holding in solution various mineral salts. Often the ore and vein stone have been found in a position so natural that but for the finding of the tools of the ancient miners embedded in the solid quartz, the fact of its being other than the primitive deposit would never have been suspected. So certain is it that many ores are thus deposited, that the operations of nature may in this respect be imitated by artificial means. M. de Senarmont has made numerous experiments with such solutions as are found in hot springs, and by ingenious combinations in vessels hermetically sealed and properly heated, has succeeded in producing not only perfect quartz crystals, but the ores of iron, copper, silver, etc.

From what I have said, it will readily be seen that what appears so very wonderful in the fact of a human body being changed into a mass of mineral, is not so very strange after all.

The place where the body was found, be it remembered, was most admirably calculated to produce such a change. Sealed up by a not uncommon accident in a cavity in the very heart of a metallic vein, and this again hermetically closed in every part by an accumulation on all its walls of pyritous concretions, while from below steamed upward gases loaded with volatilized minerals, it would have been strange if no remarkable change had been produced in the organic remains subjected to these combined influences. There is every sign that the hot springs near the mine were at one time situated as far below the lead in which the body was found as they are now above it. Hot springs are generally caused by the decomposition of pyrites in contact with water. Once this operation commences, it proceeds in pretty much the same manner as the burning of a stratum of coal, following the unburnt portions of the deposit. The course of this burning at Steamboat Springs, Washoe, is northward. Even within the memory of the present generation, certain hot springs in California have moved several rods up the ravine on which they are situated, following the bed of pyritous matter to which they owe their existence. The strong subterranean heat of the Springs I have mentioned, during the time they were passing under the lead in which the mineralized body was found, doubtless caused immense volumes of various gases to be evolved, and this, besides the production of a favorable temperature, must most assuredly have had much to do in the production of the "Silver Man."

I might say much more in proof not only of the fact of a human body so changed having been found, but of the simple and natural causes which have operated to produce a change which at the first glance appears so wonderful; however, as many would not believe, even though I should produce the body and melt it up into buttons before their very eyes, I refrain.

In conclusion, I have only to say that in my opinion the greatest wonder that Washoe has yet produced—the greatest wonder of the age—is this marvelous "Silver Man!"

Golden Era, February 5, 1865

The Traveling Stones
of Pahranagat

One of De Quille's most famous hoaxes—"The Traveling Stones of Pahranagat"—is also the one which is by far the most extended in time. It was achieved in three stages. The first one was masked as a news story in the Territorial Enterprise sometime in 1865 or 1866. The issue in which it appeared is missing but De Quille paraphrased it, still tongue-in-cheek, in his 1876 book, The Big Bonanza (I). The story, taken at face value, seems to have spread all over the world, and for a number of years De Quille took delight in the constant stream of inquiries he received about it. By 1879, however, he claimed he had enough and exposed the hoax in another Enterprise column (II). The rediscovery this year of the third stage, in a Salt Lake City Daily Tribune column of 1892 (III), reveals him at his most proficient as a hoaxer, for in it he undertook—apparently successfully—to re-hoax an audience which knew he had deceived it before. The tip-off to the hoax is in the detail about the special action of the last stone. How can stones determine which is last and make it jump a foot into the air?

At the end of chapter 3 of The Big Bonanza, De Quille tells the story of an uninformed and novice prospector named Pike who became unduly excited when he found a ledge of what turned out to be nothing more than magnetic iron ore. Having thus, in a fashion, warned his readers, De Quille immediately proceeds, with the appearance of objectivity, to tell about the Pahranagat stones.

I

Some years after Pike's great discovery a prospector who had been roaming through the Pahranagat Mountains, the wildest and most sterile portion of southeastern Nevada, brought back with him a great curiosity in the shape of a number of traveling stones. The stones were almost perfectly round, the majority of them as large as a hulled walnut, and very heavy, being of an irony nature. When scattered about on the floor, on a table, or other level surface, within two or three feet of each other, they immediately began traveling toward a common center and then huddled

9

up in a bunch like a lot of eggs in a nest. A single stone removed to a distance of a yard, upon being released, at once started off with wonderful and comical celerity to rejoin its fellows; but if taken away four or five feet, it remained motionless.

The man who was in possession of these traveling stones said that he found them in a region of country that, though comparatively level, is nothing but bare rock. Scattered about in this rocky plain are a great number of little basins, from a few feet to two or three rods in diameter, and it is in the bottom of these basins that the rolling stones are found. In the basins they are seen from the size of a pea to five or six inches in diameter. These curious pebbles appear to be formed of loadstone or magnetic iron ore.

The Big Bonanza, p. 18

II
THOSE "TRAVELING STONES"
We Throw up the Sponge

In an idle moment, some fifteen years ago, this deponent concocted and wrote an item entitled "Traveling Stones." The stones were said to have been brought from the Pahranagat country, (because little was then known of that region and it was not easy of access,) where they were found in shallow basins in the rock. They were round, and ranged in size from those no bigger than a buckshot up to such as were of the size of ten-pin balls. They were evidently largely composed of magnetic iron ore, and when spread out on a floor or other level surface would all run and huddle together like a covey of quail, though when one was removed too far from its mates it could not get back.

The story of the little traveling stones seemed to supply a want that had long been felt—to exactly fit and fill a certain little vacant nook in the minds of men—and they traveled through all the newspapers of the world. This we did not much mind, nor were we much worried by letters of inquiry at first, but it has now been some years since we ceased to enjoy them. First and last, we must have had bushels of letters asking about these stones. Letter after letter have we opened from foreign parts in the expectation of hearing of something to our advantage—that half a million had been left us somewhere or that somebody was anxious to pay us four bits a column for sketches about the mountains and the mines—and have only found some other man wanting to know all about those traveling stones.

So it has gone on all these fifteen years. Our last is from Tiffin, Ohio, dated November 3, and received yesterday. His name is Haines, and he wants to know all about those stones, could he obtain several and how? Not long since we had a letter from a man in one of the New England States who informed us that there was big money in the traveling stones. We were to send him a car-load, when he would exhibit and sell them, dividing the spoils with us. We have stood this thing about fifteen years, and it is becoming a little monotonous. We are now growing old and we want peace. We desire to throw up the sponge and acknowledge the corn; therefore we solemnly affirm that we never saw or heard of any such diabolical cobbles as the traveling stones of Pahranagat—though we still think there ought to be something of the kind somewhere in the world. If this candid confession shall carry a pang to the heart of any true believer we shall be glad of it, as the true believers have panged it to us, right and left, quite long enough.

Territorial Enterprise, November 11, 1879

III
TRAVELING STONES

I once wrote an item about some stones supposed to have been found in Pahranagat that, when scattered about on a table, would run together and bunch up like a covey of quail. The stones were said to be rounded by the action of water, and largely composed of magnetic iron. The item was merely put forth as a "feeler." I thought there might be such rounded pebbles of magnetic iron, as I had seen a lump of such ore pick up several fragments of the same weighing as much as four or five ounces. My object was to set the many prospectors then ranging the country to looking for such things.

My item was extensively copied, and finally it became the "Traveling Stones of Australia," some papers in our antipodes having localized it by using the name of some Australian mining region instead of Pahranagat. Meantime I was so bothered with letters from all kinds of people, that I at last came out and said my item was a mere "fake," that I had seen no such stones. Hundreds wanted sample lots of the stones—small nests of them. One man desired to become my partner in the deposit. We were to run a train of pack mules as freight trains to the nearest point on the railroad, and load several cars with the stones. When I had thus assisted in "pressing the button," he would do the rest. He would first supply the demand in all the museums of this country, and would then similarly favor the Old World. I had said that the stones traveled about "with comical celerity, and finally huddled together like eggs in a nest." This caught a man who said we would supply all the saloons in the world. He also wanted the stones by the carload. Even women and children wrote for the "traveling stones."

The Traveling Stones a Reality

Shortly after I denied the existence of the traveling stones, I began to receive assurances that such stones had really been found in central Nevada. Among others who had found and owned such stones was Joseph E. Eckley, present State Printer of Nevada. Mr. Eckley has several times told me of his having owned a lot of such stones while he was a citizen of Austin, Lander county. He obtained them in Nye county on a hill that was filled and covered with geodes. Most of these geodes contain crystals of various colors. These are not the traveling kind. Those that appear to be endued with life are little nodules of iron. They are found on the hill among the geodes, and it was only by accident that Mr. Eckley discovered their traveling propensities. He had the stones he found for some months, and frequently exhibited them. This finally led to their being stolen, some one breaking open his cabinet and carrying them off. Mr. Eckley is a truthful man. He now resides in Carson City, and doubtless would be able to give further particulars in regard to the stones he discovered.

Traveling Stones in Humboldt

The other day I received the following letter about traveling stones which is self-explanatory:

Hailey, Ida., Feb. 12, 1892

Mr. Wright. Virginia City, Nev.:—DEAR SIR:—Some time in the sixties you wrote an article that was published in the *Enterprise* giving a description of some magnetic pebbles that had been discovered in the Pahranagat country in Lincoln county. In 1877 [sic] you published another article stating that there was no truth in the article and that such a thing as a magnetic pebble had never been found. I was talking with Professor W. F. Stewart about it and he assured me that you were correct and that such specimens as you described would be one of the greatest geological curiosities.

I informed him that I had seen plenty of them, and we made an agreement to go and get some of them, but kept putting it off, and never went. They are in Humboldt county about sixty miles from the Central Pacific Railroad. If they are as rare as you and Professor Stewart seem to think, Nevada should have some of them at the World's Fair. They are from the size of No. 4 shot to quail eggs and generally there will be one quite large and then several smaller ones in a depression in the rock. It seems to be a volcanic rock, with a large amount of iron in it. If they are taken away and thrown around promiscuously they will lose their magnetic quality in a few weeks, but if kept in a glass bottle will retain it indefinitely. Take a handful of them, throw them on a table or on a smooth floor and they will all run together in less than thirty seconds, and the last one getting there jumping a foot or more and sticking on the pile wherever it strikes.

They invariably gather around the largest stone. They will remind you of a lot of chickens running to an old hen when there is a hawk around. It will take three days with a team to go from the railroad and return. Yours truly,

J. M. WOODWORTH

This seems to settle the question of "traveling stones." These appear to be different from the stones found by Mr. Eckley, but act in the same manner. I have seen some of the geodes from the Nye county locality, but they were apparently of a quartzose nature and contained crystals. Captain S. T. Curtis, the well-known mining superintendent, gave me several such which he dug from the hill. As he was in search of such as appeared likely to contain crystals he probably ignored the iron nodules. Captain Curtis informed me that the geodes could be dug out like potatoes, the ground being filled with them in all sizes from those no larger than a pea to such as were as big as a man's head.

From De Quille's article "Undesirable Thriftiness,"

Salt Lake City Daily Tribune, March 6, 1892

Solar Armor

Although De Quille's "solar armor" invention is one of America's classic literary hoaxes, it has seldom been reprinted. Immediately upon publication, on July 2, 1874, it spread across the country and even overseas. By July 25, the Scientific American took cognizance of the story (vol. 31: 4, p. 51), and by early August the London Daily Telegraph reflected on it in a way that inspired De Quille to write a sequel, thus making it a double hoax. An interesting footnote to the story is that Knox County, Ohio, was the birthplace of De Quille as well as Mr. Newhouse, but De Quille was two years younger than the ill-fated inventor.

I
SAD FATE OF AN INVENTOR

A gentleman who has just arrived from the borax fields of the desert regions surrounding the town of Columbus, in the eastern part of this State, gives us the following account of the sad fate of Mr. Jonathan Newhouse, a man of considerable inventive genius. Mr. Newhouse had constructed what he called a "solar armor," an apparatus intended to protect the wearer from the fierce heat of the sun in crossing deserts and burning alkali plains. The armor consisted of a long, close-fitting jacket made of common sponge and a cap or hood of the same material; both jacket and hood being about an inch in thickness. Before starting across a desert this armor was to be saturated with water. Under the right arm was suspended an India-rubber sack filled with water and having a small gutta-percha tube leading to the top of the hood. In order to keep the armor moist, all that was necessary to be done by the traveler, as he progressed over the burning sands, was to press the sack occasionally, when a small quantity of water would be forced up and thoroughly saturate the hood and the jacket below it. Thus, by the evaporation of the moisture in the armor, it was calculated might be produced almost any degree of cold. Mr. Newhouse went down to Death Valley, determined to try the experiment of crossing that terrible place in his armor. He started out into the valley one morning from the camp nearest its borders, telling the men at the camp, as they laced his armor on his back, that he would return in two days. The next day an Indian who could speak but a few words of

English came to the camp in a great state of excitement. He made the men understand that he wanted them to follow him. At the distance of about twenty miles out into the desert the Indian pointed to a human figure seated against a rock. Approaching they found it to be Newhouse still in his armor. He was dead and frozen stiff. His beard was covered with frost and—though the noonday sun poured down its fiercest rays—an icicle over a foot in length hung from his nose. There he had perished miserably, because his armor had worked but too well, and because it was laced up behind where he could not reach the fastenings.

Territorial Enterprise, July 2, 1874

II
A MYSTERY EXPLAINED
The Sequel to the Strange Death of Jonathan Newhouse, the Inventor of the Solar Armor

The *Daily Telegraph*, London, England, appears to doubt the truth of the account we some time since published of the strange death of Jonathan Newhouse, in Death Valley, where he fell a victim to an apparatus of his own invention, styled a "solar armor." Under the date of August 3 the *Telegraph* says:

A curious story reaches us from Virginia City, which, to quote transatlantic phraseology, is the "last new thing in the town line" that the young State of Nevada has produced. Virginia City is the child of the celebrated Comstock lode, which is in its immediate neighborhood. "The city," says Mr. Ross Browne, "lies on a rugged slope, and is singularly diversified in its up-risings and down-fallings. It is difficult to see upon what principle it was laid out. My impression is, it was never laid out at all, but followed the dips, spurs and angles of the immortal Comstock." Be this as it may, the alkaline plains lying between the young Capital of Nevada and the eastern border of the State have a terrible reputation for burning heat and waterless sterility. It is not uncommon for men—and even wagons, with their teams of from eight to sixteen mules or oxen—to sink overwhelmed with heat and thirst when an effort is made to cross this desert during the height of summer. The *Virginia City Enterprise* tells us that a Mr. Jonathan Newhouse, being a man endowed with considerable inventive faculties, devised what he called a "solar armor," which he proposed to don before taking to the alkaline plains. This armor "consisted of a long, close-fitting jacket, made of common sponge, with a hood of the same material, both being saturated with water." Under the right arm its wearer had an India-rubber pouch filled with water, and connecting with the top of the hood by means of a gutta-percha tube. As the traveler proceeds and feels the sun scorching his head, he compresses his right arm and squirts water into the hood, whence it percolates through the entire jacket. Clothed in this strange outfit, Mr. Newhouse set out from Virginia City for a place called "Death Valley," which, if this story be true, has more than ever earned the name that it bears. He expected to be absent for a couple of days. The heat of the sun was torrid, and, on the second day after his departure, an Indian, in a terrible state of "scare," rushed into a camp of white men on the edge of the desert, announcing that a man was lying frozen to death, under a rock towards which he pointed his finger. Followed by his startled companions, the Indian led them to the body of poor Mr. Newhouse. It was then found that the traveler had been unable to unlace the jacket which his friends had fastened with thongs before he started, and the evaporation of moisture from the saturated sponge vestment had produced such intensity of cold that its wearer and inventor paid the penalty of his too successful ingenuity with his life. His beard is represented as having been covered with frost, and a large icicle hung from his nose and lips. The marvelous stories which come from "the plains" are apt to be received with incredulity by our transatlantic kinsmen who dwell upon the Eastern seaboard of the United States. We confess that, although the fate of Mr. Newhouse is related by the Western journal *au grand serieux*, we should require some additional confirmation before we unhesitatingly accept it. But every one who has iced a bottle of wine by wrapping a wet cloth round it and putting it in a draught, must have noticed how great is the cold that evaporation of moisture produces. For these reasons we are disposed to accept the tale from Virginia City in the same frame of mind which Herodotus, the Father of History, usually assumed when he repeated some marvel that had reached him—that is to say, we are neither prepared to disbelieve it wholly nor to credit it without question.

Had not our attention been called to the above by Mr. Duncan McKay, Superintendent of the Santiago mill, Carson River, who is in the weekly receipt of several English newspapers, we should probably never again have referred to the death of Mr. Newhouse. However, as the truth of our narration appears to be called in question, if not directly at least impliedly, by a paper which enjoys the reputation of having the largest circulation of any daily newspaper in the world, we feel that it is but right that we should make public some further particulars in regard to the strange affair—particulars which throw a flood of light upon what, we must admit, did appear almost incredible in our account of the sad occurrence as published. It seemed strange that so great a degree of cold could be produced simply by the evaporation of water, but it now appears that it was not water—at least not water alone—that was used by the unfortunate gentleman.

We are glad that the Telegraph has given us the opportunity, long awaited, of publishing in detail the sequel to the curious affair. [The Telegraph is mistaken in supposing Death Valley to be near Virginia City. It is 250 or 300 miles distant.]

A fortnight after our account of the sad affair was published we received a letter in regard to the matter from one David Baxter, who states that he is Justice of the Peace and exofficio Coroner, of Salt Wells, a station in Inyo County, California, situated at the head of the Sink of Amargosa River, at the north end of Death Valley. Mr. Baxter states that he held

An Inquest on the Body

Of the deceased, Newhouse, in due form, and that the verdict rendered was as follows: "We find that the name of the deceased was Jonathan Newhouse, a native of Knox County, Ohio, aged 47 years; and we further find that deceased came to his death in Death Valley, Inyo County, California, on the 27th day of June, A.D. 1874, by being frozen in a sort of coat of sponge called a 'solar armor,' of which he was the inventor and in which he was tightly laced at his own request, said 'solar armor' being moistened with some frigorific mixture, with the precise nature of which we are unacquainted."

Mr. Baxter further states in his letter that he had before him as witnesses the men stopping at the camp on the borders of Death Valley where Mr. Newhouse was last seen alive. These men produced what Mr. Baxter had not before heard mentioned, namely:

The Carpet-sack of Deceased,

Which he had left at their camp. In this was found, besides a few light articles of wearing apparel, several bottles and small glass jars, containing liquids and powders or salts of various kinds, with the nature of the most of which no person in the settlement was acquainted. One of the largest bottles was labeled "Ether," known to them to be a very volatile liquid and capable of producing an intense degree of cold by evaporation.

From this they were able to give a shrewd guess at the nature of the contents of the other vessels. Although it was at first stated—and generally believed until after the contents of the carpet-sack had been overhauled and the inquest held—that deceased had used water only in filling the little India-rubber sack used in supplying moisture to the armor, one of the witnesses, Mr. Robert Purcell, testified that he had observed Mr. Newhouse at a spring about fifty yards from camp, half an hour previous to his donning the armor, and recollects distinctly to have seen him handling one or two of the bottles and jars found in the carpet-sack; though at the time he thought nothing of it, and did not approach very near to deceased, as he did not wish to be thought inquisitive.

Besides the bottle containing the ether, there was another in which was a liquid labeled "Bisulphide of Carbon." There were small glass jars containing what appeared to be salts. They were labeled "Ammonic Nitrate; Sodic Nitrate; Ammonic Chloride; Sodic Sulphate, and Sodic Phosphate."

Mr. Baxter is firmly convinced that with these chemicals, either alone or diluted with water, the degree of cold was produced which caused the death of the unfortunate man. He thinks that in his attempts to reach the fastenings of his armor, on his back, when he began to experience a painful degree of cold, he unavoidably compressed the India-rubber pouch and thus constantly ejected more and more of the freezing fluid into the head-piece of his armor.

As He Stiffened

In death, his arm, under which the sack was suspended, naturally pressed more strongly upon his side and thus caused a steady flow of the fluid. Mr. Baxter is of the opinion that the frost and icicle found on the beard and depending from the nose of deceased were formed from the water mingled with the more volatile fluids comprising the frigorific mixture.

He states as a remarkable fact—and it is strange that this was not mentioned by the gentleman from Columbus, Mr. Abner Wade, who gave us our first brief and imperfect account of the affair—that the men who went out with the Indian to find the remains of Mr. Newhouse came near having their hands frozen in handling the body when trying to place it upon the back of a horse. The freezing mixture oozed out of the spongy armor upon their hands and gave them intense pain. Finally—after they found they could handle the body in no other way—they were obliged to cut the lacings to the armor; when, after an infinite deal of pain to their hands and fingers, the armor was peeled off the body and left lying in the desert, where it probably still remains.

One of the men, Alexander Martin, suffered for about three weeks from the freezing his left hand received and he came near losing the middle finger, gangrene supervening at the root of the nail.

Viewed in the flood of light which Mr. Baxter throws upon the strange death of Mr. Newhouse, we think there can be but one opinion in regard to it; which is, that he fell a victim to a rash experiment with chemicals with the nature of which he was but imperfectly acquainted.

In conclusion, it only remains for us to state that Mr. Baxter informed us that it was his intention to send the bottles and jars of chemicals to the Academy of Sciences at San Francisco; also, the solar armor, in case he could recover it. Whether or not he has done so we cannot say. For several weeks we have closely watched the reports of the proceedings of the learned body named, but as yet have seen no mention made of either the chemicals or the armor.

Territorial Enterprise, August 30, 1874

Eyeless Fish That
Live in Hot Water

A most singular discovery was yesterday made in the Savage mine. This is the finding of living fish in the water now flooding both the Savage and Hale and Norcross mines. The fish found were five in number, and were yesterday afternoon hoisted up the incline in the large iron hoisting tank and dumped into the pump tank at the bottom of the vertical shaft. The fishes are eyeless, and are only about three or four inches in length. They are blood red in color.

The temperature of the water in which they are found is 128 degrees Fahrenheit—almost scalding hot. When the fish were taken out of the hot water in which they were found, and placed in a bucket of cold water, for the purpose of being brought to the surface, they died almost instantly. The cold water at once chilled their life blood.

In appearance these subterranean members of the finny tribe somewhat resemble gold fish. They seem lively and sportive enough while in their native hot water, notwithstanding the fact that they have no eyes nor even the rudiments of eyes. The water by which the mines are flooded broke in at a depth of 2,200 feet in a drift that was being pushed to the northward in the Savage. It rose in the mine—also in the Hale and Norcross, the two mines being connected—to the height of 400 feet; that is, up to the 1,800 foot level. This would seem to prove that a great subterranean reservoir or lake has been tapped, and from this lake doubtless came the fish hoisted from the mine last evening.

Eyeless fishes are frequently found in the lakes of large caves, but we have never before heard of their existence in either surface or subterranean water the temperature of which was so high as in the water in these mines. The lower workings of the Savage mine are far below the bed of the Carson river, below the bottom of Washoe lake—below any water running or standing anywhere within a distance of ten miles of the mine.

Territorial Enterprise, February 19, 1876

The Troubles of
John Smith

Why will the Smiths, man and wife, go on naming the majority of their male offspring "John?" It is exceedingly stupid, and it is about time to put a stop to the practice. It is all very well to say to a man—"Know thyself!" but how is a man to know himself if his name is John Smith? For Mr. and Mrs. Smith to name their son John, is to send him forth nameless into the world. He is a digitless cipher. We yesterday morning had in our Police Court to report the following item:

John Smith, arrested by officers Lloyd and Iby on a charge of petty larceny; dismissed.

Then came pouring forth scores of notes from distressed and outraged John Smiths. The poor fellows are obliged to parade before the public not only their trades and troubles, but also their infirmities, in order that the public may not mistake them for thieves. The following are only a few of the notes we have received, and are taken at random from the avalanche that covers our table:

Editor Enterprise: Please state that the John Smith mentioned in your Police Court report this morning—the petty-larceny fellow—was not John Smith who does night work, and oblige
Yours truly,   John Smith.

Editor Enterprise: Will you be kind enough to state that the John Smith arrested yesterday for petty larceny was not John Smith who drives the swill cart. Yours,
John Smith.

Reporter Enterprise: Please say that the John Smith arrested for stealing was not red-headed John Smith, the tinker.
Respectfully,   John Smith.

Mr. Local: You will oblige me by saying that one-legged John Smith is not the petty larceny cuss who was in the Police Court yesterday.
Your obedient,   John Smith.

Mr. Items: Be good enough to say that the John Smith up yesterday for theft was not the Smith commonly known as "Lying Jack Smith from Poker Flat." I remain, etc., John Smith.

Local Items: Please correct your police report of yesterday morning by saying that the John Smith up before Judge Marple yesterday for petty larceny was not the John Smith lately divorced from his wife, and commonly known as "Cock-eyed Smith," and you will oblige
John Smith.

Mr. Enterprise: I am no d——d thief! I wish you to state in your paper that the John Smith pulled yesterday for petty larceny was not John Smith from Idaho, commonly called "Sore-legged Jack." Yours, etc.,
John Smith.

As may be seen by the above struggles of the John Smiths to make themselves known, John Smith is no name at all. Indeed it is worse than no name. Let Mr. and Mrs. Smith name their boy Ebenezer, Hippatodorus Gabriel, Lacedaemonious, Jedediah or Epaphroditus, but let us have no more John Smith—at least not for a generation or two, when there shall appear to be a demand for them.

For the comfort of the John Smiths who have asked us to set them right, we will state that the John Smith arrested on a charge of petty larceny is better known as "Suck-egg Smith."

Territorial Enterprise, July 8, 1874

The Boss Snorer

After the fire old man Bullard found lodgings on South C street. He got a bed in a large room containing two other beds that were occupied. Mr. Bullard is a huge, fat, good-natured and very entertaining man. The proprietor of the lodging-house was much pleased with Bullard, and laughed at his jokes the first evening of his arrival at his place till tears ran down his cheeks. The men who were to be Bullard's room-mates also thought well of him—that evening. The next morning, however, they looked sad and red-eyed. Then they went to the landlord and told him that he must find some other place for Mr. Bullard, as he was such a terrific snorer they couldn't stand him. The landlord's rooms were all occupied, and he had no place for Bullard but just where he was. The complaining lodgers left and in two or three days two other men were put into the vacant bed. Bullard made short work of them; one night let them out. The landlord sought an interview with Bullard and remonstrated with him. Bullard stoutly asserted that he did not snore—had never been known to snore. The landlord had to give Bullard up as a bad bargain and turned his attention to looking up lodgers with which to fill his vacant beds. He found men to take the beds, but again Bullard cleaned them out in a single night. Growing desperate, the landlord again went to Bullard. He told him he must either leave the house or pay rent for all the beds in the room—$45 per month. Bullard said a bargain was a bargain; he had paid $15 for his bed and he intended keeping it till his month was up, and he didn't propose to pay for beds he had no use for; he didn't snore, and the man who asserted to the contrary was a "liar and a horsethief!" The landlord felt very much depressed after this last interview with Bullard, as he saw he was determined not to be removed from his quarters. A morning or two after, as Bullard's landlord was going down town he saw standing in his door a brother lodging-house man.

"Thank heaven he's gone!" said the man as Bullard's landlord came up. "Thank heaven I'm rid of him at last!"

"Rid of whom?"

"Why, of the big fat man you see yonder waddling down the street."

"What of him?"

"Enough of him! He cleaned nearly every man out of my house before he left. They wouldn't stop in the same block with that snorting, Falstaffian porpoise, sir!"

23

"He's a good one, is he?"

"A good one? He's a perfect terror! He's more different kinds of a snorer than any man I ever heard, and every time he changes his key it is for the worse. While I had him here crowds were gathering in front of the house nightly wondering what was the matter within, and the police came in one night thinking some one was being murdered. My dog ran away, and all the cats left the house, sir!"

"And the man you pointed out to me is this snorer?"

"Yes, sir, and may he burst!"

"Good-day, sir!" and Bullard's landlord hastened down the street. * * * * * * * The next morning with the first peep of day, Bullard, puffing and blowing, rushed into the presence of his landlord.

"What are you trying to play on me?" cried he. "I never slept a wink all night. Of all the infernal noises I ever heard that man in my room got off the worst. Is he going to stay here?"

"Stay? Of course he is. Hain't he got the bed for a month?"

"Then I leave," and Bullard was as good as his word.

An hour afterward the man who had ousted Bullard arose and waddled serenely into the presence of the landlord.

"You've cleaned him out," said the landlord. "You raised him; he's gone for good!" and the landlord gleefully rubbed his hands. "Now," continued the landlord, "I'll give you a good square breakfast and then you can go."

"Go," said the fat man, "not much I don't. Didn't you say last evening in the presence of Bullard and half a dozen others that I was to stay here a month?"

"But that you know was only to—"

"I know nothing of the kind and I shall stay here. I am human; I must have some place in which to repose!"

The landlord is now trying to get some man to set up some kind of machine in his house that will oust the boss snorer, who now has the whole place to himself, except a small room in a corner of the third story where he and his wife spend their nights in a miserable way.

Territorial Enterprise, January 1, 1876

Torture Unutterable

**WHAT A WOMAN SUFFERED TO WIN $50,
AND WHY SHE LOST**

Mr. Morey had seated himself in his easy chair, newspaper in hand, to read up the Turco-Russian business.

"Just the way when I've anything particular to say to you, Mr. Morey; the moment you come into the house you take up your paper," and Mrs. Morey paused for a reply.

"Tell me of a time when you didn't have something to say—and something particular?"

"You speak as though I were a perfect magpie, or a poll parrot. I hope I may be allowed to speak once in a while. There is not a woman in Virginia City that talks less—."

"You are not talking now, my dear?"

"Not when you are taking the conversation to yourself."

"I presume it is the old subject—what your neighbors have got and what you have not got in the way of dress or furniture?"

"No, it is not."

"What then?"

"O, go on with your reading. I have nothing to say now. I should be sorry to disturb you."

"Nothing to say—for once you have nothing to say!"

"Nothing."

"That is good. Ha, ha, ha!—nothing to say! Now, look here, Mrs. Morey, I'll tell you what I'll do with you. I'll—."

"What?"

"I'll give you a chance for getting some of the fine things you are always talking about."

"You will?"

"I will. Now, provided you do not speak a word during the next two hours, I'll give you $50."

"Honor bright?"

"Honor bright!"

"It's a bargain! I am not to speak a word for two hours and you are to give me $50?"

"That's it."

"It's a bargain! It's a bargain—bargain!" cried Mrs. Morey, and she began dancing about the room.

"Let us have a fair understanding; you are not to speak a word or write a word during two hours, and if you do not I am to give you $50."

"Yes; $50."

"You may laugh, cry and dance about to your heart's content, but not one intelligible word must you utter."

"I understand—then I get the $50?"

"Of course, if you win."

"If I win! You may just as well give me the $50 now—I am sure of it. Why, I'd be sure of it were the time three hours—four hours—eight hours!"

"All right. It is now three minutes to 2 o'clock p.m.—at 2 o'clock you start in, at 4 o'clock you win—that is, provided you do not speak in the meantime."

At 2 o'clock, precisely, Mrs. Morey closed her lips hard together. Her eyes twinkled roguishly, and she shook her finger at her husband, as much as to say: "Now I begin—not a word shall you induce me to speak!"

Mr. Morey read quietly for some twenty minutes, then suddenly said: "Hattie, the children were not at school to-day. What can have become of them?"

Not a word from Mrs. Morey—only a smile and a look that said: "No you don't."

Again Mr. Morey read for some time, when he cried: "Ha! What is that I see! Your sister Ellen married to that old hunks, Hiram Todd!"

Mrs. Morey smiled, shook her head and, with her eyes, said: "Too thin—try again!" Then she laughed and waltzed about the room, as much as to say: "O, haven't I a good thing for that $50!"

Mr. Morey tried several similar dodges without avail. Nearly an hour had passed and not a word had his wife yet spoken. Her chances for winning the $50 seemed good. Mrs. Morey was jubilant and laughed, danced and snapped her fingers.

Finally Mr. Morey happened to look out at the window, and saw at his front gate Mrs. Brownson, the wife of his partner. Assuming a serious and frightened look, he ran to meet the lady. In a few words he told her that he had just started in search of her—that his wife had suddenly lost her speech, and he feared her reason as well.

Mrs. Brownson, a timid little creature, turned pale at once and looked much frightened. She even showed signs of beating a retreat, but Mr. Morey caught her by the arm and hurried her into the house, begging her to see his wife and do all she could to restore her speech and reason.

"Oh, my dear Mrs. Morey," cried Mrs. Brownson, "your husband has been telling me that you are very, very ill—that you have lost your speech."

Mrs. Morey burst into a merry peal of laughter, as though she thought it an excellent joke.

Mrs. Brownson stared wildly at her and was evidently not a little alarmed, but finally managed to say: "speak to me, Hattie, dear—tell me that your tongue is not paralyzed!"

Mrs. Morey laughed loudly and merrily, then put out her tongue to show that she had full use of that member. To further explain she went to the clock. She pointed to the figure 2, then to 4, when she took some silver coins from her pocket and made believe she was counting a considerable sum of money, looking at her husband and laughing as she did so.

"Just the way she has been going on for nearly an hour, she evidently thinks there is something wrong with the clock," said Mr. Morey, speaking in a low tone, yet so loud that his wife might overhear.

Mrs. Morey darted upon him and boxed his ears in a playful way that was meant to express some such thing as: "Why, you great story teller, how can you talk so?" Then she hugged and kissed Mrs. Brownson, to show that lady that she was perfectly sane.

Mrs. Brownson did not so construe her actions, however. On the contrary, she thought Mrs. Morey was rapidly growing violent, and instead of returning her caresses released herself as soon as possible, and throwing herself into a chair, burst into tears, trembling in every limb.

To reassure her, Mrs. Morey ran to her side, and, laughing immoderately, again tried to embrace her.

"Take her away! take her away!" cried Mrs. Brownson, springing to her feet and running to Mr. Morey for protection.

Mrs. Morey began to look serious and puzzled. Soon, however, she ran to the clock and pointing again to the figures 2 and 4, opened her mouth, put out her tongue and laughed merrily, as she thought, but insanely as a bedlamite, as it appeared to Mrs. Brownson.

At this juncture the little boy and girl of the Moreys, aged respectively nine and six, came darting in from school. Their faces were radiant with happiness, and both at once began to tell their mother some wonderful bit of news.

"Why don't you say something, mama?" cried they, looking astonished.

"Your poor mama has lost her speech—she can't talk," said Mr. Morey.

"Can't you talk, mama?" cried they.

Mrs. Morey nodded her head, laughed and kissed them, but the little ones looked frightened and clamored for her to speak to them.

"My poor dears, your mother has lost her speech," said Mr. Morey, solemnly.

"Poor little dears!" cried Mrs. Brownson, and burst into tears. Both children followed her example, crying bitterly.

It was after 3 o'clock. In less than an hour Mrs. Morey would win the $50 if she remained silent, and she determined that as she had gone so far no power on earth should make her speak. She pointed to the clock, laughed and tried all manner of pantomime in order to show that she was all right and could speak if she chose to do so, but this only served to frighten Mrs. Brownson and the children all the more. Hastily whispering a few words to Mr. Morey, Mrs. Brownson left the house. She ran to the houses of two or three neighbors and told them the terrible news that Mrs. Morey had suddenly lost her power of speech and was, beside, a raving maniac; that she had tried to kill Mr. Morey, and she feared that ere now she might have killed her children. Three or four boys were sent for physicians, and soon half a dozen women were found who had the courage to move upon the house of the Moreys in a solid body.

They found Mrs. Morey weeping and laughing by turns, while Mr. Morey, apparently utterly broken down and hopeless, sat with his face buried in his handkerchief, sobbing convulsively, as it seemed. He merely looked up when the female delegation arrived, pointed to his wife, then buried his face in his handkechief and again visibly shook in every limb.

Mrs. Morey's face was flushed, her eyes were red and had a wild look, yet she tried to laugh, and by various gestures and embraces strove to reassure her friends.

It was 3:30 o'clock. In half an hour she would be at liberty to relate the joke—in half an hour she would have the $50. It would then be a big joke on her husband and it would be a triumph for her sex—all would applaud her self-control and courage. Nothing should make her utter a word—no, nothing!

Finding that she could not be made to utter a word; that she only laughed or wept hysterically, and kept her eyes fixed upon or with her fingers pointed to the clock, the ladies, her neighbors, decided that she must be put to bed and if need be, tied there.

The ladies advanced upon Mrs. Morey in full force, Mr. Morey, poor soul, seeming to be utterly broken down and unable to do anything to assist them. They were in the midst of a fearful struggle with Mrs. Morey—who was a large and strong woman—when the doctors began to arrive. The children were screaming at the top of their voices; the women were all coaxing and scolding at once; Mrs. Morey's long golden tresses were streaming below her waist, and Mr. Morey was moaning and groaning with his face in his handkerchief, when two physicians came rushing in together.

They at once seized upon Mrs. Morey and tried to force her down into a chair. This she at first stoutly resisted, pointing to the clock and gesticulating wildly, but she was finally obliged to seat herself.

"It's in the clock—it's something about the clock that is troubling her! She's constantly watching and pointing toward the clock!" cried the ladies.

A gleam of hope passed over the face of Mrs. Morey. She thought she might in some way make the doctors understand the situation, therefore she again pointed toward the clock, though she was not permitted to rise and approach it; went through the pantomime of counting money and pointing to her husband, who was staring at her with his eyes just peeping over his handkerchief.

"Yes, it is evidently in the clock, or about money matters or in regard to her husband—they take all manner of queer cranks," said one of the physicians.

"It's strange she is unable to speak," said the other, "as I see she puts out and moves her tongue quite freely—evidently it is not paralyzed."

"The lolling of the tongue," said the first physician, "is a mere animal movement and may be quite involuntary; I've often seen 'em do it—it proves nothing."

Two more physicians arrived about this time, and soon all four quite understood each other. The poor lady was insane, but it might be only temporarily so. They would do all they could for her relief.

"Poor thing! poor thing!" moaned the neighbor women. "Oh, oh!" groaned Mr. Morey within his handkerchief.

Mrs. Morey saw that in five minutes more she would win, and she pointed to the clock and laughed loud and long. Soon she would be at liberty to speak, and O, the fun she would have.

One of the doctors whispered to a lady, who nodded and went into another room; two doctors then tightly grasped Mrs. Morey's arms and held her firmly in her chair. The lady who had left the room returned with a pair of scissors in her hand.

"It is a great pity that we are obliged to do it," said one of the physicians, taking the scissors, "but her hair must come off, her head must be shaved, a blister must be applied and she must then be put to bed and kept there."

"Oh, oh!" groaned Mr. Morey.

The doctor had grasped a large tress near the top of Mrs. Morey's head and she felt the cold scissors pushed across her scalp. In two minutes the clock would strike four and she would win the $50. She struggled to free herself, but the two strong men held her in the chair.

"O, you wretches—you fools!" cried she—"you call yourselves doctors! I am as well as any of you and have a thousand times more sense this minute. You have made me lose $50! Release me, you idiots!"

The doctors looked surprised at hearing Mrs. Morey speak, but it was only for a moment. One of them said: "Hold her fast. Her silence was only a freak. They do all manner of curious things."

The man with the scissors again had his hands in Mrs. Morey's hair, but her tongue was now free and she made good use of it. "My husband was to give me $50 not to speak a word in two hours and you four fools have made me lose by two minutes!" cried she, and then rapidly proceeded to tell the whole story.

The doctors looked confused, but still incredulous, and turned toward Mr. Morey for an explanation, provided he had any to offer.

Throwing aside his handkerchief and his lugubrious air, Mr. Morey burst out in a roar of laughter that almost shook the room, and crying: "It's all true that she says!" advanced to release and embrace his wife, declaring that she was a greater heroine than Joan of Arc or any of them; but Mrs. Morey boxed his ears and broke into a torrent of tears.

"We have heard that in Heaven there was once silence for the 'space of half an hour,'" said one of the doctors, "but, then, we don't know that there were any women there."

"A woman not speak a word for two hours, lacking two minutes!" said another of the wise men. "She has vindicated her sex—her praise should be sounded to the farthest corners of the earth. Such a thing has never before been known."

"Here are your $50, Hattie," said Mr. Morey, "I brought the money home to-day on purpose to give it to you, and without any conditions, but things happened to take that curious turn, you know."

All the women were crying in concert by this time, and retired to another room to hold a regular indignation meeting; but, sobbing bitterly as she was, Mrs. Morey first went to her husband and held out her hand for the $50.

Territorial Enterprise, October 14, 1877

Tom Collette's Bath

HUMORS OF THREE JOLLY PROSPECTORS

Had you ever traveled the same trail with Tom Collette you would have been aware of the fact.

Tom is a cowboy, miner, mail carrier, prospector or anything else that is necessary when he finds that his pocket is empty and his larder lean. But wherever found and whatever engaged in Tom is sure to be at the head of all the deviltry and reckless "horseplay" that is going on. He counts no labor pain when it gives promise of resulting in a telling practical joke on some one—though it be his dearest friend, he cares not.

On one memorable occasion, however, Tom suffered equally with his victims, though had he failed to find victims his pains and pangs, both physical and mental, would doubtless have been far less endurable.

This was when out on a prospecting trip with two of his dearest friends and chums, Joe Carah and Jake Nordine. Mounted upon mustangs and having with them two or three heavily loaded pack mules, they were making a slow and painful journey across one of the great desert regions of Nevada. The men had started from Pine Grove, in Western Nevada, and were headed for the Osceola placer mines, in the eastern part of the State, close to the Utah line.

The month was July when all the deserts are like a blazing furnace and when the flying clouds of alkali dust fill the hair, beard and every pore of the sweltering traveler's body.

One afternoon the little party camped near some hot springs in the neighborhood of Walker Lake. Discovering a large pool that was full of cold water and convenient to one of the hottest of the hot springs, the boys turned the hot water flowing from the spring into the pool, until the hot and cold water blending made exactly the right temperature for a comfortable bath. This done, the three men plunged into the pool and enjoyed the delicious water as only those can who have traveled for days over dusty alkali plains in hot weather.

When supper was over and the three men had lighted their pipes, the theme of conversation for a long time as they sat smoking was the delightful bath they had taken, and the wonderful sense of refreshment it had brought them. Full of the joy of their bath in the wilds, the trio spread their blankets on a thick carpet of grass beneath a clump of willows a few yards distant from the spring and soon all were wandering in the land of Nod.

Tom was up with the dawn. Recollections of his glorious bath of the previous evening were still fresh in his mind. So, bounding up from his blankets, with a hop, skip and jump, he ran and plunged into the swimming pool up to his middle. With a groan of agony he sprang out again with the agility of a wildcat. The little dam in the trench leading from the hot spring had dissolved away and boiling water had been running into the pool nearly all night. Hours before dawn the cold water pool had been rendered almost as hot as the boiling spring itself. Brief as had been the period between his entry and his exit, Tom's fair skin was changed to the hue of a boiled lobster. He was soon in a terrible state of torture as the skin was almost sufficiently cooked to peel off.

With infinite care Tom drew on his pantaloons and boots, though he felt as though the cooked flesh was peeling off in strips wherever his clothing touched him. Biting his lips and forcing back the tears of anguish that were welling out of his eyes, Tom crept back to camp. Though it was a difficult thing to do, he put on his usual frank, good-humored smile as he neared the sleeping place at the willows, for Jake Nordine had awakened and was sitting on his blankets, gaping and stretching.

Seeing Tom approach, Jake asked where he had been—if he had been out looking after their ponies. Tom replied that he had so enjoyed the bath of the evening before and had so much benefited by it that he could not think of breaking camp without repeating it.

"Jake," said he, "the water in the big pool is fine this morning—it's just lovely!"

Jake did not wait to hear more. Bouncing up from his blankets he rushed away toward the pool.

As swiftly as he could move, considering the tender condition of his skin, Tom followed and dodging behind a convenient clump of willows kept covert watch.

Jake threw off the few "duds" in which he had slept then bounced into the pool. Instantly he uttered a cry of mingled anguish and rage, then clawed his way out upon the green turf with the celerity of an otter. As soon as he stood erect he began to make swift application of his open hands to various parts of his body to arrest the pain, each particular inch of his hide seeming to hurt worse than the other. All this time he was swearing a blue streak.

Louder and louder rose Jake's voice, as light began to break in upon his mind, when Tom stepped out from his hiding place crying: "Hold your howl! Will you bellow like one of the bulls of Bashan and give us away, when that other son of a gun up in camp is not yet cooked? You and I have had our dose, man, we must now cook Joe Carah or we shall never hear the last of our bath."

Soothed by this proposition, Jake carefully drew on his duds and the pair proceeded leisurely to camp.

By this time Joe had commenced to rouse up. Seeing Tom and Jake approaching he asked if they had "found the stock—the ponies?"

"Ponies, no," said Tom—"We haven't been looking for the animals. We have been taking a bath. Do you think," said he, as he stood holding his pantaloons away from the rear of his person—"do you think we'd break camp without one more magnificent swim? Not much!"

At this Joe sprang up crying: "By Jove, that's sense! I'll go and have another swim myself," and away he dashed toward the little pond.

As Joe disappeared behind the willows, Tom sprang for his pistol and took off all the caps. He and Jake then secured their own revolvers, Tom crying: "Get your pistol, Jake, and be quick. There'll be business when Joe comes back."

In about three minutes Joe did come back. He was howling and cursing furiously and, all naked as he was, never stopped running until he had got his six-shooter in his hand.

"Drop it!" cried Tom, "I have a dead bead on you and so has Jake. Besides, I've taken all the caps off your gun."

The difficulty was amicably settled as soon as Tom and Jake had related their experience. The trio took breakfast standing that morning, and—to spare the ponies—did not ride much for the succeeding three days.

Tom says his system received such a shock on that occasion that he has never since ventured to take a bath.

First published in the *Territorial Enterprise*, December 2, 1877. This hitherto unpublished revision is taken from a manuscript, courtesy of the University of Nevada–Reno Library.

II
HISTORY AND
DESCRIPTION

De Quille was a reporter as well as a literary artist. Much of what he wrote was a record of what went on around him. His most famous book, The Big Bonanza (1876), is largely historical. It would be easy—and worthwhile—to collect other groups of factual articles he wrote for newspapers or magazines and put together informative books out of them.

The first four pieces in this section are illustrations of his ability to record history dramatically. De Quille was probably the most knowledgeable writer in the Old West on the subject of prospecting and mining. In these articles, he vividly portrays from his intimate familiarity with them types of men once common but now, sadly, extinct. "The Tricks of Miners" and "A Superintendent Who Was Fatherly and 'Smooth'" are factual glimpses of the battle of wits that frequently accompanied the physical struggles for wealth. The unnamed superintendent in the latter sketch is actually James G. Fair. This true story suggests how Fair got to be and remained one of the "Silver Kings" of the Comstock.

"The Wealth of Washoe" is an unusual firsthand account of the awesome phenomenon of Comstock mining in 1861, in its early days just after the mines began to develop advanced new technologies. "Old Johnny Ranchero," despite its obvious humor, is actually another revealing view of the Comstock seventeen years later, when it was at its very peak. At the time this story was written, Virginia City was honeycombed with at least 750 miles of tunnels, and it was possible to travel underground from Virginia City to Gold Hill—four miles away. In its humorous way, the story depicts the extent of underground development and also records some of the problems which eventually became the bane of the mines and forced their closure. As the mines delved ever deeper into that volcanic region both heat and an inflow of hot water increased to the point where mining was made unprofitable despite the continued richness of the ore.

Although De Quille is usually associated with the Comstock, he also spent important years of his life in Ohio and Iowa. All during his writ-

ing career, he would periodically publish anecdotes of life in what was once pioneer country. The two pieces included here are among his best accounts of the frontier. "The Wolf and the Wild Hogs" is extraordinarily gripping; it exhibits a literary realism akin to A. B. Longstreet's 1835 collection of stories, Georgia Scenes, that was seldom seen again until the end of the century. "Trailing a Lost Child" is both poignant and fascinating in its recollection of a historically authentic incident. Recent biographical information has confirmed that De Quille recalled the search from personal experience.

The Typical Prospector

When it was proposed to erect the Colorado Mining Stock Exchange building, the editor of the *Industry* was asked to suggest a fitting emblem to surmount the tower. He suggested a bronze statue of a prospector, as a type of the best form of honor and the great occupation the Exchange was founded to aid. It was put there. We made a mistake. We should have suggested a statue of a man whose hand was in some one else's pocket. But it is more pleasure to write about the prospector than the other fellow, so we write about him, hoping that some time in the future the bronze may be a true and fitting emblem of what it was intended to be.

It is said that there are certain peculiarities of disposition and character belonging to each calling, profession or trade. The observing reader of human nature knows that to be the case. The teacher, lawyer, preacher, railway man, carpenter, miner and prospector, and men in every trade, carry with them their brand of occupation. Among them all not one is more peculiar, and in most ways more interesting and admirable than the old-time typical prospector. He is rapidly going out of existence now, as the conditions which made his life possible are disappearing with the march of civilization, and he will soon be known only in story as the pioneers of the Daniel Boone type are known.

No other occupation ever bore the peculiarities which prospecting possesses. It is an existence supported by hopes, and day dreams of undiscovered riches, and of wealth to be won. It is devoid of the grind of humdrum trade, and the sameness and saving of daily life in business. It is a game of chance, and it carries with it its brand of open-heartedness, generosity, love of fair play and contempt for meanness.

It is not a gamble, though, where he matches his skill against that of another, and where what he wins is another's loss. What he wins is from Nature—from the wealth that the great Creator hid away as a reward for the labor and trial and skill of the one who discovers it. His success benefits the world, and robs nobody.

Necessarily he is an optimist and enthusiast. Were he one who saw and measured the chances as they are, he would quit his occupation for another that promised better rewards. To him hope tinges everything with a golden hue. Darkness and the blues are not his companions, though if the blues ever come to him, they come with the power to kill. No matter if he goes to bed weary and disappointed, he gets up in the morning as ready for the day's work as though success was surely in his grasp before night. And so the long days and weeks and months and years go on, and the sanguine heart seldom despairs.

He is a trusting mortal, as an optimist is quite apt to be. He sees the good side of everything. He is not trying to live by getting the best of a bargain with his fellow-men. Business with him is not trying to beat some one, and the absence of the strife leaves an impress on his face. The events of daily life do not warp his nature from its natural tendency to open-hearted trust and faith, and he believes in man, in fairness and in justice. He respects the location stake of another, and is ready to mete out to one who will not be fair the exact justice of a miners' court. The tools, supplies, provisions, tent or cabin of a brother prospector is as sacred to him as he wishes his to be to others, and in the new camp he joins with his fellows in saying "woe be to him who will not obey the unwritten code of justice." It is the tenderfoot and not the typical prospector who tries the robbing game. In the camp, where courts and lawyers have not yet penetrated, justice presides and equity is law. In the prospectors' camp far away from railways and cities and so-called civilization, the perfection of government is found. Every man's tent is his castle, and his ounces of gold dust are as safe unhidden there as they would be in the city safe deposit vault.

There is a good deal of poetry in his nature, though perhaps unsuspected. Sleeping with the sky and stars as a roof, daily seeing the crimson, gold and purple sunsets flush along the white snow-banks, and tinge the many-hued rocks and cliffs with countless shades of color, is an existence that touches the artistic, poetic chords of his nature, and shapes it somewhat despite all other influences. His pretty camp fire, throwing dark shadows beyond in the pines, and a near-by rippling mountain stream running darkling down into the willows singing a good night lullaby, aid more in shaping a lovable character than all the glare of gas or electric lights and pulpit or theater shows.

His trust makes him a victim of sharpers. When he is successful and is followed by the gambler and the saloon keeper, he becomes an easy sucker. The life they introduce him into is quite too apt to have a strong attraction, and he is led into many a trap. But when he has lost his dust or the few hundreds he obtained for some prospect hole, he returns to his tent and tramps the hillsides and gulches again, blaming no one but himself. Every camp and mining town is full of accounts of men who squandered fortunes in the strange and alluring attractions of the gambling den and its accompaniments. Bassick, who discovered the Bassick mine in Custer county, and began taking out money almost too fast to count, was tapped and bled for many thousands. It is said that when he was about to leave his mine to visit Pueblo or Denver, the fact was tele-graphed ahead and he was cordially met upon his arrival and greeted and wined and dined and artistically bled by gamblers. But he quit in time and was not ruined. Another quite noted prospector who made a fortune at Leadville, started out to see the world, and at Paris let a woman swindle him out of every dollar he owned, and was sent home busted by a collec-tion taken up among the fraternity.

Geo. H. Fryer, who gave the name to Fryer Hill, Leadville, after making a couple of hundred thousand, "blew it in" and died a pauper. Pat Casey, the first prospector to make a pile in Colorado, about 30 years ago, died without a dollar. So one might go on and give instances without number, all illustrating the ease with which old prospectors fall a prey to gamblers or schemers. The typical prospector gets rich occasionally, seldom keeps it long and generally dies a violent death in some form.

It is a rather strange thing that the great majority of well, or best, known prospectors have died tragic deaths. George Fryer died from an overdose of morphine.

Old Virginny, after whom the "Consolidated Virginia" was named, came to his death by an overdose from a bucking mule near Dayton, Nev.

Bill Bodie, the discoverer of the great Standard mine in Mono county, California, slept his life away in a snow-storm, while making his way to the mines.

Col. Storey, who gave his name to the county in Nevada where the Com-stock is situated, was killed in battle by the Pyramid Lake Indians.

Thomas Page Comstock died a beggar in a strange land. "Old Pancake," as he was known in the mining camps, committed suicide at Bozeman, Montana, by shooting himself. He was the leader of the famous Big Horn expedition that was sent out by Nevada capitalists in search of the Lost Cabin mines, supposed to be somewhere among the Big Horn moun-tains. The expedition was a failure, and Comstock, whether from disap-pointment or some other cause, while encamped near Bozeman, drove a pistol ball through his head and died instantly. He was buried there and his grave is unmarked and unknown.

Near the spot where, twelve years before, the hidden treasures of Alder Gulch were first revealed to him, William Fairweather was laid down to rest. Like poor "Old Pancake," this erratic soul stranded on the shoals of dissipation, although each in his day had turned a key—the one silver and the other golden—which unlocked millions for others, but nothing for themselves.

William Farrell, who "struck" Meadow Lake, died a victim to remorse in one of the leading hospitals of San Francisco, "haunted by the spirits of one thousand deluded pioneers and prospectors passing and repassing his dying bed." The locator of the famous Homestake, in the Black Hills, is said to have afterward turned road agent. Times going hard with him he attempted to stop a stage loaded and prepared for just such emergencies, and he was planted alongside the road by the tender-hearted express agents whom he had tried to rob and kill. Homer, of the Homer district, followed in the suicidal tracks of Comstock. After squandering a small fortune he shot his brains out in the streets of San Francisco. "Doughnut Bill," "Old Eureka," Kelse Austin, Lloyd Magruder, "Nine-Mile Clark," and scores of others, died violent deaths in one way or another and reaped nothing from the rich finds each had made in his day. Doughnut Bill was planted in the Lone Mountain cemetery in Utah, in 1858; a lone grave under a white pine tree in a frontier mining town of California tells where poor "Old Eureka" sleeps his last sleep; Kelse Austin was killed and buried in Elko county, Nevada, 15 years ago.

Lloyd Magruder, while conducting a number of wagons loaded with treasure from Virginia city to the nearest railroad, was murdered and robbed by his teamsters, who were Plummer's outlaws in disguise.

So one might go on telling a story that would hardly have an end.

There is as wide a difference between prospectors and miners as there is between their occupations. The former find mines and the latter work them. Genuine prospectors never mine. It is seldom that they dig a hole more than 25 feet deep, and very few have ever dug more than 10 feet. They find properties to sell. That is their business. They cannot content themselves with the daily humdrum life of the miner underground. A tent is their natural house, and a windlass is the only mining machinery they care to know anything about. Like the birds, they are never so happy as when on the wing to some new, untried and wild region.

When the story of the mountain regions is told, and the development of civilization is followed, the old prospector will occupy the place of grandeur, standing as the pioneer and the representative of honor and generosity in the grandest work under the sun. Song and story and history will preserve his deeds as the ever-enduring bronze on the tower of the only Mining Exchange building in the world preserves his form.

The Mining Industry and Tradesman, c. 1892

The Old California Prospector

The old California prospector, the veteran of the prospecting race, still "lags superfluous on the stage." He is the hoary-headed father of all the present tribe of hunters after the precious metals. There is now little in his line to be found, for, true to his first love, visions of rich gold placers still haunt his mind. He has never recovered from the "days of '49." He was thoroughly inoculated with the golden microbe of the placer, and its virus is still in every drop of his blood. In the "days of '49" he was in his prime. Then no toil could exhaust and no danger intimidate him. He rejoiced in the very wildness of the mountains—in the great forest, the dark cañon and the thundering waterfall. The desire of his heart was to penetrate wilds virgin to civilized eyes. It was in such places he pictured gold-paved lakes and gold-ribbed mountains. Neither the whoop of the savage Indian warrior nor the growl of the fierce grizzly monarch of the mountains could turn him from his path; in the glitter of his golden visions all dangers were obscured—became mere shadows.

The prospectors of those old days were merely searchers after the secret hoards of nature. For untold ages before the foot of the first white man pressed the soil of California, Dame Nature had been playing miner in all the mountains of that country. Countless millions of tons of auriferous gravel and earth had been sluiced down through every gulch, cañon, creek and river that crossed either the channels of old dead rivers or veins of gold-bearing quartz. Thus the golden accumulations of ages strewed the rocky channels of the streams and filled to overflowing all their holes and crevices. The first-comers found little to do but to help themselves to the gold which the mining processes of nature had stored up.

However, in a few years these heaped hoards of nature were exhausted, but this fact the genuine old-time prospector cannot be brought to believe even to this day. All cannot be gone; he will not hear that said. He still believes that somewhere a great hoard of golden nuggets is reserved for his special benefit. Having feasted from the golden fleshpots of the old days, he cannot content himself with the hermit fare of these frugal times. If there is nowhere still a golden treasure to be unearthed, then his occupation is gone—he is ready to lie down and die. It is in the hope of finding this secret hoard that he lives and wanders.

In California the ancient prospector has a modern successor who gives more time to searching for gold-bearing quartz than to hunting for placers. He is a cabin-dwelling animal; has something of the instinct of the hermit crab. He takes possession of any cabin he finds vacant and from it as a base of operations scouts the country for miles in all directions, carefully working over every rod of ground. If he finds nothing he looks for another vacant cabin some miles away, moves into it and begins the exploration of a new region.

The genuine old time prospector, however, does not settle down. He is always moving along in some direction—is a veritable Wandering Jew. He may halt for a few days in some ancient camp, and do a little panning and crevicing to put a few dimes in his pocket, but his dreams of gold urge him on. Again he is seen toiling over the hot and steep mountain trails toward some camp known to him in the old golden days, which seem to him as but yesterday. In mind and heart he is still young. He has grown old and feeble in body without realizing the fact. This is probably because his plans for marrying and settling down in life were all dropped at the time he left kith and kin to become a gold hunter, and as he has never since taken them up, he has come to think that his growth of years and all else pertaining to him as a social being, stopped to await his finding the golden hoard always seen as a sort of will-o'-the-wisp dancing along just a little before him.

The old prospector will creep along mountain trails for days in order to take another look at the ground about the head of some gulch which he knows to have been very rich when it was worked in the olden times. He thinks that at last he shall be able to solve the problem of whence came the gold found in the gulch. He will find at the head of the gulch the continuation of the golden gravel in the side of some hill or mountain. But when he reaches the old camp he will find everything torn to pieces and turned upside down. He will not even be able to distinguish his ravine. Then he will say the Chinese have been there before him, and he will heartily curse them. The Chinese are the plague of his life. On his death bed he will say he failed to find the golden hoard for which he sought because it was discovered and stolen by the prowling Chinese.

In the old golden days our ancient prospector scoured the mountains, mounted on a splendid and powerful mule; later he was contented with a burro, but now increase of poverty has rendered him independent of even the slight encumbrance of a donkey. The old prospector is no new-found friend of mine. I have known him for years and years and have encountered him almost everywhere on the Pacific coast. He is always the same wherever seen. He bears upon his back the same roll of well-worn blue blankets; the same old slouched hat shelters his gray, straggling locks; the same no-colored woolen shirt does duty as both coat and vest, and the same old greasy leathern belt still serves to carry his venerable Colt's six-shooter and to prevent his baggy canvas pantaloons from subsiding wholly into the tops of his huge boots, where about one-third of the length of the legs have already taken up quarters.

The old prospector does not like large towns and seldom visits them. In large places outside of the mining regions he is looked upon as a curiosity. He attracts a crowd and is stared at as the representative of an almost extinct race, one of a type soon to be classed with the mastodon and the dodo. He keeps to the mountain camps. A town, according to his ideas, is only of use as a place in which to obtain supplies. If the place contain one or two saloons, as many provision stores and a blacksmith shop, it is as large as he would have it.

After he has found a saloon that suits him, has deposited his roll of blankets and other "traps" in a corner, taken his "tod," as he calls it, and seated himself for a "whiff" of his pipe, the old prospector is in a humor to be approached. He may then be drawn out and will even become quite garrulous. Still you must be careful in your advances. He does not like a loud-talking man. He has been subdued by the silence of the mountains, and his voice attuned to the murmur of the lone brooks along which he wanders. He never talks so loudly himself as to be overheard in a mixed company; his voice has the muffled, monotonous flow of a gentle mountain stream. No longer ago than yesterday I again encountered the "old prospector." He had found his saloon and was snugly settled for a rest. I took a seat beside him and greeted him as an old friend. He did not seem in the least surprised. He is well aware that he is known to thousands on the Pacific coast whose names, faces and places of residence he cannot recall. The old man at once began to talk about Downieville, no doubt thinking he had seen me at that once famous California camp.

"I was back in Downieville three years ago," said he. "I went up there from Sonora to take another look at the old 'Blue Banks.' I thought there might be a back channel there; I believe I once explained to you my theory of the back channel of the Blue Banks. Downieville was a wonderful camp when I first saw the place. Lord, the gold they used to take out there on Zumalt Flat, Jersey Flat and all about there on the Yuba. Why, right in town was what they called the 'Tin-cup Diggins,' because every night they used a tin cup to measure and divide the gold taken out during the day. I only stopped three or four days at Downieville. No chance at the Blue Banks; blamed Chinamen there. I went up the North Fork to the mouth of Sailor Ravine and looked at the place where they got the 40-pound nugget in the early days; looked about Slug Cañon a bit, then shouldered my blankets and struck out up the South Fork of the Yuba toward Charcoal Flat and Sierra City. Blamed Chinamen all the way along up the river! Then I crossed over by Milton to the Middle Yuba and on down that way; blamed Chinamen everywhere!

"Beer? Thank you, a drop wouldn't go bad just now," said the old man, knocking the ashes out of his pipe and refilling it.

"Well, do you know," resumed the old prospector, after a whiff or two at his pipe, "about two months ago I was again back on the South Yuba, at the old town of Washington. Yes, and being there I thought I'd go up to Phelps' Hill, where I mined thirty years ago, and where I took out the only pile of money I ever made in the country.

"Well, I climbed the mountain straight up from the river—awful big and steep it used to be!—and at last reached the site of the old mines. All was silent and deserted; not even the crumbling ruins of a building remained; not a living soul was in sight. I hardly knew where the town had stood. Hills and trees had been swept away, and great stone piles, overgrown with brush and brambles, filled their places. I could no longer locate the spot where were once my old diggings. I stood on the brink of a circular pit half a mile in diameter and nearly two hundred feet in depth, resembling the crater of an extinct volcano. In that vast stony pit lay all that remained of Phelps' Hill. A buzzard that soared above the tops of the tall pines encircling the great sink was the only living thing in sight.

"I threw my bundle of blankets on the ground at the foot of an old live-oak tree and seated myself in the shade. Looking down upon the chaos of brier-grown stone piles, I sat thinking of—of what might have been. Again I counted over all the gold I had dug in the place before me. It was thousands, but I then thought it was not enough. Now I am sure that a certain young girl who was *then* waiting for me in the old Buckeye State would have said it was a great fortune. As I sat and sadly reflected upon the past, I felt that the loss of the gold was not so much as the loss of what 'might have been.'

"I had just lifted a tear off my cheek, and was gazing at the drop glittering on the tip of my forefinger as a friend I had not seen in many years, when a slight crackling of brush attracted my attention. Raising my head I saw a strange apparition peering curiously out at me through the parted undergrowth. Holding apart the bushes with both hands stood an old man, with straggling iron-gray locks and a long flowing beard that was almost snow-white. On his back he had a roll of blankets and some prospecting tools. His patched canvas pantaloons were of the color of clay, and the broad brim of an old wool hat flapped about his eyes. He seemed posed as the 'owl in the ivy bush.'

"For some moments the old man stood and gazed at me, evidently astonished at seeing a human being in such a lonely spot, then timorously advanced toward the tree at the root of which I was seated.

"When within three paces the old man halted and solemnly said: 'Stranger, this is a deserted and desolate-looking place.'

"'It is, indeed,' said I.

"'Thirty-three years ago this spot was all life and activity.'

"'Yes, stranger, it was,' said I, 'and I was here.'

"'I, also,' said the old man, 'and for years I have been thinking I would like to see the old camp once more. Now I wish I had not come; it makes me sick at heart.'

"'Friend,' said I, 'by what name may I call you?'

"'Edward Hamilton; but in the old days,' said the old fellow, with a faint smile, 'the boys always called me *Dandy* Hamilton.'

"'Why, Dandy!' cried I, jumping up and grasping the old man's hand, 'Dandy, old pard, is it possible?'

"Dandy stared at me as though I had been a ghost come up out of one of the old stone piles. 'And what was you called in those days?' he presently asked.

"'Slim Jim,' I answered.

"'My God!' cried he, looking at me from head to foot, 'my God! is it possible? And now so old and gray!'

"'Ah Dandy,' returned I, 'you, too, are gray and old—are no longer the dandy I once knew.'

"'And here,' huskily said my old partner, 'here, impelled by the same curiosity—perhaps by the same impecuniosity—we meet after a separation of thirty years!'

"'Yes,' said I, 'hither our old legs have brought us—in this desolate spot we meet.'

"My old partner was gazing down into the dreary pit where once had stood a town—vacantly staring down upon the huge stone heaps, upon the scattered patches of chaparral and upon the crumbling banks of red clay surrounding the whole place, forming the rim of the unsightly sink. He was thinking of what might have been. His chin was quivering, and brushing a tear from his cheek he said in a low and choking voice: 'Let us go—let us leave this place.'

"'Yes,' said I, drawing my sleeve across my eyes—'yes, let us go.'

"We camped together that night by the river at the foot of the mountain. In the morning we shook hands and parted, as thirty years before we had shaken hands and parted near the same spot.

"When my old 'pard' and I meet again it will probably be in a better place—a place floored with gold and where there will be no more parting."

"Well, friend," said I, lifting my glass, "many happy days!"

"Yes," said the old prospector, pointing upward, "many, many happy days—up there. The gold of that land is good: *there* is bdellium and the onyx-stone!"

The Engineering and Mining Journal, November 14, 1891

The Tricks of Miners

Among those who came to the Comstock camps in the rush caused by the silver excitement were many mere adventurers—men who knew next to nothing about mining, and who had no intention of settling down to hard work of any kind. They came over the mountains from the California towns and camps because they thought the newly discovered silver mines offered a promising field for all manner of trickery, and such swindling operations as are practiced by men who live by their wits. The one thought of these fellows was to make a "raise" in some way and then "skip" the country. Probably there were also a considerable number of men who at first hoped to make a big strike by honest prospecting, in whom were presently developed streaks of latent trickery when they found themselves unsuccessful and flat broke.

There were in the new camp a set of fellows who might be termed "owl" prospectors—men who haunted the saloons and gambling games all night and then retired to their dens and slept during the greater part of the day. Toward evening, when the miners were coming into town from their work, the "owls" would make their appearance amid the throng that filled the main street, pretending to have just come in from a prospecting trip among the hills. Dressed as miners, they would have their canvas overalls and woolen shirts freshly daubed with yellow clay, and would drop mysterious hints of being on the track of a big thing. Soon they would have "on their string" some of the men of money who were on the watch to cheaply get hold of mining property. These mine-hunters were many of them in business in San Francisco, Sacramento and other California towns, as keepers of stores, shops and the like, and knew nothing of mines or mining; therefore were just the men to be caught by the pseudoprospectors.

At that time a man had only to take from his pocket a piece of quartz and pretend to be examining it with a magnifying glass in order to at once become the center of an eager crowd. Such being the case, the owl prospectors had no trouble in hunting up subjects. They came of their own accord. They would almost force their eagles and double eagles into the hands of the pretended prospectors, saying: "You may need this while tracking up your vein, and if you need a little more let me know. All I ask is for you to give me some kind of a show when you make your location and record your claim."

Once the bogus prospectors had thus tapped a few purses they reported progress daily in the work of tracing up their rich "float," and took up regular collections for tools, powder, fuse, and all manner of imaginary expenses. Once a man had begun to contribute, he continued to do so in the hope of presently getting his money back. The sham prospector, therefore, always felt sure of his victim as soon as he had made a first bleeding.

Men might in those days be heard to say: "I am doing no prospecting myself, but I have a dozen men out scouting the hills in various directions," little suspecting that their men were snoozing in dug-outs, brush shanties and old tunnels, studiously keeping out of sight during working hours.

The owl prospectors always had in tow plenty of men who were ready to treat all the "chain lightning" they could hold; indeed there were men who were jealous of the privilege of "filling them up" and who were suspicious and distressed if they saw their pet prospectors accepting the alcoholic hospitalities of other parties.

In those wild and exciting times men were to be seen on the streets holding piles of twenty-dollar pieces that reached from their waists to their chins, shouting their offers for "feet" in various mines. At that time interests in mining claims were sold by the foot—men talked of "feet" instead of "shares." The streets were full of men anxious to buy feet in almost any kind of vein that yielded a prospect in silver, however small. They had come over from California to invest, and did not wish to return without being able to boast of having an interest in a silver mine. Big prices were then paid for "feet" in many outside claims that never yielded a paying amount of either of the precious metals, for at that time people, even the best of miners, saw no reason why almost any of the big quartz veins of the country should not turn out to be as rich as the Comstock when properly explored. Men then said: "As all quartz veins on the western slope of the Sierras are gold bearing, so all on the eastern slope carry silver."

As all the country eastward to the Rocky Mountains and northward to the Arctic was then a virgin mining field, honest but impecunious prospectors willing to venture out into the wilds of the mountains and deserts could have any kind of "grub-stake" they asked for. They were in demand. In the rocky wilds of the great mountain ranges seen towering through the purple haze far to the east of the Comstock camps, there were possibilities that might exceed the imaginings of even the most sanguine. It would be almost like exploring another planet. In finding the Comstock, near the base of the Sierras, we seemed to have just touched upon the edge of a vast unexplored mineral world. But those who went forth into the unknown wilds would be obliged to brave the danger of being killed by the Indians, and a whole legion of other dangers.

However, if they were ready to risk their lives, many others were very ready to risk the money required. The prospectors could have the best of riding horses, all the pack mules they wanted, the best of weapons and the choicest of provisions—outfits good enough for so many English lords. Money with which to fit out a party of half a dozen men in the very best style could be raised in 20 minutes any day, if it were known that the prospectors were going into some new and unexplored section of the country. The men who undertook these distant and dangerous expeditions were almost, without exception, courageous and honest; they always did the best they could for the men who sent them out. Yet there were a few parties who obtained splendid outfits and then slipped back over the mountains to California, being too cowardly to venture into a region where there was danger of losing their scalps.

The tricky prospectors were found among those who had not the courage to strike out into the virgin wilderness. Their operations were conducted within a circuit of 20 or 30 miles of the Comstock towns. A trick of these was for a pair of them to take up a mining claim in some out of the way place, putting into their location notice the names of eight or ten men known to have money. They would then start a shaft or tunnel and this done would every month call upon the men they had selected for partners and collect from $10 to $20 from each. The men selected to be thus assessed were business men and such others as could not well spare time for a trip of investigation to a distance of 15 or 20 miles into rugged mountains. Some pairs of such prospectors would make three or four "wild-cat" locations and collect money regularly from as many different sets of partners. Occasionally they would do a little work on one or other of their locations—just enough to swear by—but most of their time was spent in reading blood-and-thunder literature, hunting or loafing in neighboring camps.

There were some men who while thus drawing money, provisions and supplies on a worthless wildcat location would be working and spending all on a mine some miles away which they individually controlled.

A man who was supposed to be developing a promising quartz vein in the Como Mountains, twenty miles east of Virginia City, who brought in ore samples and made collections of coin fortnightly and who seemed fast nearing a bonanza, was finally ascertained to be giving his individual attention to wood-chopping. He was doing nothing at all at mining. During a whole summer he regularly collected assessments, loaded his burro with provisions, jingled the extra double-eagles in his pockets and meandered up through the mountains to his Como wood ranch. He was cutting wood for sale to the mining works and once in two weeks, when on his way to the city, stopped at an old tunnel on Gold Cañon and procured samples for the delectation of his milch kine in town.

A druggist in Silver City paid a fellow assessments regularly every month for over a year, under the impression that he was delving in a tunnel on a claim near Genoa, where he had set him to work, whereas he was all the time at work on a claim of his own twenty miles away, in quite another direction.

Very little successful "salting" of claims was done in the early days. There were men among the adventurers who understood the various dodges of planting gold dust in placer mines, as practiced by miners in California inclined to such rascality; but to "salt" a mine with silver was impossible. The trick was tried in several ways, but the ore of the Ophir and other leading mines, which it was necessary to use, possessed an appearance and characteristics so peculiarly its own that it was everywhere recognized almost on sight—it contrasted too strongly with the quartz of outside mines. The few attempts made were by dumping quantities of the very lowest grade of Comstock ore into the bottom of shafts or winzes where a strong flow of water had been struck, and whence it could only be fished out in small quantities. But nothing was made at such games by those who attempted them; they found themselves objects of ridicule and their mines stood condemned by their own action.

In one instance, in 1863, a quantity of silver coin was melted, granulated by being thrown into cold water, and then tamped into holes made in clay seams at the bottom of a shaft by driving down a drill. This was in an outside mine called the North Ophir. For a day or two there was a big excitement about free silver having been found in the bottom of the shaft that could be panned out in grains and nuggets the same as gold, but the trick was exposed before much had been done in the way of disposing of stock in the mine. The assayers at once found that the metal produced contained precisely the amount of copper that is used as an alloy in our silver coins, and it was even reported that the date was found on one piece of coin that had not thoroughly melted.

Before buying a mine off (or outside of) a well known vein—as the Comstock or other large lode—mining men claim the right to explore it in their own way. They pay no attention to either the decomposed ore or the solid quartz already dug out. Their examination is extended so far into the firm and virgin quartz as to make sure that they are obtaining reliable samples. The mining "pig" cannot be sold in the "poke."

There were some in the early days who tried salting their claims by pulverizing the rich ore of the Comstock and mixing it with decomposed material in their shafts and tunnels, but the trick was discovered as soon as it was found that nothing of value could be obtained from the solid quartz. Such an attempt always gave a mine a "black eye," as the miners phrased it, and soon the game was given up as a losing one.

Men of the confidence stripe sometimes played off as coming from mines found in some distant and secret place small pieces of the richest Ophir ore, obtaining from credulous persons loans or gifts of money, "square meals," or drinks, according to what they thought their dupe would stand. Those who practiced this game were generally careful to select samples that contained no quartz. The peculiar grain and crystallization of the Comstock was not easily mistaken—was too well known—but a lump of pure sulphide of silver from one place would be much like a lump of the same ore from another locality. Men who played this dodge would claim to have found the ore they exhibited in some wild region, from which they had been obliged to retreat on account of Indians or some other trouble or mishap.

Able and accomplished liars at times appeared in this line who were capable of holding a long list of gullible contributors for several weeks with no other aid than a few well selected pocket samples of Ophir ore. They were never quite ready to head a party to visit the scene of their find. First they must have money to pay a big board bill they pretended to owe; then a horse and weapons, and finally when they could invent no new excuses, and were about to be cornered, they skipped between two days for California. Even the Piute Indians got hold of this game and managed to draw from their white brothers presents of blankets, coin and other good and useful things. Indeed it was at one time supposed that the Indians knew of whole mountains of silver to which they could lead the way could they be induced to yield up the secret. In some instances Indians did lead parties of miners on wild-goose chases through the mountains, guiding them hither and thither while the "grub" lasted and then disappearing in the wilds.

A trick was successfully played upon a party of San Francisco men in 1861 by some Silver City miners who were prospecting a vein of gold-bearing quartz. The vein was very "spotted" and the pockets when found were small. The miners had a shaft down about 25 ft. on their vein, and having reached a rich pocket that covered the whole bottom were anxious to sell, as they might sink 50 ft. further without finding another spot as rich. In Virginia City they found three men of money from San Francisco who wished to invest in a mine, and who were well pleased with the samples of ore shown them. The San Franciscans agreed to go to Silver City in a few days and examine the mine, when, if they found all satisfactory, they would pay the price asked—$20,000.

With the San Francisco trio was a fourth man who was impecunious, but not contentedly so. This man "approached" the miners on the sly, and saying he had great influence offered to talk the San Francisco men into buying the mine, provided he were given a share of the spoils. It was agreed that he should have $500 if a sale were made. Then it was arranged that on a certain day the Silver City men would not go near their mine, that they should be at work at another place a mile away. On that day their confederate was to take his friends, the San Francisco capitalists, to the mine on the sly and assist them in prospecting the bottom of the shaft in the most thorough manner; he telling them he had ascertained that the owners would be at work on another claim for a day or two.

The three San Franciscans bit at once. They thought it would be a clever trick to steal a march on the "honest miners." They dug into all parts of the bottom of the shaft and obtained wonderful prospects. Free gold was visible in almost every piece of quartz they dug out. In short, they readily paid the $20,000 asked for the mine and set to work in the shaft expecting to get their money back in less than a month. They had not gone down over 2 ft., however, before they were in barren quartz. They did much work but never found anything except a few insignificant pockets. The worst of it was that they dared not complain of their bad luck, for as soon as they had secured the mine they had boasted to many friends of the cunning way in which they had prospected the bottom of the shaft. It was long before they heard the last of their mining venture. When they talked of there being a big thing in a mine their friends would ask them if they had been prospecting it "on the sly." The $500 which their honest friend received changed his luck; he remained in the country and presently secured a fat State office.

The Engineering and Mining Journal, June 11, 1892

A Superintendent
Who Was Fatherly
and "Smooth"

In after times, when all was deep mining on the Comstock, the roving, tricky fellows of the earlier days were noted for "soldiering." They carried their tricks into the drifts of the lower levels and managed to loaf four hours out of the shift of eight. We had one mining superintendent, however, who was a match for them. On one occasion this superintendent came upon a party of the "soldiers" in an out-of-the-way drift in his mine so unexpectedly that all were caught sitting and lying about. Being always "fair," he said: "Taking a rest, my sons? Well, the rock looks very hard." Taking a candle he then pretended to be examining the rock in the face of the drift. While he was thus engaged he managed to smoke a line across the roof of the drift, just at the face.

"Yes, yes, the rock is terribly hard," said he, as he replaced the candle, "and it is too bad, for we can't expect to make much headway in such rock. Well it can't be helped—we must take things as we find them in mining," and he turned and marched back along the drift.

What a pleasant-spoken, good, easy-going superintendent he seemed. When he popped in upon them the "soldiers" had been a good deal alarmed, but as he took his departure they felt quite at ease.

The next day the superintendent again made his appearance in the drift, but the men had been on the watch for him and were not caught napping. Taking a candle the superintendent again examined the face of the drift and in so doing noted that it had not been advanced more than a foot beyond the mark he had made the day before.

"Well, well," said he, "the rock is as hard as ever, my children. It must be very hard work to make any progress in such rock?"

"O, yes it is indeed!" cried all the "soldiers."

"I'm afraid it is almost too hard for you," said the superintendent—"I hardly know how we are to get ahead with this drift."

"O, we'll worry through with it, sir!" cried all the "soldiers."

"An easy going and fatherly superintendent as I ever saw," said one of the men when the superintendent left. "Yes, we've got a soft snap here," said another and all hands became very merry as they softly said to one another—"The rock is hard as ever, my children."

After leaving the drift, the superintendent went at once to the surface in search of his foreman. As soon as that officer was found he said to him: "Do you know the men who are at work in the old drift north on the 1,200 level?"

"Yes, sir."

"Well, they are not worth their salt. Discharge every son of a—of a gun of them the moment they come off this shift!"

"Yes, sir."

A day or two after the superintendent saw one of the discharged men loafing on C street. Going up to him he said in his soft kindly way: "How is this my son—how is it that I see you here? I thought you were at work in a drift on the 1,200 level—the one where the rock is so hard?"

"Well, sir, I was at work there until your foreman discharged me."

"What! Did my foreman discharge you? Well, well, that is just his way. I don't know what I am to do with that foreman of mine. If I ever get a good honest, hard-working man in the mine my foreman is sure to discharge him. I am getting to be a mere figure-head about the mine." And scowling at the thought of the way in which he was being overridden by his subordinate, the millionaire superintendent turned and strode away, leaving the "soldier" a good deal bewildered.

From "Tricks and Humors of Miners,"
The Mining Industry and Tradesman, c. 1892

The Wealth of Washoe

A DAY IN THE SILVER MINES

On a sunny Saturday morning, not long since, I concluded to take a stroll to Virginia City. Without incident or accident I reached the famed Comstockian city, and soon after "sighted" and "bore down" upon my friend Perry C., who was cruising in the vicinity of Paster's. Having no objection to a more extended voyage, we set sail Ophir-ward, taking an outside peep at the mine and making arrangements for an underground survey at 2 o'clock. We then for a time wandered and chatted promiscuously, viewing and noting the improvements in the town—which are indeed numerous and substantial. There are new mills, splendid new buildings and many improvements in and about the various mines.

After perambulating the streets somewhat at random for the space of an hour, and arriving at the conclusion that Virginia was really fast becoming a city, my friend informed me that Mr. B——, of the *Era*, was in town, and proposed calling on him at his hotel. It was with many misgivings and much trepidation that I consented; for I pictured a fierce-looking personage with great, shaggy, gray eyebrows overhanging a pair of piercing, greenish-yellow eyes, with a pair of huge glasses astride a ponderous trumpet-like nose; grizzly hair, standing erect as the bristles of an ireful coyote; a sallow, wrinkled face a yard or more in length; two huge, discolored tushes protruding from his upper jaw, and a perfect *chevaux-de-frise* of pens bristling above his formidable ears—judge, then, how agreeably I was surprised at finding a brisk, jovial, little man, with blue eyes, round face, rosy cheeks, smooth, brown locks and a nose which would be utterly worthless as a pumpkin-splitter. After a half-hour's chat, during which the virtues of a patent beefsteak, invented by an ingenious cis-montane *chef de cuisine*—came in for a liberal amount of praise from Mr. B——, he having conceived a *passionate* fondness for this *chef d'oeuvre* in cookery whilst wandering in the region of the West Walker, my friend and I took our departure for the purpose of visiting the Gould & Curry mine.

"GOULD AND CURRY" UNDERGROUND

Mr. Strong, the superintendent, was absent, but we found John on hand, ready and willing to show us through. In front of the mine is an embankment or terrace, some five rods in length by three in width; and inclosing the mouth of the tunnel is a spacious framed building with rooms for storing ore, after being sacked, and for breaking and assorting rock, also a neat and substantial dwelling house. John presented me a large and beautiful specimen of sulphuret of silver, or silver glance—called here black ore—also a splendid specimen of a brownish quartz completely covered and resplendent with flakes or scales of metallic silver. From a heap of ore in the assorting room, I selected a very handsome specimen of sulphuret of silver, containing numerous showy veins of green carbonate of copper and glittering spangles of gold. John now procured candles, and each with his candle in hand, passed through a door in the back part of the building and entered the gloomy portal of the mine. We proceeded along a smooth, straight tunnel, in a westerly direction for a distance of 250 feet, when we arrived at a point where a north and south tunnel cut across this main one at right angles; taking the south branch we soon reached a vast cavern of darkness. Here a large amount of very rich ore has been quarried, and though we were at length enabled, with the combined light of our three candles, to see and make out the dingy walls immediately in front of us, yet above, our feeble light failed to reach the elevated roof, nor could it penetrate the vast profundity of darkness below, which, for aught we know, might be the bottomless pit itself. But John, being posted on all of the heights and depths of this bewildering maze of shafts, drifts and tunnels, came to the rescue and informed us that this vast collection of double-refined darkness extended downward a distance of eighty feet, and that out of this "chimney"—as it is called in miner's phraseology—they had obtained some of their best ore. We now returned to the main tunnel, crossed it and followed a passage running northward through the heart of the lead—which is some thirty feet wide—for a distance of about one hundred feet, passing between walls of ore which will pay from three to eight hundred dollars per ton in silver and gold—though the appearance of the rock in this part of the mine is rather gold-bearing than argentiferous. In the end of this tunnel a shaft has been sunk to the depth of eighty-four feet, and in a number of places drifts have been cut across it at right angles through the lead.

A DEEPER DEPTH

We now descended a perpendicular shaft, by means of a ladder, to the depth of eighty feet, and passing through a tunnel to the southward for some 60 feet, struck into a passage running west, which leads again to a dark, yawning abyss of unknown (to me at least) depth, completely studded with cross-ties and braces on which rested planks, at very unequal elevations. Now we were stooping to crawl under a tie, again taking a tremendous upward stride, and anon casting timid glances into the dark, profound below, and mentally wondering whether we would ever stop falling were we once precipitated into the dismal chasm, and if we should happen to come to a halt somewhere in the vicinity of the center of gravity, whether John knew of a rope about the establishment long enough to fish us out. But at length we are over, and turning to the east through a large passage, we stand on the verge of that same huge, consolidated chunk of midnight we had been peering into above—i.e. the "chimney." Here we see some very rich veins of silver ore, mostly the sulphuret or "black ore," alternating with decomposed vertical strata of auriferous quartz. We passed back again over the gloomy chasm, upon the rugged plank pathway, but in what direction or where we went next is altogether impossible for me to say, and I hope John will excuse me if I do not make the attempt—indeed, I am not as sure as I would like to be that I am right so far. But I am very positive that we did go somewhere else, and "kept a doin' of it" for some time; and am just as positive that John told us where we were going, how far, and all about it; but about all that I can now recollect is that we passed through a multitude of passages, some of great length, and saw a vast amount of gold-bearing rock; from this I conclude we were in some of the more northern galleries, as there the auriferous ores predominate; then we saw in other parts of our bewildering peregrination, veins that were indisputably silver-bearing.

HOW WE DID IT

Our gentlemanly and attentive guide now piloted us up to a diabolically dark-looking shaft, and announced that we were to make another descent toward the lower regions of only one-hundred and four feet! Another of those confounded ladders!—Lord, how I could feel my hair stiffen beneath my hat whenever I thought of the cleats giving way! In passing down the eighty foot ladder above, I carried a candle in one hand and in the other a walking-stick, which I had thoughtlessly brought into the mine, and when having made about ten feet of the eighty, it caught between the slats and came within a hair's breadth of sending me to the bottom. Having now another *big climb* to make, I determined to leave my stick 'till we returned, and thus have at least one free hand. Our guide started down first, my friend next, and your correspondent, though at the "top of the ladder," brought up the rear. I was careful to secure this position, for the reason that besides the thought and prudence necessary to make a safe descent, I imagined it would be a decidedly unpleasant thing to have the additional fear of being knocked into eternity by the fall of a *compagnon d[e] voyage* from above. I thought of what was told the traveler, visiting the Kurprinz copper mine at Freiberg, who asked his guide,—who had just been telling him that only a few days before a man had fallen to the bottom of the deep shaft they were about to descend— "What became of the man?" "Ah," replied the guide, "he instantly became pan-take-r!" Now, having not the least desire to become "pan-take-r," slap-jack-r or even to be stove-up short-cake-r, I chose such a position that while apparently *first*, I was in reality *last*, and went down the shaft in the same manner that that most sagacious and rather jocose rattle-snake—we read of—went into his hole—namely—pshaw, you know? I think my friend and our guide were a little troubled at having me clam-bering and clawing above them, as they appeared painfully alive to my every move, and were continually calling out: "Long steps here, be care-ful!" "Stick close to the ladder, here!" "Don't bump against this beam!" But, great Moses! they needn't have been alarmed! Four of the best mules in Utah couldn't have snaked me from that ladder! I'll bet you fifty feet in the "Live Lion" or the "Lame Gipsy"—take your choice—that the im-pression of my fingers is to be seen on every cleat on that ladder, and at least three finger-nails are sticking somewhere between the top and bot-tom step.

LOWER DOWN—A NEW LEVEL

On reaching the bottom, we found ourselves in a long passage running north and south, with a great number of drifts and tunnels running across it at right angles and piercing through the lead. We had now de-scended to the water level, and the floor of this part of the mine was quite wet—varying from mere muddiness to a depth of one or two inches. Shafts have been sunk in the termini of the majority of the tunnels and drifts above; but here the amount of water, percolating the strata, pre-cluded operations of that kind, and before the mine can be profitably worked to a greater depth a new level will have to be run in—such a tun-nel is now being driven in by the company. The new tunnel will be about two thousand feet in length and will strike the lead two hundred and twenty-five feet below the present level. Passing through this part of the mine, a marked improvement was observable over that visited above; though we were shown veins and branches of excellent ore above, yet these deposits had an unstable look—shifting apparently from side to side of the lead and showing, notwithstanding the richness of the deposit, that the metal had, as yet, assumed no fixed position in the lead, and that a greater depth must be attained in order to secure that degree of permanence and concentration necessary to insure successful scientific working. But, in the lower part of the mine, not only was the quality of the ore better, but the general appearance of the mine was much more favorable. There was a very flattering increase of metal throughout the lead, filling up between and connecting the hitherto scattered deposits, and showing the most unfailing signs of assuming a position of permanence and perfect consolidation of the contained metals at no great depth below the present water line.

BRILLIANT PROSPECT—BLACK ORE—SILVER PURE

The great tunnel, which the enterprising proprietors of this mine will drive in two hundred and twenty-five feet below the present greatest depth, cannot fail to reward them with a concentrated vein of ore of equal, if not superior, richness to that of any mine in the Territory. In this part of the mine we were shown a vast deposit, in a vertical stratum, of the "black ore"; but owing to the presence of water it is impossible to sink upon it. From a large pile lying near, I obtained a beautiful specimen. We now visited a part of the mine wherein is located the vein of pure, metallic, leaf silver. The vein is cut across at nearly right angles by a drift from the main gallery, and is near four feet in width. Glittering in the light of our candles, it presented a most beautiful appearance. The rock in which it is contained is quite soft, and I scratched out a handful of the glittering "root of evil"—not that I exactly wished for the specimens, for John had given me a specimen of this same ore, which in its perfection was all that heart could desire; but then, standing before a vast bed of silver one likes to be digging at it—you know?

THE RUBY VEIN—RETURN

What a shrine, this, for a miner to worship at! Here he might drill in a hole, and crawling into it, literally roll in wealth. Our guide now pointed out a small vein of what he called ruby silver ore, said to assay at the rate of $10,000 per ton in gold—from this fact I am inclined to consider the vein decomposed auriferous sulphuret of iron rather than the ruby ore, or pyrargyrite of mineralogists. Having now visited all there was to be seen in the mine, we began to think of getting out to daylight. There were two ways to do this; one was to go up the ladder as we came down, and the other to go out through a long tunnel. It did not take me long to make up my mind as to which route I should prefer; but there was my stick. How was I to get that? John decided this matter by kindly offering to go out that way and bring my cane to me on C street, where he would find my friend and myself after we had made the trip through the tunnel. Passing out at the tunnel, on an east course, we at last emerged into the broad dazzling light of the sun, some distance below town, and on going up to C street, found John already there with my stick. After a lunch at Winn's, and a whiff at the "Indian weed," we betook ourselves to the works of the "Ophir."

INTO THE OPHIR—A 2:40 PLUNGE

As at the "Gould & Curry," there is on the "Ophir" a roomy terrace in front of the mine, on which and in front of the mouth of the tunnel are spacious buildings for storing and assorting the ore. Being introduced by my friend to Mr. Deidesheimer, a foreman in the mine and a most gentlemanly man and accomplished mining engineer, who politely volunteered to show us through the works, we mounted into the car for a ride into the bowels of the mine. The car is worked by a steam engine, which also operates a pump when there is an influx of water. Perry stowed himself in the bottom of the car, which stood on a track having an inclination of over forty five degrees, and I "piled in" on top of him, with one knee stuck into his ribs, an arm clutching the top of the car and the other round his neck, with my chin *hooked* over his head. I now supposed we were about as snugly stowed as possible, when there came an order from above to—"Put in that knee!" Finding I was the possessor of the straggling member referred to, I planted it with its mate in the ribs of my fellow passenger with such celerity as to draw from him a grunt of huge disgust, and we were as snugly packed as a pair of sardines. The word being passed to "let'r rip," we went rumbling down this literal "underground railing" at a 2:40 pace.

We went thundering along, and I managed to twist my head half-round and see out of the corners of my eyes, as we rushed through the dazzling flash of an occasional lamp fixed on the roof, that the passage down which we were coursing, was ceiled with plank kept in place with beams and braces, and that it would not be necessary to raise my head to any great altitude to get my scalp taken. It was at one instant a blinding flash of light, and the next a bunch of dark, of consistency to lift one's hat; another flash and more dark in alternate layers to the bottom. As we went rolling down, said my friend: "Well, this is a little, I imagine, like the descent into the fiery, infernal regions! Can you see anything, Dan?"

"Nary a thing! except a red streak of lamps and a blue streak of night!"

"Well, don't you think we must be near the bottom?"

"Can't be over two miles, now! without we have taken the wrong shoot and are going down the bottomless pit!" Bump! and the car has stopped. Hearing a considerable amount of loud laughter, I raise my head and open my eyes during the latter part of my journey. Lights are glancing and glimmering in all directions through the great chamber in which we have landed, and some half-dozen bearded miners are standing about us with candles flashing and flaring in their hands, all laughing fit to split their sides—what at, I didn't know at the time, nor am I better posted yet; but it is barely possible that they may have discovered something ludicrous in the manner in which we were stowed away in our box, and in our lying as still as a pair of pet kittens for some time after the car was down—waiting to be sure the "thing had lit!"

THE "PAY STREAK"

Scrambling out of our carriage, we found Mr. Deidesheimer by our side. How he came down, you can't prove by me. He must have either slid down the cable, or took a deck passage on the car—most probably the latter—but at all events, he was on hand, ready to show us the wonders of the mine. Having each received a lighted candle, we started on our subterranean tour. Near the spot where we landed, we entered a series of regular and roomy chambers of a square form, made by the removal of ore. Corresponding with the rooms, are huge, square pillars, left for the support of the roof. This part of the mine is under the supervision of Mr. Deidesheimer, and evinces a superior knowledge of mining. The timber work is substantial, and most scientifically arranged, and in every department there is sufficient room for carrying on work in the various branches, without crowding or confusion. The "pay-streak" is here thirty feet in width, and has been opened a distance of one hundred and twenty-five feet along the lead; thus exposing ready for removal, a body of ore one hundred and twenty-five feet in length by thirty in width. The floor, walls and ceiling of this part of the mine, are solid ore, averaging $1,500 per ton. In gazing upon these dingy walls one can hardly realize the immensity of the wealth by which he is surrounded. Here are black and apparently valueless masses of rock, which, touched by a magic wand, are suddenly changed to glittering, metallic silver. The storied splendors of the palaces of the Oriental world would be surpassed by the glitter of these galleries. In the dull, unattractive form of ore, the silver is there, and the metallurgist with his furnace is the magician who is able to bring forth the glittering metal; and allowing that we are not able to see the walls hung with a silver web, or silver stalactites pendant from the roof, yet, in the solid bars he is able to produce, we have weighty and tangible evidence of the almost incalculable riches hidden beneath the dingy, soot-like covering of these ores, and learn to look upon the sulphurets, arseniurets, chlorides and seleniurets with almost the same favor as though they were coined dollars. The very floor on which we walk, notwithstanding its dinginess, is one of silver; the very dirt and dust that receives the imprint of our footsteps, surpasses in richness the famed Pactolian sands.

The lead might be said to be sixty feet in width at this point, as, for that distance there is a preponderance of quartz in veins alternating with streaks of "cassing" or "cab." Some of these veins are from two to three feet in thickness, and are within themselves, very respectable leads, and exhibit a very good show of ores. The ore quarried in this part of the mine is wheeled to the incline and hoisted up in the car by which we descended. To show the facility with which the ore is obtained I will mention that on Thursday, late in the evening, an order was received for a lot of ore, and by nine o'clock on Saturday, it was on the backs of a train of mules, on its way below. This lot weighed 7,510 pounds, and was all picked, or dug, by two men. The lot would average $1,500 per ton. We now visited a point in the northern part of this section of the mine, where some men were taking out ore. They do not dig it up from the bottom of the vein, but commence what is called a chimney, and work upward by digging the ore down from overhead. In the chimney we visited, the workmen had reached a height of sixty feet. On the sides of the chimney a frame-work of hewn timbers, put together with mortice and tenon, and as strongly braced as the towers of a first-class bridge, is carried up as the work progresses, and while it serves to support and strengthen the walls of the mine, also affords a scaffolding for the workmen. The reason for working upward is, that every particle of ore as soon as loosened, falls below, out of the way, and the miner, having no loose dirt on his work, can put in every blow to the best advantage, and is not under the necessity of touching the ore after it is dug out.

A SILVER WALLED PALACE

After wandering through a great number of passages, and entering divers rooms and chambers, some of which reminded me of rooms in the

The Friends of the Southfield Public Library
are pleased to present:

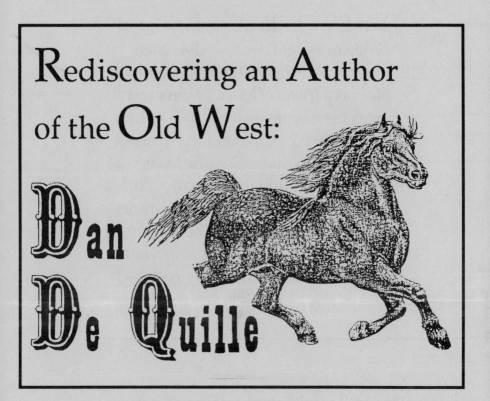

Rediscovering an Author of the Old West: Dan De Quille

featuring

Dr. Lawrence Berkove

Professor of English, University of Michigan - Dearborn

Tuesday, November 13, 1990
7 p.m.
Marcotte Room

Dan De Quille (the pen name of
William Wright) was a well-known
19th century American author and journalist.
He was a friend of Mark Twain's and
was his roommate from 1863 - 64.
De Quille lived for almost forty years in
Virginia City, Nevada. Because he did not
collect and re-publish the many stories
and essays which made him famous
in his lifetime, most of them were
lost until the past three or four years.
His reputation is now being restored.

De Quille published stories, sketches,
and essays in scores of newspapers
and magazines from coast to coast.

One of his ambitions was to publish
a book of his best work.

He never succeeded in
doing it during his lifetime.

The Fighting Horse of the Stanislaus is
the anthology De Quille would
have wanted published.

Chronology

1829
Born near Fredericktown, Knox Co., Ohio

1847
Moved with his family to farm near West Liberty, Iowa

1853
Married Carolyn Coleman. They had five children,
two of whom died in infancy.

1857
Left for California to prospect for gold. Wandered area
between Death Valley and Lake Tahoe.

1860
Arrived in Virginia City, Nevada Territory,
where silver and gold were being mined.

1861
Joined Virginia City Territorial Enterprise, one of the great papers
of the West. Worked as reporter, local editor, and mining editor.

1862
Mark Twain joined Territorial Enterprise.

1864
Twain left for California.

1875
De Quille visited Twain in Hartford, Conneticut,
to write a book about the Comstock Lode.

1876
The Big Bonanza was published. (It is still in print).

1893
Enterprise closed down.

1897
De Quille, poor and sick, returned to West Liberty.

1898
Died.

great cave at Cave City, in Calaveras county, we came back to the point at which we first landed, and taking passage on a ladder—which mode of underground travel I believe, on the whole, I prefer to the car—(a fellow feels as though he could help himself when he has a tight grip on the slats)—taking our way down the ladder, we at length reached a lower section of the mine. Here the chambers were not so numerous or extensive as above, though still of sufficient magnitude and extent to create surprise. The vein is still of the same size, and the quality of the ore equally as good as above. Here, in one place, we ascended several steps cut in the heart of the lead, to a chamber cut for some distance in the solid rock. Think of passing up a flight of silver stairs to a silver walled palace! The very walls, floor and ceiling of this chamber, with the steps leading to it, might be dug down and shipped, for it is all ore, worth at least $1,500 per ton. Viewing the cubic feet, yes, cubic rods, of silver stored in this wonderful vein—the "Comstock"—one feels that the wealth of an Astor, or even a Rothschild, is but mere pin-money in comparison. Why, the 1,400 feet owned by the Ophir Co., would of itself, were its silver made into bricks, build a fair sized city—with enough left to put a brick into the hat of each inhabitant!

RICHER STILL

We next visited—after numerous turnings and windings through tunnels, passages and chambers—a part of the mine in which some workmen were engaged in sinking a shaft in the floor of one of the rooms. All of the ore thus excavated was of the best quality; but there was a vein passing through the shaft of almost pure silver. A number of boxes stood near the shaft into which this was thrown as taken out, and the lumps had the weight, glitter and appearance of pure metallic silver. Indeed, just as thrown up from the shaft it would average two-thirds silver. Mr. D. showed me a bar, worth $8.25, which was extracted from nine ounces of this ore, and these nine ounces were taken from one pound of ore, as it came from the mine, there being a few ounces of rock thrown out in assorting the ore previous to melting. The part of the mine we were now in is two hundred feet in length and lies between the Central on the south, and the Spanish, on the north: north of the Spanish the Ophir Co. owns 1,200 ft. more.

THE SPANISH AND OPHIR BEYOND

Our guide now led us through the Spanish claim to the Ophir ground lying beyond. Our way was along a large tunnel or passage, and over yawning chasms, packed full of the very blackest kind of night. Then we were obliged to cross on poles, often a single pole or narrow plank; and in some places where the inclines crossed our way, the path across them was four or five feet higher than that in the tunnel, and we were obliged to seize hold on the timbers and draw ourselves up somewhat after the manner of climbing up the under side of a ladder. In one or two instances I managed to twist myself into such a position that I must inevitably have tumbled into the "dark profound" but for the ever ready hand of Mr. Deidesheimer, which was always extended just in the nick of time. In passing over these incline chambers in the Spanish mine, which were generally 12 to 15 feet in width, we noticed in all them the notched poles up which the Mexican miner, with his rawhide sack of ore on his back, makes his way with perfect facility, but down which I would hardly have ventured empty handed for fifty feet in the Ophir. The vein in the Spanish is hardly as large as in the Ophir, but is well defined and the ore very black, with vertical ribands of pure white quartz passing through it at intervals. No great amount of work has been done on the northern section of the Ophir, and after examining the lead, which presents about the same appearance as the Spanish, we returned to the southern section, visited a number of chambers on the west side of the lead and met with more ticklish climbing. In a number of places through the mine, we were shown shafts reaching the surface above the mine; some of these were dug in the early days of the mine and are not now used.

A SET OF SPECIMENS

We now visited a tunnel which has its outside terminus somewhere down in town; near which was a huge deposit of ore to run out in cars as soon as the track is in order, when most of the ore will pass out through this channel, as it will be more expeditious than hoisting by means of the car and more hands will be worked. The number of men at present employed in the mine is thirty-five. We did not visit the "deepest depths" of the mine, as there was only a ladder trail and nothing very different from what we had seen above. In going up we did not make use of the car, but mounted to daylight by means of the ladders, which—as they stand at an inclination of nearly forty-five degrees, and you go on the upper side—is not a "hard road to travel." On reaching the upper regions, we were conducted by Mr. D. to a room in one of the Company's buildings where we were shown beautiful specimens of the varieties of ore found in the mine, and I was kindly presented with a complete set, for which I can hardly feel sufficiently thankful: as, if there was any one thing I particularly desired, it was these very specimens, which, if others could not be procured, I would not part with for their weight in gold.

ONE FOOT OF OPHIR

After having "done" the Ophir, we felt that we had seen the elephant in the line of silver mines. No one can form an idea of the wealth contained in this mine until after passing through it and having been inclosed within its silver walls. But few of the citizens of Virginia, even, are fully aware of the extent and almost incredible richness of the mine, and some who have lately been persuaded to "go through," were very greatly astonished at what they beheld. It is said that the Company is now free from debt, notwithstanding their vast expenditures in roads, mills, and other improvements; and now, having everything ready for cheap and speedy transportation and working of their ores, with the mine in such shape that an almost unlimited amount of ore can be raised, they cannot fail to realize immense fortunes. In one pile of third-class ore, which will be worked at the Company's works on Washoe Lake, is a fortune for a dozen men of moderate desires. This heap contains 12,000 tons of ore, which at the lowest estimate, will yield $300 per ton. This mine has never sold for a price even approximating to its real value and there is "big money" in it at present rates. Recollect that in buying one running foot of Ophir, you get what is equal—in solid ore—to fifteen running feet on a two-foot lead.

In conclusion, I would say to parties visiting Virginia city, "do" the Ophir, and you will say that the half has not been told. It is impossible to convey on paper an adequate idea of its wonders. If you should be so lucky as to secure Mr. Deidesheimer for your guide, you will find him indefatigable in pointing out and explaining whatever is worthy of notice, and withal good humored, pleasant and gentlemanly, with no end of patience in answering questions. He intends getting up a model of the mine, showing every cut, tunnel, shaft and chamber, to be sent to the office in San Francisco, where, by building on the model in such parts as they are informed of the progress of the work in the mine, one may see as well in San Francisco as in Virginia, in what part and to what extent the works are progressing.

Golden Era, March 31, 1861

Old Johnny Ranchero

WHAT HE SAW IN THE LOWER LEVELS,
AS HE TELLS IT

"Yes," said the old man, "I went in and went clear to the bottom. When I went down thar to the Con. Virginia works I made up my mind I'd see it all—that I'd go as far into the bowels of the yearth as it was possible to git 'thout diggin' any new holes. I'd never bin in a mine afore and might never go agin, so I told 'em I'd jist take in the whole show.

"When that thing at the top of the shaft, what they call the 'cage,' give its fust little jog down'ard I jist thought the bottom had dropped out'n the whole country for miles around.

"Steam and hot air was pourin' up like we was hangin' over a big pot of bilin' water. The guide to the lower country grinned at me and said: 'Hold fast.'

"I was holdin' fast, but I held faster. Down, down, down we went, seein' nothin' but flashes of light and flashes of dark, and hearin' nothin' but the buzzes of noise and the buzzes of silence, as we passed by the winders cut in the sides of the upright hole we were fallin' through.

"I ain't easy skeerd, but I thought we might be goin' down some faster than the business we were on required, so sez I: 'Hez the trace chains broke, the belly bands busted, or the breechin' give way?'

"'It's all hunkey,' sez the man, an' we then went on about a mile further before thar was any conversation of interest.

"It begun to seem to me like we was gittin' past all the good stoppin' places. Even if that air rope we was a-spinning out behind us, as a spider spins his line out at his tail, was all 'hunkey,' as the feller called it, I was afeerd thar was no end to it and we might go right on through to Chiney.

"I begun to try if I could think of any prayer among them of my airly days that would kiver the case, when the thing we was a-ridin' on stopped with a bump that snapped my teeth together and made me feel up in s'arch of the top of my head.

"We'd struck bottom at last. How many miles down it was I don't know, but I guess about fourteen—mind, I'm only givin' you my impression, gentlemen; I tuck no measurement down thar below.

"At first a great blaze of light blinded my eyes and I felt like an owl out of his hole in the middle of the day.

"'Come along,' sez my guide, and we went into a big country tavern-lookin' place that they sed was the 'station.' It looked a good deal like the inside of some of them stations they us't'r hev up in the Sierrys, on the Henness Pass road. Thar was boxes o' taller candles settin' about, ropes, boxes o' sope, barrels o' whiskey, gin, merlasses, vinegar and other sich stuff I reckon, but I seed no regular bar.

"Ther was lots o' fellers thar that seemed to belong close about, but nobody sed 'Take a drink?'

"We soon left them onsociable cusses and went out into the open country. All lighted up, it was, for mor'n a mile round with candles, lanterns an' bonfires. It was as fine a 'lumination as I ever seed anywhar. Jist as I was admirin' of it I heerd several cannons go off, one after anothur, somewhere up the valley, and I sez to a crowd of men we met: 'Who's elected?'

"'What?' sez he.

"'Is the percession movin' this way?' sez I.

"'Percession?' sez he, lookin' puzzled.

"'Is it under way yit?' sez I.

"'What under way?' sez he.

"Then I drapped on it that he was one of the defeated party, and was takin' no stock in the jollification, so we went on up the valley.

"Men was at work in the fields all about, and trains of cars was runnin' in all directions. The country seemed to be very thick settled.

"It was summer down thar, and the weather was devilish hot. The doors all stood open, and the folks had nearly all ther clothes off—the men, I mean; the women and children I didn't see—all kept inside, I guess.

"We went on up country 'bout four miles, keepin' the main road most of the time. We stopped at several stations. Everybody was a-drinkin' ice water—blamedest people for ice water I ever seed. Plenty barrels and kegs around, too, but nobody offered to treat, but all swollered ice water for dear life.

"While I was watchin' these proceedin's I heerd more cannons go off. Sez I to one of the fellers that had some clothes on half way between his head and feet: 'Temperance celebration, sir?'

"'All cold water men down here,' sez the feller, grinnin'.

"'I see; at first I thought it was on account of your 'lection,' sez I.

"'Had the 'lection long ago,' sez he.

"I see he was a man inclined to be friendly and I asked him how his ore crop was this season. He grinned and sed: 'Above the average.'

"'Where is it raised, anywhere in this neighborhood?' sez I.

"'No, it's all raised out that way,' and he pointed down the valley.

"Next we got on another of them kind of railroads that stands on end and went to a settlement about three miles below. The weather was hotter than it had been up in the valley. I sez to the guide: 'I think we'll have a shower.'

"'Not now,' sez he, 'we'll give you a shower when we go above. Allers git a shower when you go out.'

"What he meant I don't know, for I saw no rain that day, though at times ther was a good deal of thunder over head.

"The last place we went to was the Geysers. All was bilin' hot in that section. Ther was nothin' thar but hot rocks and bilin' water and steam and yearthquakes, so we didn't stay long. We seed only half a dozen or so of naked, half-starved settlers thar that was camped on a small island by a big bilin' spring, which they was tryin' to pump dry.

"Ther may be finer sections of country down thar than I seed, for as I got thar in the night I didn't go far out in the settlements, but for hot weather it beats Aryzona all holler. I wouldn't live thar if they give me a thousand acres of the best silver bearin' land they've got. Fact is I want nothin' to do with silver farmin' and wouldn't stop in sich a place to dig the crap if it was already raised, ripe and ready for the hoe."

Territorial Enterprise, November 18, 1877

The Wolf and
the Wild Hogs

"WALHONDING'S" ADVENTURES IN THE
WHITEWOMAN RIVER

A night or two since some members of the Buckeye Club were telling stories about hunting and other adventures in early times in Ohio. Finally wolves were brought to the front, when it was observed that old "Walhonding" began to grow fidgety. Evidently he had, coiled up in his brain, a wolf tale that he was anxious to unfold.

At last he saw an opening and thus filled the breach: "When I lived on the Whitewoman river, back yander in Ohio, thar was lots of wild hogs in the bottoms. They lived thar on wild plums, hickory nuts, roots, akerns and the like. The starter of 'em no doubt strayed off of farms, but the old ones had pigs out thar in the woods, and finally all got to be about as wild as anything you ever seed.

"We used to build log pens over their nests of leaves, in the fall of the year, when they was fat. The pen would be sot up on a prop, like a bar trap, and to this prop would be fastened a long grapevine; then, when the hogs came in at night to sleep, we'd jerk out the prop, and down would come the pen over the whole family—Lord, what a 'booh! boohin'!' thar'd be for a time!

"But what I was goin' to tell you about was not trappin' of hogs, but a big piece of fun I had one day when out huntin' on the Whitewoman bottoms.

"As I was slippin' along, hopin' I'd see somethin' to shoot, all to onct I heerd, away off through the woods, a awful roarin' and 'booh! boohin'!' of hogs. I didn't know what in thunder was up with 'em, but I determined to find out. It was a wet, drizzly kind of day, and I could git along over the leaves and not make a bit of noise. I scooted along from tree to tree, and at last I come to a place where thar was about two acres of hogs.

"Sich a sight of hogs I never did see. Thar they stood and squirmed about, kiverin' all the ground. All had thar bristles up an' all was a 'booh! boohin'!' at a fearful rate. Thar was white hogs, black hogs, sandy hogs, spotted hogs, and hogs of all sizes, colors, and degrees of cussedness. Mad! they was jist bilin' mad—frothin' at the mouth and champin' their teeth fearful. A sort of steam rose up out'n the wet hair of that mass of ragin' beasts, and filled all the country round with an overpowerin' smell of mad hog.

"What was a causin' of all this commotion I was not long in seein'. Thar, in the middle of the great convention of hogs, stood a big oak stump, about five feet high, and in the center of the stump stood a big gray wolf—a gaunt, hungry-lookin' devil as ever I seed.

"He was handsomely treed and wasn't in any pleasant fix, as he was beginnin' to find out. All about him was a mass of uneasy hair, devilish eyes, frothin' mouths, and gleamin' teeth. Poor devil! thar he stood—his tail tucked close between his legs and his feet all gathered into the exact center of the stump—and Lord, wasn't he a sick-lookin' wolf! He seemed to be thinkin' that he had sold himself awful cheap.

"Right close about the stump, and rairin' up against it was a crowd of some of the biggest and most onprincipled old sows I ever sot eyes onto. Every half minit one of these big old she fellers would rair up, git her fore feet on top of the stump and make a savage snap at one end or 'tother of the wolf, her jaws comin' together like a flax brake.

"The wolf would whirl round to watch that partickerler sow, when one on 'tother side of the stump would make a plunge for his tail, an' so they kept the poor, cowardly, cornered critter whirlin' round and round, humpin' up his back, haulin' in his feet and tail, and in every possible way reducin' his general average. I'll bet his entire innards was drawed up into a bunch not bigger'n my fist!

"Almost every instant thar was a charge made on him from some quarter, and sometimes from three or four directions to onct. Lord, wasn't it hurryin' times with him then!

"When he had a moment to rest and gaze about, all he saw was them two acres of open mouths, restless bristles and fiery eyes. His long, red tongue hung out of his open jaws, and as he moved his head from side to side he seemed to have about the poorest conceit of his smartness of any wolf I ever seed. He had got himself into a nice pickle by tryin' to steal a pig, and he knowed it jist as well as if he'd been human, and was ashamed of himself accordin'. No quarter could he expect anywhere in all that sea of open, roarin' mouths.

"Sich was the noise, and chargin' and plungin' and surgin' to and fro that I hardly felt safe behind my tree, 100 yards away.

"I determined to try an experiment on that wolf. I raised my gun and fired into the air. At the report the critter forgot himself. He bounded from the stump with the crack of the gun, but he never touched ground. Half a dozen open mouths reached up for him, and in them he landed. There was jist one sharp yelp, then for a rod around was seen flyin' strips of wolf skin, innards, legs and hair—for half a minit was heerd a crunchin' of bones, and then them old sows were lickin' ther chops, rairin' up onto that thar stump and prospectin' about for more wolf.

   "'Bout that time I concluded the neighborhood was likely to prove onhealthy, and I got up and peeled it for the nearest clearin's."

Territorial Enterprise, October 21, 1877

Trailing a
Lost Child

To-day I saw in a Pacific coast newspaper an account of a lost child. It brought freshly to my mind a search for a lost child in which I participated forty years ago. It was the only case of the kind with which I ever had anything to do. Children are often lost in large towns and cities, to the alarm and grief of their parents, but the straying of a child in a place thronged with people is not so serious a matter as is the wandering away of a little one into the boundless wilds of an unsettled country. The police are notified, advertisements inserted in the daily papers, and as some one is pretty sure to have found and taken care of the little waif, it is soon restored to the arms of its parents, except in the rare cases of kidnapping. In wild regions, however, when a child is known to be lost, it is necessary to at once organize searching parties and scour the country for miles in all directions. Nothing more quickly arouses the people of a settlement in one of our western wilds than the news that a child has been lost. The sympathy of even the most stolid in the community is awakened. In isolated settlements all are drawn together as a sort of class or large family, each member of which is familiarly acquainted with every other member, both great and small. This being the case, when a child is lost by one of the families of such a community, it is only necessary to mention its name to bring its image to the mind's eye of every one; besides, there will be scores of persons who have fondled and dandled the missing little one, looked into its innocent eyes and listened to its pretty prattle.

My experience in hunting for a lost child was had in Iowa, in 1851. It was in what was known as the Wapse-noe-nock (White Earth Creek) settlement, half way between Muscatine and Iowa City. To the southward was a heavy body of timber, a mile or two in width and extending for thirty miles along the creek—the Wapse-noe-nock—while to the west and north lay the wild and boundless prairie.

One night, late in October, I was aroused by a cry of "Hello! Hello! The house!"

It was about ten o'clock at night. Springing out of bed I raised a window and sang out: "Hello!"

"A child is lost—William Henderson's little Lizzie. They missed her about sundown, and since then we have been searching everywhere. Come and bring all the help you can. I am going to carry the news to the other neighbors in this direction," and the man, a neighbor, whose voice I at once recognized, galloped on.

The farm of William Henderson was two miles away, on the edge of the boundless prairie lying to the northward. My brothers and every man about the house turned out and began dressing, for all had heard the alarming news and all knew the lost child—a little four-year-old. Without waiting to go out upon the prairie to catch up horses, we all struck out on foot for the Henderson farm. When we arrived at Henderson's house, we found it filled with women. Mrs. Henderson was wild. She was determined to rush forth into the prairie, despite the darkness of the night. "The wolves! the wolves!" was her constant cry. "The wolves will kill my poor child!" Twenty women were present, and all nearly as frantic as the mother. The house was a perfect bedlam.

It was not without reason that the mind of the mother was filled with fear of wolves. At that time the prairies were full of coyotes, bands of which nightly prowled about the outlying farms, ready to slip in and carry off lambs or fowls. When intent upon such thieving they are quiet enough, but if balked by the flashing of lights or an unusual commotion, they stand off at a distance and yelp out their disappointment and anger. This evening the hungry brutes, owing to the stir about the farm, had been particularly noisy and indignant. The howl and yelps were torture to the poor mother. Some boys had two or three times gone out into the prairie back of the fields with dogs, but the wolves were in such force that they each time turned and followed the dogs in as soon as the boys turned about. Whenever the wolves began yelping, the poor mother would make a rush for the door, but four or five women, who had resolved themselves into a sort of body-guard, always piled upon her and dragged her back. As the mother was an unusually large and strong woman, these struggles were so fierce as to frighten the fifteen or twenty youngsters collected at the house and set them all to screeching at the top of their voices.

After witnessing a skirmish or two of the kind mentioned, and being unable to obtain any useful information at the house, we beat a retreat. The men were all out in a stretch of prairie that lay east of the farm. Toward them we hastened. Before us was a beautiful sight. Not only all the farmers but all the residents of the little village of West Liberty had taken the field. About sixty men on horseback, each with a huge torch, were seen moving slowly in line across the prairie. The horsemen were about fifty feet apart, and between each pair was a footman. They swept over a wide swath, and when out a mile from the fields would turn, form again and move back again over new ground. In order not to trample the child under the feet of their horses, they did not move out of a walk. At the fields a number of old men were splitting up fence-rails and making torches. Thus they were going over the prairie nearest the house, almost foot by foot.

This unusual sight stirred up the impish coyotes, and they could be frequently heard yelping in the prairie to the northward of the farm, quite heedless of the gun and pistol shots when they raised their infernal howl. The father of the lost child was among the mounted men. He was calm, but his face looked like that of a dead man in the glare of his torch. We had failed to obtain any useful information at the house, and when the father came to the fence where the torches were renewed, a cousin who was with me approached him. "Mr. Henderson," he said, "keep up your courage. Your child will be found; if not to-night, then surely very soon after daylight. What kind of shoes did she have on?"

"A pair of little buckskin moccasins," said the father.

"That is all I wanted to learn," said my cousin—"Take courage, Mr. Henderson."

My cousin then went to a man from the village who had a bull's-eye lantern, and borrowing it, started off alone in the direction of the house. This cousin—Milton Moore by name—had recently returned from the pineries of Wisconsin, where for three years he had been lumbering on the Chippewa river. He was a great hunter, and had been much among the Chippewa and the Winnebago Indians. In his hunting expeditions among the Indians and with their young braves he had become an expert in the art of trailing. I think few Indians could have beaten him.

When he left with his lantern, I asked no questions. I knew he was off on business; I also knew that he did not like questions. Although only twenty-four years of age, he had the gravity and stoicism of an Indian brave. A few years more among the red men would have fixed him in their ways for life. As it was, he did not get the Indian out of him for about three years; he would every once in a while take his gun and slip away to join some roving band of Indian hunters, presently returning a painted brave and adorned in all the finery of a young red man, every stitch of his civilized dress swapped off for fringed and beaded buckskin, and many dollars given to boot.

In about an hour my cousin came back. A large bonfire of fence-rails had been made, near which I was standing. Seeing my cousin come into the edge of the circle of light thrown from the fire and make me a sign, I went out to him and we withdrew into the dark.

"Well, what news?" I asked.

"Bad, bad!" said he. "The child has gone into the hog-pen."

"Great God! You don't mean to say that she has been devoured by the hogs?"

"No; I hope not. I could find no fragments of her dress. But if she escaped the hogs, I fear she is drowned. At the side of the lot in which the hogs are penned is a slough-well about ten feet deep. I found the child's tracks in the lane leading from the house out to the prairie; the tracks turned and followed the fence of the field. Then she crawled through the fence and went toward the well inside the hog-pen, in a corner of the fence. There I lost the track. Don't let the father know. Take a lantern and half-a-dozen men; then quietly slip away, rig some kind of grappling-hooks and examine the well. If you don't find the body in the well, search every part of the lot for scraps of the child's dress. I shall go southward along the line of the field, and if she came out of that pen alive, I hope somewhere to again find the little moccasin-tracks."

Soundings showed the slough-well to contain only about four feet of water. I would wait for no grappling-hooks. Taking a rail from the fence for use as a ladder. I slipped off my clothes, and descended to the bottom of the well. It was a very cold bath, but I examined every inch of the well's bottom, and found nothing but a drowned pig. This relieved our minds of all thoughts of the well. While I was dressing, the men with me took the lantern and began searching the corral, a lot of half-an-acre containing about sixty half-wild hogs of some unrecognizable prairie breed. While looking for shreds of clothing, the men were also to look for blood on the jaws of such of the hogs as were white-haired.

Stooping and groping up to my neck in water had so chilled me that I left the examination of the lot to the others and bent my course toward the bonfires, a quarter-of-a-mile away to the southward. Just before reaching the fires I met my cousin. Said he: "All looks well again. The child came out of the hog-pen all right. I have found the prints of her moccasins in three places in the dirt thrown out of gopher-holes. She is following the main line of fence southward among the cornfields of the different farms, crawling back and forth through the fence. I left her track in the cornfield of her Uncle John Lewis. What I want you to do is to call off the horsemen who are working southward over the prairie. I want nobody to go in that directon to obliterate the trail I am following. Make the father understand this. Tell him that, if left to myself, I will find his child. To convince him that I know what I am about, give him these threads which I found in places where his little girl had crawled through the fence," and he gave me three or four bright woollen threads from a fringed hood worn by the child.

I went toward the half-dozen bonfires blazing on the edge of the prairie, while my cousin hurried away to the southward. It was now about one o'clock in the morning and so cold that groups of men were huddled about all the fires. The horsemen soon came in when I announced the news of the tracks of the child having been found far to the southward of the hog-pen.

"The hog-pen!" cried the father. He had been kept in ignorance of the child having been trailed into the corral. When fully informed of what has been related above, the father cried out: "Thank God that she passed there in safety!" Soon, however, he said: "But are you sure her tracks have been found beyond the hog-lot?"

"Yes, sure," said I. "Here are threads from the child's hood found in places where she crawled through cracks in the fence."

The father clutched the threads and kissing them placed them in his vest pocket. "I am convinced," said he. Being informed of my cousin's wishes, Mr. Henderson then asked all to discontinue the search until further orders.

The horsemen dismounted and, tying their animals to the fence, gathered about the fires. Fence-rails were heaped upon the bonfires as freely as though they had been ordinary cordwood. The men brought corn from the adjoining field and parched it on the cob, either by burying the ears in hot embers or by toasting them on a stick. Armfuls of corn were also brought out for the horses. One seemed in a camp of Missouri jay-hawkers.

Men, on foot and on horseback, had been coming in all night, and a considerable number were still arriving, some from farms five and ten miles distant. Altogether nearly three hundred men, young and old, were in the field. There were present representatives of about twenty families, all nearly related to the lost child, with old Enoch Lewis, the Quaker grandfather, at the head.

News was sent to the mother that the child had not gone out into the prairies; that her tracks were being followed southward among the corn-fields, of the farms surrounding the village of West Liberty. This was news that would relieve her mind from fear of the packs of wolves that had been yelping in the prairie to the northward. The cowardly brutes would not venture southward past the bonfires and the crowds of men about them.

About two o'clock I stole away from the camp and went in search of my cousin. I followed the main fence leading south. I came to where the fence formed the dividing line between the Gregg and Bozarth farms, but still had not found my man. Climbing the fence of the Gregg farm into a great cornfield, I again moved along the line of the central fence. I had gone about ten rods when I was brought to a halt by the voice of my cousin, the light of whose lantern I had long been straining eyes to see.

"Well, which way?" said he. I looked about me on all sides, but in the dim starlight could see no one.

"Where are you?" I asked.

"Here," said my cousin, "sit down."

Stooping, I peered into a fence-corner and found my man lying among the grass and weeds. "What are you doing here in the dark?"

"Waiting. My lantern went out just here."

"Well, why don't you come up to the camp and get another? If the child is not soon found she may chill to death."

"O, no—she has on over her dress a good thick cloak. Her father told me that. She's all right. She's found."

"Found! Where is she?"

"Not far away. She is taking another bit of a nap just now."

"Good Lord! and you lying here to let her take a nap while her father, mother and all her people are wild about her. Where is the poor little thing?"

"Somewhere out in this cornfield. I have not yet seen her."

"If you haven't seen her, how do you know where she is?"

"I'll tell you how I know. I tracked her out of her Uncle John's cornfield to this cornfield on the Gregg farm. She first went a little way into the prairie—I don't know how far—but turned and came back to the fence, as I was sure she would, for the rise in the prairie just there would make all before her the same as blank. She would turn about in search of some object familiar to her, and seeing the fence, would come back to it. Just ahead was the cross-fence of this field, which would bar her way, so I came on and soon found where she had crawled through it, leaving behind a little woollen mitten. I trailed her along the line of fence to this spot. Here she turned into the cornfield, and I had not followed her ten feet before my lantern went out, so I just halted here on the trail and curled up in the fence-corner to wait for daylight."

"But how do you know she's alive and sleeping?"

"Well, half-an-hour ago I heard her cry for a moment, just as children do at times when disturbed in their sleep. I started up, but as she ceased crying almost immediately, I lay down again with my ear to the ground. About daylight, when a little breeze starts up, it will be colder, and she will cry again. Then I may get her; if not, I'll find her as soon as it is light enough to see the trail. She is not two hundred yards from this spot, but I don't know the direction exactly."

"You take things very coolly. Let me go and get another lantern. Think of the wretchedness of the parents. Besides, the child may chill to death."

"No fear of her death from the cold. These little prairie youngsters are very hot-blooded. I have not found it cold lying here in the weeds and grass. I told the father I'd find his child, and I'm not going to have all that rabble rushing down here, tearing through the corn like wild men. Now, go back to camp. About daylight let the child's uncle, Clark Lewis, come on his horse to the cross-fence. Then you come on here, and we will go and get the child."

"But the father, what shall I tell him?"

"Give him this little mitten; tell him that I have not lost the trail and that he shall have his child before the sun is an hour high. But tell him to keep this news to himself and remain quietly at camp. If the men up there want to ride about the prairies, let them go—I don't want a crowd down here in this cornfield."

I went back to the camp and, taking the father aside, gave him the little mitten and as much comfort as I could. A great fear that his little girl was dead immediately seized him, however. "No," said I, "she is sleeping quietly enough."

"Quietly sleeping! How do you know that?"

For answer I repeated what my cousin had told me. When I mentioned the crying of the child, the father wanted to at once rush away to my cousin. "No, let him go on in his own cool, slow and sure way. You will make him nervous and hasty."

Next I sought out Clark Lewis, and by the time I had told him what was required of him signs of dawn were visible in the east. He wished to set out immediately, and while he was getting his horse, I borrowed a lantern containing half a candle, in order to begin the trailing at once; for until after sunrise the light would be dim among the tall corn.

Clark Lewis halted at the cross-fence while I went on and joined my cousin where he was literally and very comfortably "camped on the trail." He was glad to see the lantern, being tired of doing nothing. Besides he had again heard the voice of the child for a moment. "It has about had its sleep out and is beginning to fret because of the cold," said he.

I wanted to rush ahead with the lantern, and prosecute the search, regardless of the trail. "No," said my cousin, "for I am not sure of either distance or direction, except that the faint wailing cries came from the eastward. Slow and sure is the plan."

The old-fashioned tin lantern was found a poor thing for our use. It was only by opening the door of it that a sufficiently broad light for trailing could be obtained, and then it fell far short of the bull's-eye.

Between the rows of corn the ground was covered with pumpkin-vines, fox-tail grass, and weeds of various kinds. I could see nothing. My cousin, however, saw everything. When shown, I could see where a pumpkin-vine had been dragged out of place by the tired feet of the little one, but I could not see the moccasin-prints, and failed to note bent and crushed weeds. As the ground was thickly covered and hidden in most places, it was practically by what he saw among the weeds and plants that my cousin followed the trail.

It was slow work, but by flashing the light ahead to where a vine had been dragged, or a corn-blade broken off, we occasionally went forward ten feet at a bound. The trail, too, zigzagged about—did not go straight ahead between any two corn-rows.

"She cannot be far away," said my cousin.

"She has here been wandering in the dark. Darkness came upon her about the time she turned away from the fence. All looked alike to her, or she would have still held to the mark which had guided her so far—the fence."

Daylight found us still puzzling over the windings of the trail. In eccentricity it reminded me of the trails of the opossums I had followed in boyhood. Not a sound had we heard from the child. This worried me, as I feared she had chilled to death.

"Nothing of the kind," said my cousin. "She has heard us and is lying low. She is in a condition to be afraid of every noise she hears."

Sunrise came and we made better progress. The trail had turned and was leading back toward the fence. My cousin, who was about ten feet in advance, suddenly turned and motioned me to move forward. When I came up to him, he pointed in silence to a spot about three steps beyond where we stood. There in the midst of a mass of pumpkin-vines I saw the lower part of the child's red dress, but her head and the upper part of her body were hidden under some large vine leaves.

The sight gave me a great shock. "My God!" cried I, "she is dead! The poor child has perished."

At the sound of my voice up came the child's head. For a moment she stared at us with wild eyes, then on all fours she began to scuttle away, keeping her little body close to the ground, like a cat when in pursuit of game. In a moment my cousin had her in his arms. She clawed and fought him like a wildcat but not a word of sound escaped her lips.

She had got back to within fifty yards of the fence. As we carried her out of the field, we tried to soothe her, but she would not speak and was constantly struggling to escape. When we had carried her to her Uncle Clark, who was waiting at the cross-fence, and he had told her he would take her to her papa, the wildness went out of her face at once and she cried: "My papa! my papa!" She was her father's pet, and it was afterward found that it was in search of him that she had bundled up and sallied forth, knowing that he had gone to a neighbor's near the village.

When half-way back to the camp we came to the father, who, seated upon his horse, was waiting to hear from us. The child had hidden its face against its uncle's bosom, and seeing it carried in that way, the poor man thought it was dead. "Dead, dead!" cried he. "My poor little Lizzie is dead! Oh, I feared it!"

"Dead!" cried the uncle. "No, she is as much alive as a little wildcat!"

In a moment Lizzie was in her father's arms and almost smothered with kisses. Still, she looked rather wild-eyed, and would not speak further than to occasionally murmur fondly, "Papa—my papa."

Wild were the cheers that rent the air when we arrived at the camp— cheer upon cheer. Then half-a-dozen young men rushed for their horses, and there was a wild race across the prairie to carry the news to the mother, and those who had all night been waiting at the house. Whooping like wild Indians, they thundered along, spurring with their heels and smiting the flanks of their horses with their hats.

The shout sent up at the camp, a mile away, was heard at the house, and the half-crazed mother at once misinterpreted it, crying: "My child is dead. Hear the shrieking! They have found her lying dead!" In vain the other women said: "They are cheering—the child is safe." It was only when the crowd of wild young horsemen came flying in with their report that the mother would allow herself to believe the child safe.

The crowding about of so many men and their wild cheering so frightened the lost girl that she clung to her father's neck and hid her face in his bosom. Then he all of a sudden caught the excitement of the moment, and spurring his horse, dashed homeward about as wildly as the young men who had preceded him.

Unidentified clipping, n.d.

III
COLORFUL
CHARACTERIZATIONS

Painting was one of Dan De Quille's pastimes; it must have been another natural expression of his love of portraying the world that he knew. Very little has survived of his work with the brush but a number of remaining pen portraits attest to his psychological insight and his ability at character delineation.

"Jones' Opinion" is the earliest represented work in this genre, and even though it is only a brief sketch it may be regarded as a sort of self-portrait. As early as 1862 the artist was able to judge himself professionally, with a touch of irony, and wryly admit the justice of a critic's negative inference, from unintended clues, about a model he had intended to picture otherwise. From De Quille's later work, we may in turn infer that he learned his lesson well.

"A Strange Monomania" and "A Dietetic Don Quixote" are portraits of extreme eccentrics whom today we would recognize as mentally ill, suffering from serious delusions. De Quille, himself an alcoholic who was institutionalized more than once, was sensitive to the disorders of the mind. He took interest in personalities his society would have dismissed out of hand as crazy and portrayed these subjects acutely and with vividness. The former story is especially skillful in the way it focuses on a monomaniac yet swiftly evolves into a compact drama of the interactions of the deluded personality with his wife, his partner, and the two doctors. As each of these characters develops plausibly— even the two doctors contrast with each other—the sketch becomes more involved and thought-provoking.

"A Dietetic Don Quixote" is unexpectedly relevant to our contemporary interest in health foods. A tale like this reminds us that "natural food" diets were also in vogue in the nineteenth century; the health books and authors listed in the story are all authentic. Jasper Perry's obsession is profound and severe. De Quille's penetrating analysis of the progress of the disorder is balanced and elevated by a sense of pathos.

"The Earth Never Dies" is one of a number of De Quille stories featur-

ing black protagonists. It is worth noting that this is not a condescending story. Despite his lack of formal education, Uncle Peter Matthias proves himself knowledgeable in some advanced scientific theories of his day. De Quille often created characters who spoke in vernacular. Few, however, were as impressively realized as Uncle Peter, whose intense vision achieves a stateliness of delivery which some readers will recognize as a scientific parallel to Ecclesiastes 1:4: "One generation passeth away, and another generation cometh: but the earth abideth for ever."

De Quille's skill at capturing character through dialogue continues to be manifest in the last three selections. Tongue-Oil Timothy is as unflappable as he is unconscionable. Though a scoundrel he achieves a kind of negative perfection; we are obliged against our will to admire his serenity in the face of danger and the success of his perfect control of phrase and tone.

The central image of "A Female World-Ranger" is the phrase which picturesquely describes her talk as being like "the snapping of corn in a popper." Facts pour out of her mouth in all directions as she flits from passenger to passenger, leaving behind her a trail of squelched conversations. This is a delightful sketch of a meddlesome and officious woman who minds everyone's business but her own. Its understated irony comforts us with the hint that justice still works in the world.

"Rev. Olympus Jump" is another sketch whose appeal derives in large part from its use of colorful mining vernacular. This tale is in the tradition of the story of Buck Fanshaw's funeral in chapter 47 of Mark Twain's Roughing It (1872), in which colloquial speech also simultaneously provides humor for the reader yet demonstrates its serious value as the best way to communicate with uneducated people. The story's open preference for the rough simplicity of a folksy pastor like Rev. Jump over the "new-fangled" clergymen, the "highly eddicated, rose-water, butter-mouthed sort," undoubtedly indicates De Quille's own sympathies.

Jones' Opinion

I was writing a little sketch the other day when my friend Jones happened to drop in. One paragraph I prided myself upon—thinks I, "Jones has a pretty clear head. I'll read it to him and get his opinion on it." I had said of a married lady: "There might be but little flour in the barrel, not a joint in the larder, and no sugar in the bowl, yet her temper never lacked sweetness and she always had a smile in store for her husband!" "Hem," began Jones, "hem, fine woman, splendid woman! but got a good-for-nothing, lazy cuss for a provider!" Now I had endeavored to picture out the husband as being a most excellent fellow, a model man, and Jones' opinion had so much weight with me that I scratched out the paragraph—it really did not present my model in a very handsome light.

From "Letter from Dan De Quille," *Cedar Falls Gazette*, January 17, 1862

A Strange Monomania

A MAN WITH A BEEF'S LIVER IN HIS NOSE—
HIS SUFFERINGS AND HOW HE WAS CURED

A late resident of Owen's Valley, who arrived in this city a day or two since, tells a remarkable story of a curious monomania which took possession, some weeks since, of a man who was his partner in a ranch in the valley named.

The case is so curious that we think our readers will not find fault with us if we relate it as fully as it was detailed to us by the gentleman mentioned above, who observed it from first to last.

The man first began picking at his nose one evening while seated on the porch of his dwelling after finishing a hard day's work in the fields. He was then in excellent health and spirits. He remarked to our informant, who was seated near him, that it was curious, but there was some little thing in his nose that annoyed him greatly, yet he could not get it out nor move it in any direction. During the evening he spent a good deal of time picking at and blowing his nose, and finally went to bed grumbling about being unable to get rid of the substance, whatever it was. The next morning he was still picking at his nose, and worrying because he could not remove the obstruction.

However, after breakfast he went out into the fields as usual. Before noon he left off work, and going home, got his wife to look into his nose, to see if she could discover the nature of the thing which was annoying him. She could see nothing, and told him so. He did not seem altogether satisfied, but said nothing, and presently went off to the barn to work, taking his little boy with him.

Half an hour after the boy came back and said: "Mamma, when I was at the barn

Papa Made Me Look in His Nose

Ever so many times, but I couldn't see anything." This somewhat alarmed the wife, and she went in search of her husband. She found him seated beside a horse bucket partially filled with water. He was gazing down at his face as reflected there, at the same time distending his right nostril—where his trouble was—with his thumb and finger. He appeared a good deal ashamed when he saw his wife, and pretended that he was trying to adjust the bail of the bucket, which had, as he said, got "out of fix."

For two or three days he moped about. He would go out into the fields to work, but in an hour or two was back looking terribly melancholy and distressed. At last he one morning

Made a Clean Breast of It.

Calling his partner—our informant—and his wife to draw near to where he was seated on his porch, he said: "I know I have not long to live. My dear wife—" Here he burst into tears and broke down for a time, but he soon rallied and continued: "My dear wife I fully appreciate your goodness and the kindness of your intentions when you told me you could see nothing in my nose. You did not wish to distress me, but I know now that you saw it. I knew you was deceiving me, so I looked in a bucket of water when I went to the barn to water the horses and there for the first time I saw it—saw it distinctly. I didn't know what it was then, it was so small, but since then I have looked in the looking-glass and seen it. It is growing all the time and filling up my nose so that I cannot get my breath. It is a—oh! It's horrible to think of!—

It Is a Beef's Liver!

How it got there I don't know, but that is what it is. I must soon die. I shall suffocate. It's a mere matter of time!"

All arguments were vain. No reasoning could convince him that there was not a beef's liver growing in his nose. His wife at length became so much alarmed that a doctor was sent for. He proved to be a rough and gruff old fellow and, besides, was a good deal intoxicated when he arrived. He looked into the sufferer's nose and told him it was

"All D——d Nonsense!"

There was nothing in it—not even a pimple; let alone a beef's liver. In short, the doctor went away leaving the patient worse than he found him. He knew the liver was there—that the doctor had seen it and that he was incurable.

What to do next they did not know. The case stood thus for several days. The husband expecting every day would be his last and frequently calling wife, children and partner to his side to give them his dying instructions.

The partner was a single man and was living in the house. The husband took it into his head that on some occasions he had seen things—looks and actions—which showed that his wife and partner were a little inclined to be fond of each other. His hobby in giving

His Death-Bed Directions

Was to get the pair to agree to marry as soon as he had shuffled off his mortal coil. He would tell his boy that he knew John—his partner's name—would be a good father to him. "And, Maria," he would say, "I know John will make you a good husband. He loves you! I have seen it!—I have seen it!"

These scenes were most annoying both the wife and the partner— particularly to the wife, who was so shocked and shamed on the first occasion of the kind that she could hardly hold up her head.

The house was near a road a good deal traveled, and persons passing were calling several times every day. The husband was very cunning when any strangers were about. He suddenly pretended to be feeling in excellent spirits. He would smile and walk about whistling cheerfully—as gaily as any lark. As soon as he could find the opportunity he would get one of the strangers off about the grounds under pretense of showing some tree, plant or other curiosity, and the next thing would be to get him to look into his nose. When the stranger could see nothing he would leave him abruptly, rush into the house and hastening to his bedroom would throw himself upon the bed. Then he would bury his face in the pillows and sob for hours. He would say he knew the stranger had seen the liver in his nose but would not tell him, because he was incurable and it was "too horrible." When told that his nose was too small to con- tain a thing as large as the liver of a beef, a new notion took possession of him. He declared that

His Nose Was Swollen to a Prodigious Size,

And asserted that he knew they could all see it and that they all knew it to be the case. After this he tied a handkerchief across his nose, saying that its weight hurt him without this support.

He was all the time preparing to die and thought every day would be his last on earth. When he found that he was still alive the next day he explained that it was because the liver had shifted in position at the last moment. He was in this condition when his partner encountered, one day while in the town of Independence, a young physician who had heard something about the case and who seemed much interested in it. After hearing full particulars, the young doctor said he believed he could cure the man.

That same day he went out to the ranch to see the strangely afflicted man. He asked his patient very particularly all the symptoms of his dis- ease, listening gravely to all that was said. He then informed him that the disease was by no means new to him; that in Texas, where he had resided for some years, it was quite prevalent among those who had much to do with cattle. He gave the particulars of several bad cases which he had successfully treated while in Texas.

While the physician was talking the sick man was constantly glancing triumphantly at his wife and partner. When the doctor at last looked into his nose and declared that there was plainly to be seen in it

A Liver of the Largest Size,

The patient could no longer restrain himself. "I told you so!" he cried, glancing first at his wife and then at his partner; "I could not be mistaken! I knew all the time it was there, and so did both of you, but you feared to tell me so."

Seeing the doctor's drift, the wife and partner owned that they were well aware of the existence of the liver in the patient's nose and had watched its growth from the very beginning in great alarm, but had thought best to assert to the contrary.

The doctor finally arranged to come the next day armed with proper instruments for the removal of the hideous parasite.

When the wife pretended to fear that the operation would be dangerous the doctor cried: "Perfectly safe, madam! perfectly safe! It amounts to no more than the prick of a needle."

At this the afflicted man laughed aloud, for he felt confident he had found a man who would cure him.

Before leaving, the doctor took the partner aside and told him to secretly convey into the house the fresh liver of a beef, so that it might be there in readiness at 10 o'clock the next morning, when he would arrive with his instruments.

At the appointed hour the next day the doctor made his appearance with a most formidable assortment of surgical instruments—almost every instrument he had in his office, in fact. The man with the liver in his nose was observed to grow somewhat pale as this grand

Array of Ugly-looking Tools

Was spread out before him upon a table.

In accordance with the doctor's instructions, the patient was placed in a large rocking-chair. The chair was then tilted back to the proper angle, when it was blocked up in the desired position. The patient was then securely tied to its back—the doctor saying that he wanted his man in such shape that he could not move a single muscle.

After the patient's arms had been pinioned and his head drawn back into the proper position the doctor looked into his nose and declared that he could perceive that the liver had slightly increased in size since the previous day.

He then ordered a large wash-bowl to be brought and held under the patient's chin, in which to catch the liver when he should detach it with his instruments.

This being done, the doctor selected

A Long, Slender, Glittering Knife,

Which appeared to be as keen as a razor. He took hold of the patient's nose, and opening his nostrils made a movement as though about to insert the instrument. He then declared that his patient had winced, and said he would not undertake to operate until his eyes had been bandaged.

A strip of cloth was then procured and tied over the man's eyes.

When this had been done the doctor said he was ready to begin the operation.

Two or three men from neighboring ranches had been called in to assist in performing the operation, and while one of these held the huge bowl under the sick man's chin the partner brought in a large fresh beef's liver.

He had received his instructions from the doctor. Holding the liver over the bowl he stood ready to act his part.

Taking a small instrument shaped like an awl, being slightly crooked at the point, the doctor inserted it in the man's nostril, and after scratching about for a time gave the inside of the nose a smart prick, at the same time crying out in a tone of exultation:

"There, I've Got It!"

At this the liver was dropped into the bowl, and all present uttered loud cries of astonishment. They talked about its great size and declared that after all it was a real liver.

They said they had not expected this, but had thought it would prove to be a mass of flesh somewhat resembling a liver.

The monomaniac all this time was clamoring to have the bandage removed from his eyes that he might feast them upon that which had so long tormented him.

After some delay his wish was gratified, and he was shown the

Liver Lying in the Bloody Bowl.

He uttered a fervent "Thank God!" and then began to pour out his thanks to the doctor.

The doctor cut him short by thrusting into his nose a bit of sponge fastened at the end of a slip of whalebone, and containing some kind of wash composed largely of ammonia.

After a sufficient delay to prevent his observing that the liver was cold—for he was supernaturally cunning—the patient was released from the chair, and examined the contents of the bowl with great satisfaction. At last, at the suggestion of the wife, a hole was dug in the garden and

The Ugly Liver Buried Out of Sight.

From the moment the man was released from the chair he was as well as ever he was in his life and has so remained ever since.

He is perfectly sane in every other respect, but still thinks a beef's liver was cut out of his nose, though it was observed after a week or two that he did not like to hear it mentioned and at length would blush deeply when it was spoken of.

After the light he had obtained, during the leave-taking scenes, the partner thought it not well to remain longer with the family and so sold to the cured monomaniac his half of the ranch and left to push his fortune in this part of the State.

Territorial Enterprise, September 13, 1874

The Earth Never Dies

WHAT A COLORED PHILOSOPHER HAS TO SAY ABOUT THIS MUNDANE SPHERE

Uncle Peter Matthias, an old colored man who does odd jobs in the Comstock towns, is of a philosophic turn of mind. He has given much thought to what he calls the "univarse" and the "yelements." He has made such great strides in science that he is not at all abashed when he is addressed as "Professor Matthias." He accepts the title as his just due. Uncle Peter lived in slavery all the morning and part of the noon of his life. Could he have enjoyed the advantages of a proper education early in life, and had he in due time been placed in some suitable educational institution he would now probably rank as the Newton of his race.

Professor Matthias is obliged to do a good deal of spelling when he reads, and after he has done the spelling is generally obliged to go on long prospecting trips and delve laboriously into the bowels of Webster's Unabridged for the meanings stored up therein. The words used in explaining the meaning of his first word often keep him hunting and digging this way and that till he is like one lost in a jungle.

He says in regard to this business: "De fac' is, sah, dat when I gits ter peramberlatin' fru de vocabulary along wid Mistah Webstah, I hardly ebber gits back to de startin' pint. I gits so many interestin' definitions while in pursuit of de subjec' dat I'se done forgat all about de word dat I start out arter by de time I culls off de dogs an' stops de hunt."

Lectures suit Uncle Peter better than books. At a lecture the nut is cracked for him and the meat put into his mouth. He never misses a scientific lecture. Whether the subject be Astronomy, Geology, Zoölogy, or what not, Uncle Peter is sure to be on hand. "Radder go widout eatin' for free days, sah," said he on one occasion, "dan to miss yearin' dat talk to-night."

The next day after listening to a lecture on "Reason and Instinct" the old man said proudly: "I don't like to put myself forard, sah, but I could have tole dat man a mighty sight dat he don't know 'bout de queer doins of de 'coons, de 'possums, de squirrels, de owls, crows, buzzards, hawks and de jay-birds. You see when I wur a boy, back in Car'lina, I study all dem creeturs all de time—daytime an' nightime. Den I hear all de stories 'bout de birds an' de animals like de ole folks tell in dar cabins."

90

Of late, in some way, either from reading or from what he has heard in lectures, the old man has got a new hobby and is never tired of riding it. This is that the earth will finally destroy itself, but it will be a case of "the King is dead, long live the King!" or rather of renewed life from death, as is fabled of the Phoenix. The earth will not be blotted out; all that it now contains will remain, but it will be an uninhabitable waste of water—water will everywhere cover its surface to a great depth. The constantly increasing rotundity of the earth will destroy it. The attraction of gravitation will finally do the work.

A few nights ago Professor Matthias got a crowd of his people together and gave them his ideas in a lecture. As it was understood that it was to be a lecture on the "End of the World," a very attractive subject to his people, there was a large attendance.

The "Professor" at once pitched into the very heart of his subject. Said he: "Now you jist look a-heah—jes look about you an' see what is gwine on; jes look an' see what's gwine on under yer eyes every day o' yer lives. Look whar de water runs in de gutter; look whar de dust blows off'n de hill—off'n de side of Mount Davidson—look whar de boy fro dat rock an' see whar it stays. De sand an' de sejiment don't run up hill in de gutter; de dus' dat blows off'n de mountain don't never go back up dar; de stone what de boy fro's don't roll up de hill when it stops—even if de boy fro it up de hill, it makes a little run on its own account to go down again.

"Now dese little instances what I puts out afore you fust is but some of de smallest an' de mos' unsignificant. Look at de work whar it's gwine on big. See de mighty mass of de landslide; de big rocks tumbled down by de avalanche, an' de square miles o' sile dat's all de time floatin' down de ribbers. All is gwine down, down, down. De frost an' de sun, de wet an' de dry, makes de hardes' rock come to pieces, an' even if it's only a grain at a time dar's a drop o' water to help dat grain long down into de ocean.

"Nuffin can't go up on 'count of grabitation, darfore, course o' time dis heah yeath gwine to be perfec'ly roun' an' smoove as a billiard ball. All de holes and de hollers in de yeath an' in de ocean, an' in de seas an' lakes bein' filled up dar is gat to be a place for de waters, an' de waters dat already cubbers two-third of de planet will get on top and cubber it all. Dats what we'll all see jes as soon as dis heah yeath wears down smoove an' gits to be perfeckly roun'. Dar's no help for it! de water is bound to keep on de top, an' in de course of time it gwine to be everywhar. Dis heah yeath den will be whirlin' round fru space nuffin' but a big ball of water to all 'pearance—de water will kiver it all ober, jist as de peel kivers de orange.

"It's gwine to be a long time 'fore dis knobby ole footstool of de Mearster gits to be perfeckly roun' an' smoove, but it's gat to come—it's a mere mattah of time. But when it's all groun' down smoove, an' all cubbered wid water, dat ain't de end of it. No, sah! De world nebber, neber die. When de yeath is all ober water den will come de mighty tide—de tide dat will roll round and roun' de globe. Dar will be nuffin' to stop and nuffin' to break dat tide; it will grow bigger an' bigger, an' de waters will be sich a mighty mass dat dey will draw all arter dem. Fust de sand an' de seji-ment will start, den de bowlders an' de loose rocks will begin to trab-ble—all dat is loose will foller and begin to roll roun' de yeath wid dat tide. Dey will grind down de rocks as dey trabble ober dem; what is lef' of de roots of de mountains will 'gin to split an' come to pieces, an' all will go on grindin' an' grindin' in dat big tide till dey's groun' to powder, jist like de ore in de arastra, an' still on till all de water gits to be mud, and on till de mud gits to be so thick dat it can't make any more tide.

"At de end ob dis operation you'll have a great ball made up of a mixtur of all de iron and all de sulphur an' all de yelements an' chemickals in de yearf. De sulphur an' de iron, an' all de chemickals, den git into a ferment and heat an' take fire, den de whole yearf gwine to be a blazin' sun, jist like it's been many times befo'. Finally it'll burn out, an' de waters dat's been up in de air in de shape of wapor will settle back on de yearf into de big holes an' hollers left by de 'ructions dat's bin goin' on in de yearth while it was a coolin' down.

"Den dar will be rains and seasons. On de high parts grass and yarbs will begin to grow, an' livin' things begin to appear, an' so on for ages till we again gits to be what we is now. Den de yearth begins to wear down agin an' goes on a-wearin' down till it goes fru anoder fire an' gits born agin. Dat's de way de business goes on. De world nebber dies—nebber, nebber dies."

From a manuscript in the William Wright Papers archive, courtesy of the
Bancroft Library, the University of California–Berkeley

A Dietetic Don Quixote

STRANGE DISCOVERY NEAR THE COMSTOCK

**HOW JASPER PERRY OF MASSACHUSETTS DIETED HIMSELF
TO DEATH—MEMORANDA FOUND IN HIS HUT—FIGHTING TO
THE DEATH**

Virginia City, Nevada, Aug. 28.—Last week Jasper Perry, an eccentric being, known to few persons in this community except by sight, was found lying dead in his cabin, situated six miles north of this city. News of the man's death was brought to town by some wood cutters. These men say that Perry was a strange, melancholy man, who had always lived alone, and for whose society none of them much cared, as he was ever preaching to them, and groaning over the ignorance of mankind in general, in regard to matters pertaining to diet. He constantly asserted that all were debasing themselves, and lowering the intellectual standard of the race by their grossness in feeding—by gormandizing on flesh, meats, and many other kinds of stimulating food which bloated up the mere physical man at the expense of the spiritual. He was fond of quoting the German punning proverb—"Der Mensch *ist* was er *isst*" [man is what he eats]. He claimed that he was pursuing a dietetic course which was strengthening, and expanding his spiritual nature, and declared that if all mankind would but follow his rules, there would be no more wars or contentions in the world. All would be peace, and the "lion and the lamb would lie down together."

Perry's strange appearance never failed to attract much attention as he passed through the town. He was always seen driving before him three venerable and dilapidated donkeys—animals that looked as if forced to conform to some of their master's notions in regard to dietetics. Jasper Perry was a tall, gaunt, hungry-looking man, apparently about fifty years old; though his sallow complexion, his wrinkles, his deep-set eyes, and his long, tangled beard and iron-gray hair may have given him the appearance of more years than he had seen. His little train of donkeys always came into town laden with wood and went out bearing bundles of hay, topped out with bunches of turnips, beets, radishes, and onions. His few garments, ancient in fashion and coarse in fabric, hung loosely about his lean body and shrunken limbs, seeming to rest here and there upon some gristly protuberance of his angular frame. Even his long and peculiarly shaped head appeared to have shrivelled away like a gourd prematurely gathered, and his old-fashioned, napless plug hat was every moment slipping down over his eyes and ears, while in the ample circumference of his boot tops his churning legs had great latitude for play. As the grim, hollow-eyed shadow stalked along the middle of the street, goadstick in hand, turning no look to right or left, you were strongly reminded of the figure of the Knight of La Mancha, as that famous champion of the weak and distressed appeared when dismounted.

From Coroner Miot and his assistants, who went out into the hills to get the body, we have obtained some particulars in regard to the dead philosopher's cabin and its contents. In one corner of the earth-floored hut was spread a rude couch, the mattress made of old sacks filled with hay, and resting upon a few pine boughs and bunches of sage brush. Upon this lay the body of the dead man. Near his head stood a small pine box which had served as a candle stand.

As to the reason of the bed being placed on the ground, Perry's neighbors, the woodchoppers, explained that he had peculiar notions in regard to the beneficial effects of sleeping on the ground, "on the bosom of his mother," as he expressed it. He said the earth was man's first couch, and his natural resting place. He claimed that by sleeping on the ground he absorbed a proper supply of electricity, and that salutary emanations from the depths of the earth ascended to his nostrils, which, being inhaled before too much diluted with the common atmosphere, exerted a benign influence on his brain.

Several long shelves were fixed against the logs of one wall of the cabin, all of which were loaded with dusty books, magazines, and pamphlets. Upon opening a large trunk that stood at the foot of the couch, it was found to be completely filled with a queer collection of literary rubbish. All the books were gathered up and brought to town; also a great scrap book and a sort of journal or diary, in which are found recorded the results of experiments made and various thoughts upon dietetics. Over the fireplace was nailed the skull of an ox, resting upon which was a human skull—evidently that of a Piute Indian—with the inscription, "The Eater and the Eaters."

The books brought in and which are now at the office of Coroner Miot, appear to be all, or mainly, such as treat of dietetic matters, the titles running as follows: "What to Eat," "Mace's Servants of the Stomach," the "Vegetable Advocate," "Dietetic Reformer," the "Vegetable Messenger," "Mace's History of Bread and its Effect on the Organization of Men and Animals," "Butter Chemically Considered," "What We Eat," "How to Detect Adulteration in Our Daily Food and Drink," "Plain Thoughts on the Art of Living," and a hundred others of the same kind.

The old gentleman was evidently misled by the title of the volume last named, as it proves to be a series of lectures on the moral and religious topics delivered to young men and women by the Rev. Washington Gladding. One may easily imagine the vexation of the poor fellow when he came to examine the book.

Strange to say, we found among the books the "American Home Cook Book." On the first blank leaf, however, Perry had recorded his protest. "A most pernicious volume." It was evident that he had read much that is contained in the "vicious" work, as beneath several of the most valuable recipes are found written such comments as "Noxious mess, a delusion and a snare, a device of the devil, sugar-coated and lollipopped death!"

All that was found in the cabin besides what has been mentioned was a table, a bench, a camp kettle, and an old cast iron tea kettle. Nothing in the way of food was found save a few withered turnips and a sack containing a few pounds of what appeared to be a mixture of graham flour and sawdust, with part of a cake baked in the ashes and more resembling sandstone than bread. The cake was found lying on the stand beside his candlestick, and marks could be seen showing where he had tried to gnaw it.

Outside of the cabin was found a furnace roughly constructed of rocks and mud and containing a rude kind of still, made of old kerosene cans and a tin pipe, where the neighbors said the old man boiled or distilled all the water he used. He had much to say to those of his neighbors who found him at this work of the danger to be apprehended from bacteria and beheld all things in nature swarming with bacterial life. Micrococci, bacilli, and the like were ever present in his mind. He waged a never-ending war against all manner of infinitesimal creatures. They were in the air, the water—everywhere. He could escape danger from meats by not eating them, yet the *contagium* virum was vigilantly to be guarded against in many other directions. This *contagium* virum gave him great concern. In his diary, where he speaks of the completion of his boiling furnace and still, he says:

The theory of a *contagium* virum is fortified by the fact that boiling takes away the power to do harm from the infected fluids.

Just below this he says:

Dr. Sangrando of Valladolid was right in causing his patients to drink hot water or water that had been boiled, but his practice of blood letting was all wrong, and caused him to lose many patients, as we are informed by his assistant, Gil Blas.

All the water used in making his unsavory bread was either boiled or distilled. In his journal he attributes a fit of sickness with which he was stricken to his having mixed his bread with water that had not been boiled. He gives two or three pages to the matter. For a long time after using the impure water he was of the opinion that the animaliculæ that survived the baking were still in his stomach, where they were growing into monsters.

His scrap book is ponderous, pasted full of paragraphs clipped from newspapers, all of which have some bearing on his hobbies. He seems to have been early afflicted with a great dread of trichinæ and other pernicious parasites infesting the flesh of various living animals. There is in the scrap book the substance of almost everything that has ever been written in regard to such things—rinderpest, animaliculæ in water, in milk, in vinegar, and in everything else, down to potato rot. He also greatly mistrusted the air, and had a wholesome dread of atmospheric germs, being ever in arms against bacteria, which were, in his eyes, more formidable than were dragons to the knights of old. His book is full of Dr. Sansom's speculations on the subject. In one place in his diary he writes in despair:

> There seems to be no escape from the conclusion that the germs of fungi everywhere exist in the air.

Perry seems long to have been in the habit of jotting down his resolves and reflections, but without date and without much order. In beginning his diary he says:

> It is now twenty years since I ceased drinking liquor—fifteen since I have tasted tea or coffee, or any other such enervating slops, and over ten years since I have eaten meat. I made a great mistake in continuing the use of milk for nearly a year after leaving off meat. I agree with Schrodt, the Swiss dietist, in what he has set down in his "Natur Heilkunde," when he says that our natural food is such vegetables as can be eaten raw, cereals, nuts, roots, honey, and all kinds of fruits; but I am shocked that he should allow milk and eggs. We cannot be too careful if we would attain to spiritual and intellectual perfection. Dr. Radcliffe, the great English physician, speaks like a god when he says: "If we could solve the problem of diet, it would almost amount to a rediscovery of paradise. Wrong eating and drinking, and the breathing of vitiated air (which is gaseous food)—these form the triple fountain head of nearly all our diseases and our misery."

Immediately following the foregoing we find:

Thoughts on flesh eating.—He must have been a bold and a bad man that first killed and ate an animal. If he had any idea of a Supreme Being he must for a time have been troubled with guilty fears, and must have been ashamed to reveal to his fellow men what he had done. The Almighty never intended that man should eat flesh. When He gave him dominion over all things He said nothing about his eating them, but said: "Behold, I have given you every herb bearing seed, which is upon the face of all the earth, and every tree, in the which is the fruit of a tree yielding seed; to you it shall be for meat." May not the eating of meat have been the original sin? * * * Two hundred million Hindoos abstain from animal food.

Further on he writes:

I have this day taken possession of my cabin. It is no palace; what of that? I must live alone to carry out my ideas. At the restaurants they would poison me with milk and the fat of animals—grease in the vegetables, grease in the very bread. Good God, to think that but eight years ago I should have had the weakness to grease the sides of my bake kettle with a filthy bacon rind! * * * *Lotophagi* (lotus eaters)—A stranger living with these people a short time cares not to return to his home and kindred, so kind and gentle are these vegetable-eating tribes.

Further on he says:

To-day I discontinued the use of salt. It is a mineral and a poison. The stomach of man is no assayer's crucible to be filled with minerals. Soda I have not used in some years. What nutriment can there be in minerals? Clearly, none!

Turning to the middle of the book we find:

I am in doubt as to the minerals in water; but as I now distill all I use I am of the opinion that the minerals are left behind. But ah! the air! The air! The air is far from what it should be. All the scientists find it bad: some in one respect, some in another. It is much tainted and filled with corruption. Having been used over and over again for ages on ages by millions on millions of human beings and other breathing creatures (serpents, poisonous reptiles, and insects), it can but be in a foul and unwholesome condition. * * * * Of late years they have discovered that the air contains an ingredient called ozone. This ozone I greatly distrust. I think it indicates putrefaction—shows that our atmosphere is growing too old—is wearing out. I must contrive some plan whereby I may purge and purify the air I am obliged to breathe. It is very dangerous and filthy stuff—breeds germs. Some kind of respirator in combination with a vegetable disinfectant, like onions or garlic, may answer. The quantity of air inhaled by an adult in twenty-four hours amounts, on an average, to 300 cubic feet, or 2,000 gallons, or 730,000 gallons a year. My God! to think of the bacteria that may be contained in over half a million gallons of air! * * * Dr. Max von Pettenkoffer has wisely said: "Clothes are the weapons with which civilized man fights against the atmosphere as far as it is inimical, the means by which he subjugates this his element. Ornament must be the minor consideration, and the tailor ought not to hold his scissors as a sceptre over the hygienic purposes of dress." Clothing, however, cannot defend us against the air we are obliged to breathe.

Perry had even been through Burton's "Anatomy of Melancholy," and pages of his journal are filled with lists of articles of food that are unwholesome. There we discover why he ceased using milk:

Burton says: "Milk, and all that comes of milk, is bad. It soon turns to corruption, and produces an unclean stomach, headache, and other disorders."

Following are specimens of other jottings:

Cyrus, King of Persia, according to Xenophone, was brought up on a diet of water, bread, and cresses, till up to his fifteenth year, when honey and raisins were added. * * * "Do you know," asked Cyrus, "how invincible men are who can live on herbs and acorns?" * * * Corsican farmers live all winter on dried fruit and *polenta*—chestnut meal. * * * Shamyl, the heroic Circassian, for the two years preceding his capture, defied the power of the Russian empire on a diet of water and roasted beechnuts. * * * Silvio Pellico, the Italian patriot, subsisted seven years in an Austrian bastile on coarse rye bread and water. * * * Jews prohibited eating pork, rabbit flesh, &c., may try grasshoppers, as they are not flesh meat. The Piutes eat them, but will not eat pork. * * * Mem.—To inquire of some German with regard to the work called "Der Geist der Kochkunst."

Not to weary the reader with the odd notions and wild speculations of the strange being, we will turn at once to the last page or two of his diary. There he writes:

Strange that I should now be ill—should be stretched out on my bed—should feel this deathlike weakness! I have procured and read all the best works on dietetic and hygienic subjects, and have implicitly followed their rules. One by one, most relentlessly, have I given up, year by year and month by month, every article of food that any one of them has spoken of as being injurious or unwholesome. I have even this day eschewed turnips, and now eat nothing but my black bread. I cannot have failed in diet. The philosophers of antiquity were wont to say: "God needs nothing, and he is next to Him who can do with next to nothing." * * * I feel that I have not failed in diet. For some days I have strongly suspected that in my clothing lies the fault. My shirt and drawers are woollen. Wool is animal matter and of the rankest kind—as bad as flesh, if not worse. This animal matter I have absorbed through the pores of my skin. It has penetrated my whole system—has even forced its way into my stomach. I feel it there and in my duodenum, where it now struggles with the bile and the pancreatic juices. It is sapping my very life. Oh, that I had in time adopted a purely vegetable dress!

Finally, we read what was written by the poor deluded man in his last hours, when the fingers that held the pencil were beginning to stiffen:

To-day I have been much distressed; also was last night. I am troubled with visions! Why do I imagine that I see tables loaded with meats? At times I am almost persuaded that I smell the breath of fowls. Strange that these things should smell savory—so savory! My God! have I been wrong all these years? But, no, it cannot be. No; it is a temptation of Satan! I have followed all I could find in my books. I must rise superior to dreams and visions—to my weakness. Ah! this faintness—this chilly sinking! Alas! my woollen clothing. I have erred in no other respect. Yes, yes. I here record with my failing, dying hand that it was the clothing—the rank, fatty, animal matter—in the—in my—in my—

Here the pencil evidently fell from the hand of the poor wretch, and the record ends.

At the inquest held by Coroner Miot a post-mortem examination showed that the stomach of the deluded man contained nothing save a round lump of husky matter about the size of a billiard ball and almost as hard as wood. The verdict of the jury was that "The deceased, Jasper Perry, was a native of Massachusetts, aged about 45 years, and came to his death from starvation, self-imposed, in the belief that he was following dietetic rules that would preserve his health and improve his intellectual faculties, and not with the intention of committing suicide."

New York Sun, September 13, 1885

Tongue-Oil Timothy Dead

INTERESTING INCIDENTS IN THE CAREER
OF A WESTERN GAMBLER

THE PROFESSIONAL CAREER OF A MAN OF GENIUS—
HOW HE SOOTHED A GANG OF SOUTHERN GAMBLERS—
HIS SWINDLE OF WASATCH SAM

Virginia City, Nev., Nov. 20.—A letter received months ago from a friend at Butte, Montana, informs me of the death in that place of "Tongue-Oil Timothy," a former Nevadan, and in his sphere a great and a good man.
My friend says:

> He died in bed, with his boots off, passing away peacefully with the sweet month of June.

The departed was a man of genius in his walk and way of life. His like "we ne'er shall see again." It being the rule to give no word of encouragement to a man of genius during his lifetime, I feel at liberty—now that Tongue-Oil Timothy can in no way be benefited by what I shall say of him—to drop at least one leaf of "Daphne's deathless plant" upon his tomb.

In oily smoothness of discourse and plausibility of manner he was a man without compare. Virulent polemics were by him detested. His occupation, that of a dealer of the noble game of faro, was one that furnished him endless opportunity for the exercise of his peculiar talent of tongue. He was so smooth and oily in all his walks in life that it is hard to find anywhere in his career a protruding point on which to lay hold. He seems at the first glance a promising subject, but, like the Irishman's flea, when we put our finger on him he is not there.

TONGUE-OIL TIMOTHY SOOTHES A DEN OF LIONS

Tongue-Oil Timothy generally dealt his own game, moving from town to town as the grass grew short. I shall give a brief account of Timothy's professional visit to Sulphuropolis, a well-known Nevada town, which would smell the same by any other name.

Timothy had heard much of this town as being one in which shekels abounded; but he had also heard from the few of his fellow craftsmen who had lived to leave the place that its inhabitants were not such as yielded tamely to the hand of the spoiler. It was the great stronghold in the State of men born south of Mason and Dixon's celebrated line.

As the gentle dove goes cooing into the strange dovecote, so Tongue-Oil Timothy entered the town of Sulphuropolis. Unostentatiously he secured a large room in the rear of the barroom of the principal hotel, and smilingly he spread forth his net.

The people came—for it had been long since the beast of the jungle had ventured to show himself in the town—the people came, they saw, and were conquered. Smilingly Timothy raked their shekels into his drawer. With oily tongue, and in a saddened and sympathetic tone, he deprecated their losses, and almost tore his hair when one that he was cheering on and in whom he seemed to feel an almost fatherly interest was a continual loser.

The majority of those gathered about the lair of Timothy's pet Bengal were fiery sons of the chivalrous South; men of the half-horse, half-alligator strain. To guide his bark and ride serene in the midst of this turbulent element taxed the peculiar genius of Timothy to the utmost, yet he was equal to the situation. As they saw their golden pieces depart and their piles of silver melt away, not unfrequently was there heard among those surrounding Tongue-Oil Timothy's hoard the sound of grinding teeth. Sighs that shook strong frames forced their way from brazen breasts, and often great hairy hands, twitching nervously, went back and toyed with the buckhorn of a bowie, or rested upon the ivory hilt of Colt's incomparable invention.

At such times—times that try men's souls—Timothy shone forth in almost God-like greatness. He saw nothing. A serene smile of peace and good-will toward all mankind played upon his lips, and his eyes, soft in their gaze as a maiden's, glanced from face to face as in mellow tones he discoursed of other scenes in other lands. Not a thought gave he to the board or the piles of gold before him. His heart was not in them, but absent and roaming in the sunny South, where he thought it well to locate the home of his childhood. Amazed and dumfounded at beholding this exhibition of child-like innocence and serenity, the wretched and ruined men would stand and impatiently gaze into one another's faces, the long, knotted fingers would slowly relax their grasp upon the hilts of gleaming weapons, and a perfect calm would ensue. The troubled waters acknowledged the soothing oil.

Thus time—a whole month—passed on, and there, in the day and in the dead vast middle of the night, sat Tongue-Oil Timothy, smiling, cooing, and raking in the spoils of the toiling sons of Sulphuropolis. At last he had gathered in the last slick quarter. The town was cleaned; the grass mown to the very roots. Timothy had packed his apparatus, and was prepared to set out in search of fresh fields and pastures new. On the eve of his departure he was far from being easy in mind. It had been wafted to his ears that before he left he was to be made to smell something savoring more strongly of the infernal regions than did the furnace fumes of Sulphuropolis.

The stage which was to bear him away, and with him his heavy sacks of coin, was soon to drive around to the front of the hotel. Many—alas! all too many—of his old customers thronged the barroom, and war was in their eyes. Timothy made them a little speech. He spoke of the terrible stories he had heard against them previous to his coming among them, and wound up by declaring he was happy to be able to say that he was now convinced that these were all malicious lies; that more pleasant or agreeable gentlemen it had never been his good fortune to meet with than those whose acquaintance he had had the pleasure of making in the enterprising little town of Sulphuropolis. The stage driving up at the moment, Timothy with his gripsack in his hand, was anxious to be off, for his speech seemed to have fallen upon hearts of stone. Throwing a twenty-dollar gold piece upon the counter, he told the landlord to treat all hands. A dogged and ominous silence prevailed. Not a man moved toward the bar where he had thrown his gold piece, with the same design as that with which the Russian unfreights his sledge when pursued by wolves.

As Timothy made his way toward the stage the men of Sulphuropolis began to throng about him. He smiled in various directions, nodded, and spoke pleasant words; but no word was spoken in return, and no answering smile met his gaze. Glad was Tongue-Oil Timothy when he was safely ensconced within the coach, for he liked not the fierce and sullen look of those who escorted him or of the many others who came crowding up, but he made it appear in face and manner that he understood all to be filled with grief at parting with him. Just as the whip of the driver cracked and the unwilling horses began to feel their way into their collars, Timothy heard a gruff voice say in anger-thickened tones:

"Just thar what he said 'More pleasant and agreeable gentlemen he had never met' is whar you ought'r struck him!"

Timothy felt in his inmost soul that he had made a narrow escape. But, true to his nature, as the coach rolled away from the gloomy group of coinless men, he bent forward from its window and with his lily hand waved them from his benevolent countenance a smiling farewell—for he was still within reach of a pistol bullet, and the words, "Just thar is whar you ought'r struck him," were still humming in his ears.

TIMOTHY SHEARS A SHEEP OF HIS OWN COLOR

On one occasion Timothy of the oily tongue made his appearance in the brisk little town of Smelterville, famous for its many furnaces and the richness of its argentiferous ores. He walked about the town in an apparently gloomy and dejected manner, yet was he happy as he was unctuous to the core; and, even as he seemed to sorrow, the oil of gladness was oozing from his every pore. In the town was only one room in which, suitably and to the full, could be displayed the attractions of the royal beast of Bengal. This room was occupied by a brother sport, who was driving quite a thriving trade. To obtain possession of this room was the secret desire of Timothy's soul; but there was "Wasatch Sam" in full and flourishing possession. Haman looked not on Mordecai sitting in the king's gate with more envious eye than did Timothy observe Wasatch Sam, seated, behind his green baize, offering forth his layout.

At the first opportunity Timothy, in tones all greasy with grief, informed Wasatch that he was dead broke. He was even then, as he said, on his way to the Comstock to raise a sum with which to start afresh in the world. It was hard, he said, for a man like him, who had always rejoiced in the possession of almost unnumbered shekels, to be reduced to this extremity; but to this complexion must sometimes come those who tempt Dame Fortune too far. He then descended to particulars, and informed the sympathetic Sam—for so Sam strove to appear—that he had been in the town of Chloridetta, where he had spread forth his lure. The town was full of pigeons ripe for the plucking. Coin abounded in every man's pocket, and was rattling in every man's hand. There seemed spread abroad and ready for the sickle of the reaper a harvest of not less than $30,000 or $40,000. But, alas! the run of the cards was villainously against him. No expedient served to give him a turn of luck. Fortune favored alone those who fought against him, and at last his bank was broken, his last dime gone, and his fangless tiger grinned ghastfully through naked gums.

As Timothy concluded the story of his woes tears stood in his angel eyes. He heaved a heart-broken sigh, affectionately wrung his dear friend Sam's soft hand, and rushed away to his room to hide a smile of exultation. It was late—was somewhat beyond that "witching time of night when churchyards yawn"—and Sam's game had closed. Gazing in the direction taken by the departing Timothy for some seconds, Wasatch began assiduously to pace the floor of his place of traffic, meanwhile vigorously puffing a fragrant Havana. The mind of the man was busy.

"The saffron morn," as Homer hath it, had long passed, and the sun rode high in the heavens, when Timothy made his appearance the following day. A sort of premonitory symptom of a smile for a moment fluttered upon his full, ripe under lip, as a flaw of wind is sometimes seen to ripple the placid surface of a lake, when it was told him that, through some sudden and unaccountable freak, Wasatch Sam had given up the room in which he was wont to exhibit his small but energetic menagerie and departed, bag and baggage, by the early coach for some place to friends and foes alike unknown. This bit of news was imparted to Timothy as he imbibed his morning cocktail at the bar of the saloon, in the rear of which was situated the coveted faro room.

The man who furnished this intelligence was proprietor of the place. After about three flourishes of Timothy's oily tongue the landlord deposited in his till a month's rent in advance, and our gentle hero, with hands in trousers pockets, leisurely viewed his newly acquired quarters and estimated the capabilities thereof.

Now turn we to Wasatch Sam. Arrived in the town of Chloridetta, his first care was to secure a spacious room suited to his purpose, making sure of it by planking down the rent for a month in advance. Until he had done this he said not a word of his business or his intentions to a living soul. All being made sure, however, he presently strolled forth to view the bleating herds of the place, form estimates of the weight of the fleeces, and begin in anticipation the pleasing task of the shearing. Sam had none of the faults of "the weak, the vain, the vacillating good." He meant business, and he was in a hurry to set about it. He had not sauntered far along the principal street of the town before he met a brother sport.

"Hello!" cried this cheerful member of the confraternity. "Hello, Sam! what brings you here? Thought you had a good, easy-going game down at Smelterville? I had about made up my mind to go down there myself."

"Nonsense! Don't think of it!" cried Sam. "Don't think of it! for from what I hear it is ten times better picking up here. I just landed this morning, and I've got me a room already, and am going to open my game tonight."

"The bloody blazes you are!" cried the cheerful sport. "What to, I should like to know? There's not a 'splitter' left in the town. Tongue-Oil Timothy left here only four days ago, and he carried away with him the last slick quarter in the place!"

"That oily-tongued devil!" yelled Sam, "the infernal, tear-shedding crocodile! the heart-broken, sobbing, thieving liar! Why, he told me he got broke here; that the town was jingling and lousy with money, and that he could have won $50,000 if luck had not turned against him. He shed tears by the gallon! The groaning, lying, smooth-faced scoundrel! just see what he has made me do! Town tee-totally cleaned out, hey?"

"Cleaned and scraped—the last battered old dime gone, I tell you! Look at all the 'huskies' going round here with the corners of their mouths drawn down and their backs humped," said the cheerful man in his most gleeful manner. "Look at 'em! Not one of 'em has had a square meal since Tim Tongue-Oil left town. By the great bull of Bashan and everything else that roars and rumbles, even my belly is beginning to believe my throat is cut, so long has it been since any communication between the two has taken place. There is not money enough in the town to buy a flea a pair of boxing gloves."

"D—— Tim Tongue-Oil!" cried Sam. "Good day, old pard: I've business on my hands. May the devil scorch that blubbering, hypocritical beast!" growled Sam as he strode away to hunt up the man of whom he had so eagerly rented his room in the morning. After a hard battle he succeeded in getting back $25 of the $50 he had a few hours before paid into the landlord's hands.

As he busied himself with packing his traps blood was in his eye. He was bound to be off that night by return coach, in order to settle down in his old place at Smelterville, for it was much too good to lose.

"I can't understand what put it into the head of that d—— Tim to tell me such a pack of lies," muttered he as he finished his packing.

We again breathe the stuffy atmosphere of Smelterville. How serene and smiling sits Timothy behind the baize! He is a reminder of the priest of whom old Chaucer said:

> Full sweetly heard he confession,
> And pleasant was his absolution.

To lose to such a man was a greater pleasure than to win from the average of mankind. Tongue-Oil Timothy had an immense game going—better than had been seen in the town for months, for all desired to try their luck at the new bank. He was raking in coin right royally. Just when all was going on most swimmingly Wasatch Sam arrived in the town. Without waiting to look after his baggage—at least nothing more than his bags of coin—he rushed from the coach, and in a moment was confronting his old landlord.

"The room," he cried, "the room! I'll take the room again at the same rent. Here is your money for the first month."

"I don't understand you," said the landlord. "What about a room?"

"The room I had—the faro room. I'll take it again! I've just got back, and I want the room again—to keep it right along same as before!"

"O, ah, ahem! Well, yes; but you see you went away, and as Tongue-Oil Tim said that rather than see it a-lyin' idle—and as he allers felt like helpin' of a man when he came in his way, he'd try ef he could manage ter keep it a goin' on as a sorter help ter the bar, why I——"

"You rented it to him?" yelled Sam.

"Well, yes; he put up fur it fur the first month in advance, with the refusal for as long as he wants it."

"D—— Tongue-Oil Tim! he beats me at every turn. Tongue-Oil here, Tongue-Oil there, Tongue-Oil everywhere, and 'tongue-oil' wins! May old Baalzebub get Tongue-Oil!"

So, venting his wrath, Sam strode away and took a look into the faro room where the tiger was rending its prey right and left. The evidences of prosperity that he there saw made him sick at heart. He went back to the bar and took half a tumbler of raw tarantula, sat down and mused for a time, then went and called Timothy, requesting that gentleman to come out for discourse.

Timothy called upon the man in the lookout chair to take his seat and deal, winked a friend into the lookout chair, and then, serene as a summer's morn, went forth to meet and affectionately greet his dear and ever sympathetic friend, Wasatch Sam. Most eagerly did he advance and cordially grasp Sam's half-extended hand. It was like David going for Jonathan after a six weeks' absence.

"Why, my dear friend!" cried he, "just to see how strangely things sometimes turn out. A man makes an enemy in jealously striving to prove the heart of his most loved and valued friend. Now here, you see that I had a dream in which I saw myself overtaken by the very misfortune that I related to you. I saw all who played at my game winning my gold, till at last all was gone and I was left penniless—was almost kicked out of the town. All my acquaintances shunned me. You—even you, dear old friend— turned from me. I awoke bathed in tears. The dream made a deep impression on my mind. I said to myself: 'What if it were so—really and truly so—what should I do?' Then I very foolishly resolved that I would test the sincerity of those calling themselves my friends by telling them my dream as a fact. To you, Sam—you being my dearest and most valued friend on earth—I first related as a fact what was really only an idle dream. Forgive me my cruelty, my dear boy! for as I poured into your sympathetic ear the story of my losses and my despair, I saw that your very soul was wrung— that your heart of hearts was bleeding for me! Yet I had the cruelty to rush away and leave you pained and sick at heart for your friend. No sooner was I composed in my bed, and had taken the second thought, than my heart wept for the anguish I had so jealously and foolishly caused you. More than once I was on the point of rising and rushing away to find you to tell you that it was I, Samson, who had spoiled the Philistines, and not the Philistines Samson!

"Long I lingered in my room the next morning, startled, confused, and blushing at every step that sounded on the stairs, for, said I: 'There, now, comes Sam to offer—nay, to force upon me—half of his wealth. What a sorry figure I shall cut in trying to give a sane reason for having kept him a whole night stretched upon the rack! How pitiful and small will look my joke when I tell him it was all a dream!'

"Thus I tortured myself until I could no longer endure my own society. I then sallied forth, and great was my astonishment at learning of your sudden departure. At one time I meditated putting a pistol to my head, for I thought that grief at the woes of a friend might have turned your brain; or, again, that you had gone to a distant place, there to dispose of some possessions in order to assist me—me who needed no assistance.

"To make a long story short, I then, to assist this poor man and to make him some amends for having deprived him of a paying tenant, rented of him his empty room. Thus, my dear friend, you see, from a mere idle dream came about all these perplexing complications. But let them not impair that friendship which has for so long reached out from heart to heart and grappled us together as it were with hooks of steel. With my arms about your neck, like a repentant bad child, I now have only to rest my head upon your shoulder and sob my prayers for forgiveness, bitterly repenting my——"

"Tongue-Oil!" cried Sam, aghast, as he beheld that weeping and subjugated individual advancing upon him—"Tongue-Oil, keep away from me, or so help me God, I'll give you a mash in the jaw! You played your game well. You caught my jack, and much good may it do you; but if you ever deal me such a hand again and get away with the trick, I hope that I may never again hold deuce high till Gabriel toots his old dinner horn!"

The ever-serene Timothy remained master of the situation, and long sat in Sam's warm nest behind the baize, smiling whole handfuls of gold into his capacious drawers. For this was "Tongue-Oil Timothy."

My Montana friend says of the good Timothy's last days:

Serenely as a babe he passed in his chips, assuring all those about him that death had no terrors for him, as during his whole life peace and good will to all mankind had ever been uppermost in his thoughts and had influenced all his actions. When asked if he would like to see a minister before taking his departure, he said: "Yes. Bring all who will come, regardless of denomination. I may be able to do them some good. I am not one to hide my light under a bushel. I shall be pleased to see the ministers and to converse with them of that better world to which I am going; also to counsel them to persevere in good works, that finally they may receive their reward and take up their abode with me in the realms above, among the innocent and just."

New York Sun, December 5, 1886

A Female
World-Ranger

She "Takes a Header" over Her Own Doorstep

EASTWARD BOUND
And She Lands 3,625 Feet above the Level of the Sea!

She boarded the east-bound overland train at Sacramento. She was of a
tall, commanding figure, and on entering the car she had elected to en-
liven with her presence she remained standing a sufficient length of time
to cast her all-comprehending eye over its numerous occupants. She
seemed to be satisfied with the appearance of those who were for a time
to be her fellow-travelers; she thought they would do her no discredit,
and as she seated herself she smiled her acceptance of them. That ma-
turity which is the result of the ripening suns of forty summers had given
almost unbounded powers of endurance to a naturally sinewy and ser-
viceable tongue. She was also gifted with an eager and restless brain. Her
talk was like the snapping of corn in a popper.

The moment she entered the car she took charge of everything and
everybody as the one experienced person of the party. Having announced
that she was going up to Rocklin to spend a few days with friends who
were almost sick abed to see her, she began looking about to ascertain
what she could do for her imbecile fellow-travelers. She knew it all—
everything. She knew how to open the car windows, how to turn back
the seats and understood the mystery of the racks overhead. She was on
her feet in a moment to lend assistance in all the difficult and perplexing
operations connected with the opening of windows, turning of seats and
the rise of the racks, crying: "Allow me to assist you. I am an old and
experienced traveler; I understand these things, for I am always on
the wing."

And so she went on till all regarded her with some degree of awe, as a
sort of visible and material coagulation of all experience in traveling. In
comparison with her, Madam Ida Pfeffer seemed a poor stay-at-home sort
of body—a mere timid dozer in chimney corners. Our great lady traveler
had been everywhere, and overflowed with information in regard to all

things. She could tell the people everything they wanted to know—the population of California, population of Oregon, population of Nevada, and the rate of increase of population in the several States and Territories. She then skipped across the ocean and told the number of square miles in Belgium and the number of Belgians to the square mile.

Some men were disputing about the fastest railroad time ever made. "Gentlemen," said she, "the fastest railroad time ever made was one mile in 50-1/4 seconds; three miles in two minutes and 36-1/4 seconds, and five miles in four minutes and 50 seconds. That time was made between West Philadelphia and Jersey City, September 4, 1879, Edward Osmond, engineer."

The men who a moment before had been clamorously discussing the point sunk their heads into their coat collars, closed their mouths, and did not again open them during the evening. But this in no way disconcerted our Sacramento madam. She merely caught her breath and continued: "Sound moves at the rate of 1,142 feet in a second; a rifle ball, 1,466 feet; light moves—"

"Arcade!" cried the brakeman, thrusting his head into the car and then backing out with a slam of the door.

"—one hundred and ninety-two thousand miles in a second, and electricity 288,000 miles in the same period of time."

The men who had been disputing about railroad time now pulled their hats down over their eyes and settled so low in their seats that only the tops of their heads were visible; they seemed mere pigmies.

This transformation was not observed by our traveled lady, as she at the moment left her seat and ran away to lower a window for an old lady who had lost her spectacles and a good deal of breath and temper in vain endeavors to keep the night wind and her bronchitis from intermingling. No sooner had she shut down the window that was bothering the old lady than our "traveled person" heard something said near her about Lake Tahoe.

"Lake Tahoe, gentlemen?" cried she. "Lake Tahoe is 23 miles long and 15 miles wide. It is in the form of a parallelogram, lying northeast and southwest, at a distance of three miles, as I have heard—"

"Junction!" cried the brakeman, thrusting his head into the car.

"—them say, it is from 1,000 to 1,200 feet deep. The greatest depth yet found is 1,800 feet. Lake Superior is the largest body of fresh water in the world. It is 380 miles in length by 160 in width, and its bottom is 400 feet below the level of the sea."

Suddenly turning in her seat, the "Weltbereiser," as a German would call her, cried in a patronizing way to a young lady behind her:

"'Bingen on the Rhine,' my dear? why it begins—

A soldier of the legion lay dying in Algiers;
There was lack of woman's nursing, there was dearth of woman's
    tears;
But a comrade stood beside him, while his life-blood ebbed away,
And bent with pitying glances to hear what he might say.
The dying soldier faltered as he took that comrade's hand,
And he said—"

"Rocklin!" cried the brakeman.

"'I never more shall see my own, my native land.
Take a message and a token to some distant friends of mine;
For I was born at Bingen—at Bingen on the Rhine!'

Ah! no thanks, dear; I could repeat the whole if you wished, but doubtless you know it."

Next our "Welt-ganger" caught something of what an old gentleman was saying to a young man by his side about the Alps.

"The Alps, my dear sir, if you will excuse my speaking—the Alps comprise about 180 mountains, from 4,000 to 15,732 feet high, the latter being the height of Mont Blanc, the highest spot in Europe. The ascent of Mont Blanc is difficult and dangerous. It requires two days and six or eight guides, and each guide is paid 100 francs, which is about $20. A French-woman, Madam Aselie d'Angeville, ascended in September, 1840, being dragged up the last 1,000 feet by the guides, and crying out—"

"Newcastle!" roared the brakeman.

"'—If I die carry me to the top!' When at the top she made them lift her above their shoulders, so that she might boast that she had been higher than any man in Europe."

"Where is the place they call Cape Horn?" asked an English-looking old gentleman.

"Cape Horn, sir?" cried our woman of "Weltburgerlich" knowledge— "Cape Horn is the most southerly point of America, terminating an island of its own name, in the archipelago of Terra del Fuego. *Horn* is not the proper name of the cape, but *Hoorn*, as it takes its name from that of the native place of its discoverer, Schourin, who was born in the fortified seaport town of Hoorn, in the Netherlands, province of North Holland, on the Zuyder Zee. It was discovered about ninety years later than the Strait of Magellan, and since then the course of navigation of sailing vessels has been around—"

"Auburn!" shouted the brakeman, popping his head in and out.

Breaking short off in her dissertation on the "Hoorn," the world-ranger left her place and zigzagged across to where an old gentleman wearing a red woolen night-cap under his hat was seated, near the car door, crying as she advanced and steadying herself as well as she could by the backs of the seats:

"Ah, Auburn!—

> Sweet Auburn! loveliest village of the plain,
> Where health and plenty cheered the laboring swain.

You are an admirer of Goldsmith, sir—Goldsmith, the great traveler and flutist? You were quoting his 'Deserted Village,' I think? I caught the name, Auburn—'Sweet Auburn'!"

"No, mum; I didn't kote nuthin.' 'Twan't me as said 'Aubu'n.' A brakesman or suthin' o' the kind stuck his head inter the kyar and sung out 'Aubu'n.' I s'pose, mum, we're a-makin' the town—or villidge, as you call it—of Aubu'n 'bout this time."

"Auburn! What do you mean? Why, he hasn't called 'Rocklin' yet!"

"Long ago, mum; and Arcade and Junction and Newcastle. Now we're at Auburn, mum, and next will be at Coldfaxt, mum."

"Colfax! I won't go to Colfax! Conductor! conductor! Where is the conductor! If he has carried me past Rocklin, he shall take me right back! Oh, he shall smart for this!"

"You are certainly now at Auburn, madam," said a gentleman near, "and will have to remain over till the westbound train arrives."

"I can't lie over, and I shan't get off here all in the dark. My friends in Rocklin are expecting me—are at this moment waiting for me. I know that the name of Rocklin was not called out. I'm too old a traveler not to have heard it. Conductor! conductor! Where is the conductor? He has not been in this car all this night! Will some one be good enough to find the conductor?"

A gentleman volunteered to go in search of the conductor, when the lady drew forth a route map of the Central Pacific Railroad a yard in length and began studying the stations, distances and elevations.

The conductor presently made his appearance. He told the traveled madam that the best he could do for her was to carry her to Alta, where he would meet and put her aboard the westbound train.

"Alta!" cried she, "Alta!—3,625 feet above the level of the sea! 3,356 feet higher than I wanted to go! Alta! forty-eight miles beyond where you should have let me off! Alta! 1,706 miles west of Omaha and seventy miles east of Sacramento, when I only wanted to go twenty-two miles east!"

"Cold-facx!" shouted the brakeman.

"I am sorry, madam," said the conductor, "but did you not hear Rocklin called?"

"No; it was not called. I heard Auburn and all the others, as I just now heard Colfax—but Rocklin was not called."

"If you heard Newcastle you must then have known that you had passed your station?"

"I did not hear Newcastle, now that I think of it. I'm an old and experienced traveler, sir, and if he had called out either Rocklin or Newcastle I should have heard him."

"I think you are wrong there, madam; however, I am sorry that you have missed your station. But do not let the matter trouble you; I'll send you back to Rocklin from Alta."

"You'll send me to Rocklin? Indeed, sir, you'll do nothing of the kind! You'll furnish me transportation to Sacramento—to where you took me from—to my home!" and her voice grew shaky, and her chin quivered.

"Certainly, madam, if that is your wish."

"And I'll see (bracing up) what the law will do for me. I have traveled before, sir. I'm no new beginner—I know my rights!"

"Very well, madam, as you please; to Sacramento then."

"Yes, to Sacramento; and the company will hear from me too. I have a husband, sir!"

Here an old German muttered within his beard something that sounded like—"Unter dem Pantoffel kommen!"

"Dutch Flat!" cried the brakeman.

"Leave the matter to your husband, then," replied the conductor. "Let us say no more."

"My husband shall sue for damage. Yes, sir, damage! Carried to Alta, 3,625 feet above the level of the sea! To Alta—3,356 feet above Rocklin, and 48 miles beyond!" and so she ran on until the conductor had passed out of the car.

"To Rocklin, indeed!" cried she, looking about the car, when the conductor had made his escape—"As if I'd show myself to my friends in Rocklin and tell them I had allowed myself to be carried past them, and all the way up to Alta, 3,625 feet above the level of the sea! I'd never hear the last of it! To go home to Sacramento is bad enough. However, I need not tell them. I can say that I met a party of friends going East and concluded to accompany them as far as Alta. Ha, ha! [y]es, that will do!"

"But then, my dear," said a venerable dame in a drab bonnet, "what will become of thy suit for damages? If thee brings suit thy mishap must be made known, and as a great traveler thee would not like that."

"Alas! yes—yes, that is true. I—an old, experienced traveler—am in—"

"Alta!" cried the brakeman.

"—a very ridiculous position," and she bowed her head and sighed.

Here the conductor made his appearance, saying: "Come, madam, I'll escort you to the westbound train. Don't feel downhearted, you are none the worse for your little ride to Alta."

"Three thousand six hundred and twenty-five feet above the level of the sea!" murmured the world-ranger as she passed out of the car.

Instantly every one that remained in the car seemed to come to life. The two "railroad pigmies," like turtles, thrust their heads forth from their shells, and, towering heads and shoulders above their seats, again appeared as men of average stature.

"'If I die, carry me to the top!'" grunted the old gentleman who had spoken of the Alps.

"Me kote po'try?—'sweet Auburn!'" cried the old fellow in the red night-cap.

"Cape Hoorn!" snorted the Britisher.

And then was heard the voice of a young lady cheerily singing:

> I never more shall see my own, my native land.
> Take a message and a token to some distant friends of mine;
> For I was born at Bingen—at Bingen on the Rhine!

San Francisco Examiner, March 11, 1888

Rev. Olympus Jump

The Mountain Howitzer of God
and His Good Works

COMSTOCK RELIGION
A Man with a Natural Gift for Converting Sinners

It was a cold, stormy night on the Comstock. A blizzard played at hide-and-seek about the peak of Mount Davidson, and splitting on the rocky pinnacle gave birth to a whole brood of frolicsome little whirlwinds. Those mischievous imps of the storm, racing to and fro under the brow of the mountain, tossed high in the air great columns of frozen and powdered snow, hurling them in blinding showers down into the streets of Virginia City, 2,000 feet below. In the town no merry jingle of sleighbells was shaken out upon the thickened air. Even the principal business streets were almost deserted. It was only here and there that a muffled pedestrian was to be seen, as with head bowed low he staggered against the driving gale. So filled with flying "dust" of snow was the whole atmosphere that gas lamps were only visible as a faint firefly glow, and about the electric lights were seen such halos as enring a stormy moon. On such a night even the shaggy coyote would seek the lee of some friendly rock.

Gathered in the "Golden Fleece" saloon, their favorite retreat, were a dozen or more old grizzled "Argonauts" of the days of "forty-nine." Snugly harbored from the storm, the veterans enjoyed their pipes, their hot toddies and their flagons of beer; also the friendship of the white-haired "Jason," who commanded behind the bar.

"Well, well!" cried old Dan Manix, as he laid aside the newspaper he had been ogling for the last half hour through the cracked and misty lenses of his iron-rimmed spectacles. "Well, well! Hit's jist the same old song back yander in the States. Alles a fussin' 'bout religion and quarrelin' 'bout the preachers. Why can't they take thare religion in the nat'ral way, like us ole fellers? They all think they've got to go to a certain place at a certain time an' git it vaccinated inter 'em like a lot o' school children in smallpox times. Let 'em take it in the nat'ral way. Let 'em lay alone on the mountain top and look up at all the millions of stars, and the light of truth will shine down into thare souls. Let 'em listen to the voice of the

114

Lord in the tops of the tall pines in the dark, still night! They all think they've goter jine church, give in thare sperience, pull long faces and put up long prayer in public—prayers sich as is more for the ears of thare neighbor than to be heard by the Almighty."

"Wall, that's 'bout so, Dan," said Arkansaw Jim. "I don't keer 'bout hearin' any manner o' prayer. A prayer that's cut out to fit the ear of both God and men ain't wuth a cent to one or t'other. My idear is that prayin' is a sort of business that lays between a man and his God."

"Anoder ding," said Dutch Jake, "I dinks it is all tam nonsense to have a burticular times and blace to bray. In mine obinion, too, it is all tam nonsense to all de time bodder de Almighty van dare is nodding burticular de matter mid me. I only ask de Lord God to help me van I git in such a scrape vare I can't bull out mineself."

"That's 'bout so, too, Jake," said Arkansaw. "I think that 'bout the best and strongest prayer I ever made wur offered up while I wur on the keen jump—jist runnin' my level best."

"Vile you vas run?" queried Jake.

"Yes," said Arkansaw, "and a big grizzly bar wur also a-runnin'—runnin' in my direction, and mighty close at my heels."

"Dat vas a goot time to bray; a ferry goot time to bray," said Jake. "On dat burticular occasion I would hafe brayed mineself. Did he get you?"

"Not quite," said Arkansaw. "The Lord heard my prayer, and I got to a tree and up it; but, for my sins, before I was high enough the bear was allowed some privileges."

"Dat so?" said Jake. "Vat vas dem brifiliges what he tooked?"

"Wall, boys, with one swipe of his paw he took the whole seat out of my trousers."

"Ah, vell," said Jake, "ve all haf our little sins."

"Well, boys," put in old Jim Hawkins, who had all this time been quietly smoking and listening, "let 'em say what they will 'bout us old California mountain men, we've got about as good religion as is goin', and about as much as some as makes more noise about it. We've had it, too, right along, through thick and thin, and I for one am goin' to hang on to the faith the Lord has given me. I'm not much on the golden harp business, but the Lord will find some quiet nook for me somewhere when I cross over to the other shore."

"'Pears to me, after all," said Texas Jack, "that us fellers out here in the wilderness has kept to the right trail better nor some of 'em back in civilization. Thar was ole Henry Ward Beecher who said there wasn't airy hell. Bob Ingersoll says there ain't no heaven, and next we know some new-fangled gospel-grinder 'll get up and knock the solid yearth from under our feet."

"Do you know, boys," said Gurnsey Bob, a battered and weather-beaten old '49er, who had all along been quietly sipping his beer. "Do you know," said he, as he thumped his glass on the table before him and called for another half-gallon of beer; "that it jist makes me sick to hear all the talk and furse they make these times about these fashionable highferlutin preachers. I tell yer, boys, they ain't deuce high 'longside the preachers we had in the airly days in California."

"In course not! Can't hold a candle to 'em! Hain't got the sand, nor the gift, nor the grit!" chorused all present, for Bob was a big chief among them, and an authority on all pioneer matters; indeed, when it came to speaking of affairs in the old mining camps in early times, his word was law. Besides, as he was this evening "putting up" freely for the beer, he was entitled to a patient and respectful hearing.

"I tell yer, fellers," cried old Gurnsey, filling his beer-mug and squaring himself for a big talk, once he found he was going to obtain the floor and have things all his own way. "I tell yer what it is, fellers, I us'ter know a preacher what us'ter ride on what they called a circle, over in Californy, in '52, as was named Olympus Jump, an' he was a roarer, you kin jist bet!

"He wasn't one of yer stuck-up, kid-gloved kind, as would be afeered they'd dirty their hands if they give the flippers of a honest miner a grip. No sir; he'd take hold of yer paw like 'er wolf trap.

"Olympus, he wasn't one of them kind as goes a snufflin' and a prospectin' about with noses in the air, a-smellin' roast chicken an' hot biskits afar off! Not at all! He wasn't one of yer yeller-legged hen kind. No sir! Olympus, he was a Godfearin' man, an' pork an' beans was the highest ambition of his meek and lowly bowels. He'd flop his lip over a flapjack with sich a Christian grace as was eddifyin' to the highest, an' gave comfort to the soul of the humblest!

"Olympus Jump, he wasn't one of yer kyoters in sheep's clothin', sich as goes a-sneakin' about among the ewes of the flock a-making more scandals in a week nor yer could wash out in six months by pipin' inter 'em all the water that could be throwed by the biggest hydraulic in all the mountains of Californy! No, sir! that wasn't his style. He walked uprightly afore the Lord, and was as happy as the day was long, with his own comely little wife and his half-dozen little Jumps.

"He wasn't one of yer highly eddicated, rosewater, butter-mouthed sort—Olympus wasn't. He had the gift nat'ral—right from the Lord—and when he unbuttoned his shirt-collar, reached up his front har an' began to sling the word in dead earnest, it made a feller think of a string of bowlders thunderin' down a ground sluice under a big head o' water.

"Olympus, he wasn't one o' yer new-fangled, oily-tongued sort o' preachers what stand up before yer Sunday after Sunday, never showin' up the

Rev. Olympus Jump

'color' of the word of God nor givin' you a single mouthful of the bread of life. Not a bit of it! He come to yer with a whole loaf under each arm—good, sound bread—none of yer butter-crackers of boughten grace or gingersnaps of six-cent salvation!

"He was a miner of the word afore the Lord, Olympus was. He'd 'drifted' and 'creviced' all through the Bible, from the 'grass-roots' down to the 'bedrock,' pannin' out bushels of 'chispas' and scores and scores of big 'nuggets' of pure gold. With these he was loaded clean up to the muzzle, an' when he turned loose and began to fire scriptur into an aujence he might'er been called the mountain howitzer of God!

"Olympus Jump wasn't one of the kind to be afeerd; he wasn't one o' yer skeery sort. He was bold as a lion in the strength of the Lord. He'd pan out and size up the man of thousands as quick as he would a faro-dealer or a monte sharp. When he went forth to labor in the Lord's diggins he spit on his hands and at every lick sent his gospel-pick clean down to the bedrock of rascality and sin. He didn't sneak round behind and fire into sin at long range. He'd weigh out a feller's 'dust' for him right before his eyes. If he found even the 'color' of gold he'd give full credit for it, but if he raked over the 'black sand' and saw 'nary color' away went the whole batch into the 'waste dump' of perdition. No bones about it!

"He was full of the spirit, and when he took off his coat and laid himself out to labor for his flock the kyoters tuck to the woods. He wasn't one o' them kind o' prayers whose prayin' is jist a little sneakin' drizzle that only wets the earth here and there, washin' away none of the dust of iniquity—never causin' a single good seed to sprout nor raisin' up the droopin' head of a single crushed or wilted plant! No. The prayer of Olympus was like a cloud-burst on a mountain; it swept down through all the dark, deep canyons an' gulches of sin, and sent all the miners delving therein end over end down through the 'tail flumes' of the devil till they was glad to grab the first branch of the tree of life that hung in reach and haul theirselves ashore, high an' dry on the Rock of Ages.

"Olympus he wasn't one of yer stuck-up kind of laborers in the vineyard as couldn't preach without a morocco-bound, gold-clasped Scriptur and a pulpit as grand as the gates of the New Jerusalem. Not a bit of it! Why, fellers, he'd jist mount a dry-goods box or a big bowlder, haul his little old greasy pack o' loose leaves of Bible out'n his coat-tail pocket, shuffle it up, give it a cut, deal out a text, and then jist hammer h——l's bells out'n every sinner from Shirt tail Canyon to Sucker Flat.

"That was a preacher for yer! You'd see his aujences rock like pines in a storm. He'd bring tears of repentance from the eyes of a three-card monte dealer, make a sluice robber moan, and even rock the sadden soul of a water agent. Then, when he'd pernounced his bennerdiction and tied up and stowed away his gospel deck, the boys would chuck gold inter his old wool hat till the bottom hung down like a strainer bag. Fill up yer glasses, boys, and let us all drink to the memory of the great and good Olympus Jump; now safely landed on the other side of Jordan, high up on the golden shore!"

San Francisco Examiner, April 1, 1888

IV
LEGENDS AND
FOLKLORE

⎯⎯⎯⎯⎯⎯⎯⎯⎯⎯⎯⎯⎯⎯⎯⎯

*Even before he began to work on
the* Territorial Enterprise *Dan De Quille was already making references to legends and folklore in the newsletters he sent to various
newspapers. Studying mythology and collecting folklore were lifelong
avocations in which he became impressively knowledgeable. It was
only a short step for him from collecting legends to creating them. Dives
and Lazarus and "Pahnenit, Prince of the Land of Lakes," the most am-
bitious fiction of his career, were imaginative new literary creations
largely made up of elements appropriated from a variety of myths. It is
now possible to see that these works of his last years were the culmi-
nation of a process which had begun many years before.*

*Just as De Quille's regular newspaper columns are a rich fund of
historical information about his time, so are his fanciful narratives
a significant contribution to the legends and folklore of the frontier.
Among his very best is "Lorenzo Dow's Miracle." Lorenzo Dow (1777–
1834) was a famous, almost notorious, Methodist itinerant preacher
who traveled across much of the eastern half of the country. He was
highly eccentric in appearance and habit and controversial in his
evangelical methods, and a number of anecdotes about him sprung up
in his wake. On one of his travels in 1827 it is possible that Dow visited
the Shipley settlement in the Owl Creek region of Ohio, a site that can
be identified as the outskirts of what is now Mt. Vernon, the seat of
Knox County, just a few miles from the childhood home of De Quille.
The Dow anecdote narrated by De Quille also circulated in both bal-
lad and narrative form so it is not possible to be certain whether he
adapted it from one of the Dow miscellanies that were popular in mid-
century or actually recalled a local tale from Knox County. Whatever
his source, De Quille certainly improved upon it and gave it new life.*

*Americans have always bestowed imaginative names upon pictur-
esque places in the new country which they settled: Lovers' Leap,
Castle Rock, the Grand Tetons, the Great Stone Face. Death Valley is a
site naturally conducive to the generation of legends, and on its behalf
De Quille came up with a most powerful and haunting tale. Ever since*

he prospected in the area in the late 1850s, he was intrigued by Death Valley and occasionally referred in his columns to its history, its geology, its mirages, or the strange sandspout pillars that waltz across its wastes. Although his story "Death Valley" is cast as a memoir, in the absence of biographical verification it is most likely a work of fiction. As a literary work by someone who knew a great deal about the region, however, it is an excellent example of De Quille's skill at verisimilitude, and from the dramatically described setting of its opening to its eerie climax it is composed with consummate artistry.

No one knew the history of the Comstock better than De Quille; that is why he was the one persuaded by some of the Comstock's "Silver Kings" to write the book that became The Big Bonanza. *But when he was not writing serious history, he was transmuting it into fiction. "A Goblin Frog" is one of at least two legends that De Quille manufactured about the discovery of the Comstock. The other, involving Mrs. Bowers and her crystal ball "peepstone," is to be found in De Quille's famous biographical account of "Snow-Shoe Thompson," one of the few substantial De Quille works that has continued to be reprinted. "A Goblin Frog" was one of De Quille's most successful works of fancy. The January 1876 printing of it, if not the first, was a very early version. De Quille reprinted it several more times but expanded it considerably for its 1888 republication in the* San Francisco Examiner.

"Elam Storm" is a story to be valued both for its possible relationship to Mark Twain and certainly for its insight into how De Quille—and other authors, no doubt—appropriated material from others and turned it into their own fiction. De Quille's account of how he learned of the idea for what was to become his story is itself as good as a story and in fact seems to verge upon the fictitious. In his column of August 5, 1870, in the Territorial Enterprise, *apparently written before he composed the story, he presented this colorful explanation:*

> *Mark [Twain] is now wealthy, but all the wealth he possesses is not even pin-money to the world of wealth that awaits him high up in the solitudes of the Sierras—himself and one other man, if that man is still living. To prove this we have only to tell a story which Mark has told us many and many a time, and in which he always appeared to be a firm believer: Seven or eight years ago, while in Carson City, Mark made the acquaintance of a man who took him into his confidence and made him the sole depository of a great secret— the whereabouts of one of the most astonishing deposits of gold the world has ever heard, or dreamed of in its philosophy. As Mark used to tell us the story, this friend once got lost while hunting deer or*

grouse high up in the Sierra Nevada mountains, and wandered about three or four days, till almost famished. The last day he was in the mountains he came upon a rill of water at the bottom of a deep canyon and lay down to quench his thirst. While drinking he observed a nugget of gold lying just under his nose. Securing this, he began to look about him, and found that the bed-rock forming the trough of the canyon was literally "lousy" with gold. Although weak and almost starved, he gathered several thousand dollars' worth of nuggets, then began the descent of the canyon, carefully noticing the other canyons coming in on either side, until he found himself in the valley not far from Carson. He told no one of his great discovery, intending to return and "locate" the ground in due form, but a heavy snowstorm set in—it being late in the season—and prevented his going back to his mine. He sold his gold in small lots, as his wants required, and patiently waited till the next year, when he hoped the ground would again be free from snow. But the snow did not melt away that year, and when he visited the spot the year following the ground was covered to the depth of fifteen or twenty feet with snow an avalanche having fallen upon the spot [sic]. The mine was in this condition when the secret of its existence was imparted to Mark Twain by the discoverer. Mark was shown a map of the ravines, and had the whole route by heart, but the snow never would melt away. Every year while he was in this state he hunted up his partner in the great gold mine to ascertain how the chances looked for getting in that particular season. But year after year the debris of the old avalanche remained upon the spot; stubbornly refusing to melt away. Mark grew tired of remaining upon the same spot and concluded to "rustle around on the outside," leaving his partner in Carson to watch for the melting of the snow which covered their gold mine. Last winter was a most remarkable one; less snow fell in the mountains than any previous year since the settlement of Nevada by the whites; the summer has been unusually hot and again there is a season much as that during which the discovery was made— all the mountain peaks west of Carson are clear of snow. We may expect to see Mark in our midst, as his partner has doubtless telegraphed him that at last, after all the long weary years of waiting, the last vestige of the old avalanche had disappeared.

Whether this explanation is fact, fancy, or some combination of the two is at present unknown. Twain spent less than three years in Nevada, hardly enough to give much weight to De Quille's implication that Twain waited a long time, but as stories of lost gold mines were not uncommon and as Twain himself related one such tale in chapter 37 of Roughing It, it is not impossible that he had heard of or made up another one.

The ghost story was a highly popular genre in the late nineteenth century. Mark Twain, Ambrose Bierce, Lafcadio Hearn, Charles W. Chesnutt, and even Henry James all made memorable contributions to it. "Peter Crow among the Witches" is one of De Quille's best achievements in this line and, along with "The Earth Never Dies," is another example of his use of a sympathetic black protagonist. The story reflects De Quille's knowledge of contemporary folklore—Virginia City had a great deal of ethnic and racial diversity, and he was amply provided with informants—but it also shows the careful attention to details that makes his stories gripping to the point of being believable. As a cat, for example, Peter Crow underwent a personality change; he saw nothing wrong with sucking away the breath of an infant. So confident is De Quille of the story's impact on his reader that he caps the ending with Peter Crow's warning against resisting a belief in witches: it is "'sputin' agin reason"!

Lorenzo Dow's Miracle

HOW THE GREAT ITINERANT PREACHER
RAISED THE DEVIL

THE CONVENIENT BARREL OF FLAX

AN OLD PARSON'S SHREWDNESS ENABLED HIM TO MAKE AN
IMPRESSION UPON THE MINDS OF HIS FRONTIER
CONGREGATION

Among the old residents of the Buckeye State were in circulation many anecdotes of Elder Lorenzo Dow, most of which showed that despite his many eccentricities he was not only a shrewd observer of human nature, but also a man of good, strong common sense. Men from the older States who had pushed west and settled had all either seen or heard of Lorenzo Dow, and had something to relate illustrative of his peculiarities—his eccentricities of speech, dress and manner.

In the early days Lorenzo Dow had come out to Ohio to fulfill a series of appointments to preach at various places. It was on a Saturday, late in the month of October, that Elder Dow, mounted upon a sorry nag which long had carried him and the saddlebags containing his change of raiment, was toiling along a road cut through the heart of a great primitive forest. He was heading for the Owl creek region, where he was to preach the next day at what was known as the Shipley Settlement, at We-we-hausen prairie (old Indian fields).

The day was one of those cold, dreary, drizzling ones so well known in the fall months to those living from fifty to seventy miles south of the line of the great lakes. At the time the roads through the country, where any were to be found, were during the season of rains almost one endless "Slough of Despond." As Elder Dow rode slowly along the narrow and slippery wagon track, filled with stumps and protruding roots, the drizzle increased until it became a drenching downpour. To add to the unpleasantness of the situation, frequent gusts of wind shook down upon the "man of God" from the far-reaching arms of elms and swamp oaks perfect cascades of water, which he very soon began to feel through the seams and rents of his old camlet cloak.

To the chilled and weary preacher the forest seemed almost endless. At last he broke through it into a small clearing. To his joy he saw before him, at a short distance, a little cabin, a log stable and a shed or two. At sight of these evidences of "entertainment for man and beast," the tired old nag pricked up its ears and gave vent to a glad whinny, and the preacher, now knowing that he was within three miles of We-we-hausen, with half the afternoon still before him, resolved to seek the shelter of the cabin and await an abatement of the downpour.

After tying his horse under a shed the strolling evangelist stepped across a muddy patch of ground to the little cabin, the smoke from whose stick chimney told of a good fire and some occupant at home. As he passed the one little front window in the cabin his quick eye caught a glimpse of a man in a buckskin coat and coonskin cap. After stamping and scraping the roughest of the mud off his shoes at the doorstep, the preacher knocked at the door and was bidden to enter.

The elder saw before him in the cabin a rather handsome woman, still in the prime of life and buxom, to whom he made himself known and also his business in that part of the country, then asked permission to remain in the house until the rain slackened and to warm himself and dry his clothes before the fire.

The woman at first seemed a good deal confused, but soon recovered her composure and welcomed the preacher, saying she had often heard of him. Soon the elder's old camlet was steaming on the back of a chair, and steam was also being given out by the clothes still on his back as he stood and revolved before the ample fireplace.

After the elder was thus comfortably established he began to look about for the man, a glimpse of whom he had caught in passing the window. To his surprise no man was visible. The only door in the cabin was the one in front, by which he had entered, and the only window, the one near that door. The cabin boasted no loft, and he could look directly up into the apex of the steep clapboard roof. There was only the one room, and in that very little furniture. In one corner of the cabin stood a poor and naked-looking bed, but no man was under it, as he could easily see when seated.

In the corner of the cabin, between the fireplace and window, stood on its bench a hackle, and across the bench were laid some hanks of hackled flax, while under the window stood a large cask filled with the tow combed out of the flax during the operation of hackling. Besides the articles mentioned the cabin contained little else. There were a few common chairs, a table, a stool or two, some rude shelves for crockery, pewter plates and a small brass kettle, with beneath the shelves a bench for the water bucket. Over the door were the wooden hooks for the gun, but the gun itself was absent.

Elder Dow's keen eyes had taken note of all these things almost at a glance, and he soon had the woman of the house feeling quite at ease and laughing at his quaint jokes as he added faggots to the fire and occasionally turned his faithful old cloak on the chair back.

Presently there came a heavy stamping of feet at the doorstep. The preacher turned an inquiring eye upon the woman, who, coloring slightly, and saying, "I guess my husband has come," arose and moved toward the door. At the same moment the door was thrown open, and there entered a tall and powerfully built man—a splendid specimen of the frontiersman. He carried upon his right shoulder a long rifle, from the barrel of which were suspended two fine wild turkeys.

"Elder," said the wife, as the hunter advanced toward the fireplace, "Elder, this is my husband; Jim," proceeded she, "this is the great preacher, Lorenzo Dow, that we've heard so much about. He's to preach at the Wewe-hausen Prairie settlement tomorrer and has stopped here to git out'n the shower."

The face of the hunter instantly lighted up with astonishment and delight. Shifting the breech of his gun into his left hand he advanced, holding out his huge right to welcome the preacher.

"Powers alive!" cried the brawny six-footer, "I'm glad to meet yer. For years I've heerd of Lorenzo Dow, the big camp-meetin' preacher, but I never thought it would be my good luck to shake hands with him in my own house!"

The elder explained the situation, and then complimented the settler on his success as a hunter, as he threw his turkeys upon the bench beneath the shelves constituting the "dresser," and hung his rifle upon its hooks after carefully wiping it dry with a bunch of tow taken from the cask by the window.

"Poor luck—poor luck!" said the hunter. "I went out expectin' to git a good fat buck, but nary a deer could I find. I wouldn't proverably have turned my gun loose on the turkeys, hadn't it bin that I was on my way home when I came acrost 'em and seein' two of 'em git in range I thought they'd be worth one charge of powder and ball. But, great powers alive! what a s'prize it is to find in my own house—and shake hands with him—Lorenzo Dow, the greatest preacher in all the world!"

Elder Dow merely said he hoped he had done some good in the world in his humble way.

The backwoodsman would not have it so. He insisted that Dow was the biggest of all the preachers. He had heard of the many wonderful things

Dow had said and done. "Why," cried he, "haven't I heerd of the mir'kles you've worked! Of your healin' the sick and raisin' of the dead! And, Elder Dow, it's even said that if ye're a mind to you can raise the devil himself!"

"O, as to that—as to raising the devil—that's easily done," said the preacher. "That's one of my easiest miracles. I can do that any time in half a minute and without the least bit of trouble."

"You don't say so!" cried the honest backwoodsman, staring at Dow in open-mouthed astonishment. "But you don't mean to say you could raise the old feller right here in this house in broad daylight!"

"Certainly; right here, and in less than half a minute. I can raise the devil if you really wish to see such a thing done!"

"Oh, Jim, don't!" cried the wife. "It'll be too awful!"

"Don't you be gettin' skeert afore ye're hurt, Betts!" said the husband. Then turning to the preacher, he cried: "Elder Dow, I've heerd of you a thousand times, and I've heerd hundreds of times of your mir'kles, and if you'll do one for me here in my own house, it'll be the proudest day of my life! Now, as you say raisin' the devil is the easiest one you do, s'pose you jist try your hand at that."

"Very well, my friend, but you must know that the devil has his home in the midst of flames and fire. It is only in fire and flames that I can make him appear, which being the case, you must not be frightened at anything you may see."

"O, never mind, Elder, if I am a bit skeert; I'll grin and bear it."

"But, Jim!—think of me, Jim!" cried the wife.

"Yes, Betts, I'm a-talkin' for us both, and we'll stand bein' purty badly skeert jist to be able to say we've seed sich a mir'kle in broad daylight right in our own house."

"Very well, then," said Dow, "if nothing will do you but the miracle you shall have it. Throw the door wide open, for when the fiend appears he is liable to take the side clean out of the house if he finds himself shut in."

The backwoodsman, heedless of his wife's many protestations, was determined to proceed in the business. He at once threw the door wide open, and as he did so Dow took from the fire a blazing faggot which he thrust into the cask of tow. Instantly there was a flash of flame that reached half way to the roof of the cabin. At the same moment there came from the cask a wild yell, and in the winking of an eye there leaped forth and dashed out at the open door a tall form enveloped from head to toe in a sheet of flame. Through the flames could dimly be seen the shape of a man and something of a terribly distorted and frightened looking face.

"The devil or Dave Baxter!" cried the husband, at the same time making a rush to the door and reaching up toward the hooks for his rifle—the first thought of a backwoodsman in the presence of an enemy, whether man or devil.

"Oh, Jim! Jim!" shrieked his wife, darting forward and throwing her arms about her husband's neck before he could get hold of his rifle. "Save me, Jim! It was the devil sure enough; I seed his horns and his tail, Jim."

"I seed a tail, too, an' it was all afire," said Jim, "but it was on the back of his head and looked like the tail of a coon. How is that, Elder, does the devil have his tail on the back on his head!"

"Some kinds do—particularly little ones like this I raised for you," said the complacent preacher.

"Oh, his horns!—his horns!" cried the wife, who by this time had released her husband.

"Whose—your husband's?" asked the elder.

"Oh, no; the devil's! They were like the horns of an old goat!"

Impelled by the instinct of the hunter within him, the husband was by this time out at the doorstep looking for the devil's hoofmarks. "Hah!" cried he fiercely. "Ugh! Moccasins! Why, how is this, Elder—does the devil wear moccasins!"

"Why not? Do you suppose he is proud of his cloven foot?"

"O, I s'pose not. But, I say, Elder, what if I take down my gun, track him up, and take a shot at him jist for luck—and to help along religion?"

"Oh, Jim, you mustn't leave the house! The elder's goin' away now and I'll be skeert to death to be left alone and the devil loose in the settlement. Jim, jist think a minit—think what might be the consekenses!"

"Sure enough! Well, Betts, I won't go—let the devil go to the devil!"

"Oh, ah! already I'm afeerd I've bin too much skeert, Jim!"

"In course, Betts, it wur natchully a kinder sprise, but I didn't see's he looked much wus nor some white men I know. Fact is, at the fust glimse, as he riz out'n the old meat bar'l, I thought it looked like the sneakin' blaggard Dave Baxter."

"Dave Baxter, indeed!" cried the wife, scornfully. "Here you go to beggin' the elder to do a mir'kle an' raise the devil, an' when he raises him you think it's Dave Baxter. You're makin' a puffic fool of yourself 'bout Dave Baxter and if yer don't quit it—partic'ly before company—I'll jist pack my duds and go home to my good old mammy."

"Say no more, Betts!" cried the honest backwoodsman. "In course 'twur the devil, fur how would the elder, who don't know him, ever have thought of raisin' Dave Baxter!"

"You asked me as a favor, my friend, to perform a miracle in your house, and when I oblige you then you fall to quarrelling with your wife about a person I never heard of until now. It's nearly always the way when I perform a miracle; it makes trouble of some kind. I shall be obliged to give up miracles."

"I beg a thousand pardons, Elder," cried the honest settler, "I've been making a fool of myself! Don't be takin' your cloak to go, Elder. Stay an' presently we'll have a bite o' supper. Our smoke-house ain't quite empty yit."

But the "man of God" would remain no longer. He said only a mere mist of rain was falling, his clothes were dry and warm and he would push on to the Shipley Settlement.

"If you won't and can't stay," said the frontiersman, "you must take along my biggest and fattest turkey for yer dinner tomorrer. I'll strap it on behind yer saddle for you. You preformed a big mir'kle for me right under my own ruff, and I want to do somethin' fer you."

Elder Dow accepted the turkey with thanks, and then readily obtained the promise of the husband that he and his wife would come on the morrow and hear him preach.

At the meeting the next day the man was so touched by Elder Dow's preaching that he was among the first to go forward to the "mourner's bench," and he pulled his wife along to be prayed for. After meeting he told all the settlers of the miracle the elder had performed in his house, saying that after that he felt it to be in his duty to "git religion." His wife was constantly called upon to corroborate what he said of the raising of the devil, and a hundred times she was obliged to give a minute description of the evil one—horns, tail, fiery breath and all.

On the strength of his great and well-attended miracle, performed in the midst of the people, the elder obtained many converts in the settlement.

Another occurrence was also much talked of in the settlement that Sunday. It appeared that the day before, while Dave Baxter was trying to kindle a fire, when out in the forest hunting, his powder-horn exploded, burned his cap and coat and singed off eyebrows and hair, yet did not leave in his face a single powder mark. This escape from having grains of powder shot into his face was declared by all the old and experienced backwoodsmen the "biggest kind of a miracle." So they had in the settlement at one and the same time two first-class miracles.

San Francisco Examiner, February 12, 1893

Death Valley

THE STRANGE REGION KNOWN AS THE
AMERICAN THIRSTLAND
"Uncle Bob" Sees the "Dance of the Sands"—
The Horse and the Man of the Fountain

The region of extinct lakes and inland seas of Southern Nevada and Southeastern California is the great "Thirstland" of the continent. Where immense lakes once rolled their waves are now seen naught but broad and thirsty deserts. In places the floors of the ancient lakes are as white, smooth and solid as marble. In passing over them no trace is left by either man or animals. Covered with an efflorescence of crystallized salts of various kinds, these beds of extinct seas glitter in the sun like fields of ice. Surrounding the areas of solid material are vast tracts of shifting sands. In the same region will also be found miles on miles of comparatively level land, the surface of which is a brown crust, beneath which is a gray dust resembling volcanic ashes, or a soft, clinging mud. Into this material, whether wet or dry, men and animals sink at each step to a depth of from six inches to a foot, the crust giving way beneath the weight of any creature heavier than a fox or coyote. It is this portion of the deserts that drags the life out of both man and beast.

These regions are the home of the delusive mirage and of tall revolving pillars of sand that to the number of half a dozen at a time are often seen waltzing solemnly to and fro over the level wastes. They make their appearance every afternoon in certain places, as if forming for a cotillion, and, unbroken, for hours slowly weave back and forth and around one another. These sand pillars tower almost to the clouds—a grand and striking feature of the deserts. In watching their stately and apparently intelligent movements, one is almost inclined to believe with the Indians that they are the ghost of giants that lived in the days when the dead seas were alive, or to set them down as being genii of the deserts partaking of the nature of that gigantic genius who was released from the jar by the old fisherman, as related in the "Arabian Nights."

There are in many places in the mountain ranges bordering the deserts springs and small brooks of sweet water, and those who know where to find these may safely travel through the country, braving even the broadest of the alkaline wastes; but the stranger who ventures into these arid wilds may wander for days without finding water. Parched with thirst, physically exhausted, mentally deranged, deluded by a thousand phantasms—he at last lies down beneath the blazing sun to die.

Every year there are discovered in the wild recesses and lonely nooks of the Great Basin region the bodies of men and animals, lost, no one knows how, many years ago. Desiccated by the dry, hot air, and in a manner embalmed by the many mineral salts contained in the soil, the bodies of both men and animals become mummified. The muscles and flesh acquire almost the blackness and hardness of ebony, while the skin dries and shrinks, firmly binding together the frame. In this state bodies remain for years without change and without odor. In the rainless region in which lie Death valley and the more southern of the great deserts material objects and substances long remain unchanged. At "Lost Wagons," near the north end of Death valley, where many members of a bewildered and exhausted emigrant party perished in the early days while trying to find their way into Southern California, was seen a striking illustration of the preservative qualities of the air and climate of the desert. There, about the last camp of the lost people, the tracks of men, women and children were still visible in the sand in 1860, after the lapse of ten years. All were apparently as fresh as if made only a week before.

There under the eyes of a party of roving prospectors, remained the imprints of the feet of persons dead a decade of years—the footprints of toddling little ones as well as those of men and women grown. Robinson Crusoe's eyes goggled when he saw in the sand the track of a solitary savage and he mused and marveled long thereat. But these prospectors had before them food for even more serious reflection than had the hero of Defoe. There, too, stood the old wagons with the ox-chains stretched before them; also, yokes lying across the chains at equal distances, telling the number of cattle that had belonged to each wagon. It was the disastrous misadventure of this immigrant party that gave to Death valley its present name, as it is really the ancient sink of the Amargosa river. A few of the emigrants of the "Lost Wagons" found their way through a rugged pass to California, but the majority lost their lives in the deserts, the women and children falling by the roadside and the men wandering away to perish among the lava-capped hills.

In 1859, at the then new mines at Monoville, near Mono lake, I made the acquaintance of three Kern county men, who had been all the summer vainly searching for a place called "Three Peaks," where, they said, a member of this party of lost emigrants had seen huge nuggets of pure gold in the channel of a little rocky ravine at which he lay down to drink. When these men reached our camp they were in a very dilapidated condition, and having a whole summer's growth of hair and beard, they looked more like savages than men of any civilized land.

An old Virginian, known as "Uncle Bob," was the leader of the party, and had in his possession a map of the country which he said was made for him by the emigrant who had seen the gold in the creek. A sight that Uncle Bob saw one day to the northward of Death valley caused him suddenly to give up his search for the brook of golden nuggets, and lead his companions out of the country.

Uncle Bob was one day out from camp alone. In returning toward evening he took a "near cut" across a neck of desert. Seeing at some distance an object that looked bright and red in the light of the declining sun, he turned aside to investigate. On reaching the spot he found lying on the sand the mummy of a woman in a calico dress. An old cloth reticule was hanging to one arm of the mummy, and by the other lay a big cotton umbrella. Uncle Bob did not long remain to study the face that grinned up at him out of an old-fashioned sunbonnet. He precipitately fled to his companions and the next morning broke camp and struck out for the White mountains, thence steering for Mono lake.

It seems heartless to take advantage of the soul-consuming thirst of a desert-wandering human being and make use of it for the purpose of playing off a practical joke, yet the hardy prospector of the Pacific Coast, with scarce a spark of life in his body, still has left an animating sense of humor, grim though it may be, that never deserts him. I shall never forget one instance of the "humor" of the prospecting miner which I observed some years ago and which was a little the grimmest I ever heard of.

In company with J. M. Campbell, now editor and proprietor of the Walker Lake *Bulletin*, Hawthorne, and one or two others, I took a prospecting trip through the southern part of Nevada and a portion of Southeastern California. We were on a wild-goose chase after an old abandoned Spanish mine supposed to be situated in the Death valley region, and of the whereabouts of which one of our party claimed to have exact knowledge.

We were provided with pack and riding animals, and struck out for Candelaria, to Fish Lake valley and Gold mountain, thence heading for Oasis springs. These springs are in the middle of a rocky desert region, and are the fountain head of the Amargosa river. This "river" is about two feet wide, and after running about ten miles sinks into a broad, sandy canyon, or valley rather, called the Amargosa "wash." This wash is a "wash" without water. We were obliged to make two or three "dry camps" while following it. After a long course it circles around the point of the Amargosa mountains and bears northward into Death valley, which was the sink or lake into which the river emptied ages ago, when it was a real river.

In Death valley, on the east side, is a great trough-like depression, fifteen miles in length from north to south, which is 150 feet below the level of the sea. To the southward lies the sink of the Mohave and the great Mohave desert. The Mohave river rises in San Bernardino county, California, and flows northeasterly to its present lake or sink, while the Amargosa heads in Oasis springs, Nevada, and flows, or once flowed, southwesterly to the edge of the Mohave desert, whence it turns northeast to Death valley (formerly called the Sink of the Amargosa). Ancient channels afford indubitable evidence that at one time what is now known as Death valley was the common "sink" of both the Amargosa and the Mohave rivers; and that at a time still more remote it was the deepest part of a great inland sea which covered the Mohave desert and all the smaller surrounding connected deserts. The Amargosa wash shows evidence of a once mighty river. It is from ten to fifteen miles wide, and can be traced northward to Silver Peak, in Nye county, Nevada, a distance of 150 miles. The stream rising at Oasis springs was, in ancient times, a mere tributary creek.

Before coming to the Amargosa mountains, we had made a dry camp—devilish dry—and exhausted our supply of water. It was in June, and the sun blazed in the copper-colored heavens. The rocks were so hot that one could not touch nor sit on them. Our thirst presently became terrible. In vain we looked for the little monuments of stone, which are the Indian "guide-boards" to springs. Not a sign of water could be found.

The following lines from Tasso's "Jerusalem Delivered" well describe what we then experienced:

> Heaven seems a sable Furnace: not a thing
> Speaks freshness to the sight; the frolicksome
> Sweet Zephyr[u]s, silent, waving not a wing,
> His grotto keeps; mellifluous air is dumb.
> Not a bird's flutt'ring, not an insect's hum
> Breaks the still void; or on its sultry gloom
> If winds intrude, 'tis only such as come
> From the hot sands, Sirocco or Simoom,
> Which, blown in stifling gusts, the springs of life consume.

As we crept along down the Waterloo "wash," walking and leading our animals, which were more dead than alive, our burning eyeballs rolled in every direction for some sign of water, for we were now among the first considerable hills of the Amargosa range.

"Ha!" suddenly shouted Campbell, who was in the lead. "Ha! See here!" and on our coming up he pointed to a trail that turned squarely away from that leading down the "wash." It made directly up a narrow, rocky ravine where were seen some green and waving bushes. Up that ravine must be a spring. The green foliage denoted it, and the branch trail could only mean that up there beside the big rocks and waving bushes was a fountain of living water. Behold, too, standing hitched by the thicket of green, a horse.

"A horse! See the horse!" cried all hands. The animal was unsaddled, as we could plainly see, and was standing at ease to rest, having, no doubt, traveled over a long and hard road. The bunch of grass in his mouth was apparently forgotten as he stood dreamily enjoying a welcome respite from the arduous toils of the burning desert.

It was only three hundred yards away up the little gulch to where stood the horse by the fountain. With a glad whoop and a hurrah we all turned from the direct path and took the steep trail that led up the lateral ravine.

"Water, water! Thank God; water at last!" was the general cry. Already in imagination we were plunging our faces into the fountain up to our eyes and gulping down whole rivers of the cool and sparkling element.

"Hurrah! whoop hurrah for the spring!" and up the dusty bed of the ravine we scrambled, pulling after us our unwilling animals.

"What is the matter with you, Bill?" cried Campbell to his horse. "Sometimes you can smell water a mile, but now when it's in plain sight you hold back as if you were being led into a blazing furnace."

Suddenly Campbell, who was in the lead, halted and cried: "Ha! What the devil—why, what is this?" "What is what?" said someone.

"Why, the horse. Look at the horse," cried Campbell. "If it ain't dead I'm a liar!"

"Dead! The horse dead!" was the cry as we all moved forward to take a square look.

"Dead as a door-nail!" said Campbell. And dead he was, sure enough, as we could all now plainly see, being but a rod away from where the beast stood. It was but the mere mummy of a horse—the skin and bones of a horse. Every rib could be counted, the tail was almost hairless and the eye-sockets were empty. But there the animal stood firmly braced on his bony legs and his halter tied to a bush. In his mouth, which was partly open and showed the projecting teeth, was a bunch of sagebrush. The bushes we had seen were mesquit, which grows on the highest and dry-est sand-knolls in the country, luring many a weary pilgrim from his path by its greenness.

"Some devil's crew that passed this way," said Campbell, "set that skeleton up in that way; tied him to the tree and put the brush in his mouth on purpose to fool people into coming up here in the expectation of finding a spring. Whew! the place is dry as a lime-kiln!"

On coming quite up to the horse, and making a close examination, we found that he was supported in position by two strong mesquit stakes firmly planted in the ground and cunningly concealed between his fore and hind legs as he stood broadside across the ravine. We hardly made this discovery before one of our party cried: "Great God! Look here!"

Turning quickly to where the man pointed, our hair almost stood on end as we saw seated but ten feet away under a mesquit bush a grinning human mummy. The mummy was dressed in dark woolen clothes and wore jauntily a tattered black wool hat. The skin of the face was so drawn and puckered as to expose the teeth, giving to the visage an expression of devilish glee and cunning. The mummy seemed grinning at us as if gratified at having succeeded in fooling us up the ravine.

The back of the mummy rested against the rocky wall of the gulch and it was seated on an old, weather-beaten Mexican saddle; by its side was a roll of old moldy blankets, and leaning against the rock stood an old musket, the barrel of which seemed ready to pull out of the bleached and broken stock. The bony left hand rested on the knees and held a hair rope, or lariat, which was fastened about the neck of the skeleton horse. It was a grim and terrible tableau, illustrative of the perils of the surrounding waterless wastes. Tortured with thirst as we were at the moment, the skeleton man and horse seemed to hint for us a similiar fate. The dead and desiccated mortal seemed, as if in a voice from the tombs, to say:

As I am now so you must be;
Prepare for death and follow me.

We hastened from the spot, leaving the man and the horse at the fountain as we found them, a trap for the next party of thirsty explorers passing that way. The trail up the little gulch seemed as much traveled as that down the "wash," telling that all who had passed the place had, like ourselves, been lured from the main path by the mummy horse and the equally deceptive greenness of the little clump of mesquit. It was probable, we thought, that the mummy man had himself been deceived by the mesquit bushes, and that the last struggle he and his horse made was to reach them.

A mile farther down the "wash" we found a small supply of brackish water in a hole that some party had dug in the bed of the dead river at a clayey spot. Still, before reaching Resting springs, which we did about midnight, we were again suffering terribly from thirst.

At Resting springs some men from San Bernardino were then preparing for borax mining. From them we learned that for many years the mummified man and horse had been seen just as we had found them. No one knew who the dead man was, but it was thought he was some Mexican miner who had perished there many years before.

San Francisco Examiner, January 29, 1888

A Goblin Frog

Through Its Agency the Silver Mines of the Comstock Are Discovered

O'REILLY'S GOOD LUCK
An Irishman Who Struck It after a Frightful Experience

Peter O'Reilly was a pioneer miner of Nevada and one of the discoverers of the great Comstock silver lode—one of the two men who turned up to the light of day that glittering ore which was the first of over $300,000,000 since taken from the wonderful vein then hit upon.

For years before he made the great discovery O'Reilly had been working among the gold placers of Gold Canyon, a wet weather tributary of the Carson river, in which gold was discovered as early as 1852. In this canyon he wrought with pan and rocker, and at times with much success, sometimes taking out several hundred dollars in a few days, for the ground was very rich in spots.

"Pete" was fond of rambling away alone along the meanderings of the canyon in search of the rich spots that were to be found by those who diligently sought for them. He liked to be by himself and mine in his own way. Provided he could find a few "colors" (small particles of gold), he would dig and pan away for days, quite confident that his luck would at last lead him to the right spot and his labors be richly rewarded.

Peter O'Reilly was not only a spiritualist, but also a firm believer in all manner of signs and omens. He heard voices, as did the heroes of Ossian, in the sighing breeze and extracted a meaning from all the sounds of hill and vale that reached his ear. The end of all this was (a few years after the discovery of the Comstock lode) that he became insane, and finally died in a private asylum at Woodbridge, Cal. The last mining O'Reilly ever did in Gold Canyon was when he started in to prospect a bar on which he found a previous locator in the person of a frog, which held a "squatter's" right to the place, and which frog almost immediately began to give him trouble.

Pete began his mining operations by constructing a small dam to turn the rill flowing in the canyon into a little ditch that led to his "panning hole" at the lower end of the bar.

The little reservoir formed by the dam held only about a dozen hogsheads of water. It was soon after this reservoir filled that Pete first had notice of the presence on his claim of the frog. He had sunk a pit in the gravel of the bar almost down to the bed-rock and had washed out two or three pans of dirt that yielded well. He was down in this prospect hole filling his pan with some particularly promising gravel, when he heard a small squeaky voice sing out, "Struck it?"

Pete was at the moment deeply absorbed in the work in which he was engaged, and the shrill, squeaking voice ringing out so near at hand and asking a question that so exactly chimed in with the train of thought running through his head, so startled him that his pick almost fell from his hands. He pricked up his ears and looked about in all directions to see whence proceeded the cheery little voice. Almost he expected to discover a little red-mantled fairy peering out at him from some neighboring clump of willows or some tall tuft of grass. As he thus stood gazing about in open-mouthed amazement, the little voice again piped out: "Struck it? Struck it? Struck it?"

Turning his eyes in the direction whence proceeded the inquiring voice, Pete presently descried a small green frog mounted upon a stick that projected an inch or two above the surface of the water in his reservoir. The frog was but a rod or two away and seemed, as Pete thought, to be looking inquiringly into his eyes.

"Struck it? Struck it? Struck it?" again said the frog.

"Are ye schpakin' to me, sor," said Pete.

"Struck it!" says the frog.

"It's a good omen," said Pete. "The little feller says I've sthruck it. Though he's no countryman o' mine, I belave in me sowl he manes well by me and that I have sthruck it in this very hole."

So saying, Pete carried the pan of dirt he had dug to his panning place, panned it out and did not get a "color." He was not a little astonished at this result, and was much inclined to call the frog a liar, but on turning to look for him the little fellow was gone. He went to his pit and dug another pan of dirt, listening all the time to hear what the frog would have to say about it. Not a word did the frog say, however.

Pete washed out the pan of dirt and got gold to the value of nearly a dollar. "Aha! ye little divil!" cried he, "where air ye now? Ye didn't have a word to say this time."

Well pleased with his luck, Pete began digging another pan of gravel from the place where he had got the last, expecting another rich result. He had been at work only half a minute before the little voice rang out sharp and clear: "Struck it? Struck it? Struck it?"

"O yes, ye little fool!" cried Pete, "it's aisy for ye to say, 'Sthruck it! sthruck it! sthruck it!' after ye've seen what I got in me pan."

"Struck it! Struck it! Struck it!" cried the frog in what seemed to Pete a triumphant tone.

"All right, me bye!" cheerily assented Pete, nodding his head toward the little fellow that sat winking and blinking on the end of the stick. "All right, me bye; av coorse I've sthruck it!"

Pete then picked up his pan of gravel, carried it to the water hole, washed it out and did not find a speck of gold. "You're the worst liar I iver saw!" cried Pete, rising up from his work and shaking his fist in the direction of the frog. Not a sign of the frog did he see, however, the little fellow having very prudently retired to the bottom of the pond.

Pete grumbled for a time, then went and dug another pan of gravel. As he was carrying the dirt to his panning place the frog stuck his head above the water and called out, "Struck it!" and again no gold was found. Thus it went. When the frog said nothing he got a good yield of gold, but when he made his usual inquiry—sneering inquiry—Pete now considered it to be—no gold was found.

At last Pete had washed so many pans of dirt out of which the frog had charmed all the gold that he began to grow very angry. He was also not a little discouraged. Finally, just as he began to scrape the gravel out of a very promising crevice, and just as he was beginning to think the frog would this time hold his tongue, out came the little fellow with his "Struck it? Struck it?"

Pete quietly laid down his crevicing-spoon, slyly gathered two or three big rocks, then softly, on tip-toe, began stealing toward his little persecutor, and just as the frog cried "Struck it? Struck it?" the irate O'Reilly let drive at him with a rock so huge that it could have been hurled by no lesser Ajax. The rock missed its mark, but raised a great commotion in the little pond.

Thinking he had given his bad angel a fright that would last him a fortnight, Pete returned to his work. He had almost filled his pan with very rich-looking dirt, when up popped the frog's head and out came his tantalizing "Struck it? Struck it?"

Pete threw the pan of gravel as far as he could send it and made for the frog, determined on its destruction. He would stand no more of its infernal deviltry.

Shovel in hand he waded out into the middle of the little reservoir and scooped and tore about in it with the vigor and venom of a mad bull. Once or twice he saw, or imagined he saw, the frog dart through the discolored water and brought down the back of his shovel on the spot with such a "spat" that the blow might have been heard half a mile away.

At last, not seeing anything more of the frog, Pete concluded that he had killed him. He gave the little animal a parting curse, and being wrought up to such a pitch of excitement and nervousness that he could work no more that afternoon, strode away, put on his coat and went home.

The next morning he returned to his claim and his work. He had washed out several pans of dirt and was getting good pay out of all he washed, when suddenly there fell upon his ear the shrill cry of "Struck it?"

The first note sent a thrill through Peter's stalwart frame like the sharp shock of an electrical battery; then a chill fell upon his heart and his hair almost rose on end. His evil genius, as he now firmly believed the little green frog to be, was still there, alive and at his old tricks.

"May the curse o' the Howly Saint Pathrick light on ye!" cried Pete. Then he kicked over the pan of dirt he had dug and made a rush for the reservoir, the frog "plumping" under the water with a little chirp at his approach. Again Pete went into the reservoir with his long-handled shovel. He charged about, but could see nothing of the frog, nor anything that looked like it. Being determined to do for his enemy this time, Pete went for his pan and began trying to bail out the reservoir. Finding this too great a task, he got his pick, dug down the embankment of rocks and earth forming the little dam, and eagerly watched, with uplifted shovel, for the frog as the water ran off. The water all ran out of the reservoir, but his little tormentor was nowhere to be seen.

Pete waded out into the oozy bed of the pond, digging and plowing about with his shovel; but he failed to start the goblin frog. He then arrived at the very reasonable conclusion that the little imp had gone down the stream with the body of water that rushed out of the reservoir when it was opened. He cruised about the spot for an hour or more, going down the channel of the canyon, turning over rocks and beating tufts of grass with his shovel, but saw nothing of the frog. Thinking his evil genius had been washed down through the canyon into the Carson river, Pete rebuilt his dam, in order that he might have water ready for use in the morning. This job done, he went home, feeling quite sure that he had either killed or permanently ousted his little enemy.

The next day he returned to his work. Before starting in, however, he walked round the reservoir several times, peering keenly into the water and kicking every bunch of grass about its margin. The frog was nowhere to be seen or started.

Pete then went to his prospect hole and began digging, stopping occasionally, however, to cock an eye toward the pond and listen for the frog. There was not sign of the little imp and Pete's heart grew lighter. He had dug a pan of dirt without the usual hated interruption, and was on his way to wash it out when—"Struck it? Struck it?" was squeaked from the pond by the goblin frog.

This was too much for Pete. The pan dropped from his hands, his under-jaw fell and he sank down upon the nearest bowlders. As he was wondering if it was possible for him ever in any way to rid himself of the evil thing that destroyed his luck, the frog again called out as cheerily as ever, "Struck it? Struck it?"

"May the divil burn ye!" cried Pete. "No, I haven't sthruck it, and what's more I never will sthrike it wid ye there, ye dirty little blackguard! Must I be comin' after ye again? ye unclean baste o' the divil!"

"Struck it!" said the frog.

"Ye think so!" cried Pete, sarcastically; and, catching up a pick, he ran to the reservoir and began digging down the embankment.

Soon, however, he paused in this work, and, throwing down his pick, said: "No, it's of no use. Haven't I thried to get him in all manner o' ways? No, when I get the wather off he'll be gone. He's no human frog! I'll jist let him howld possession, and I'll hunt me another place. Divil a lick will I ever sthrike here again; it's the divil's own child he is! I've heard birds talk and bastes talk, but niver wan o' thim all that could schpake so plain as this little green divil that's widout either feathers or hair—he's not human."

Pete began gathering up his tools and clothes with the intention of vacating the place, when he stepped and gazed wistfully at his prospect hole. "A promising place, too, it was in the main," said he. "Howly Mother! Shall I, a Christian and a good Catholic, be tormented away by a dirty little heretic baste like yon? No. I'll give him a warmin' yit, and all the likes of him. I'll pepper him to-morrow!" So saying, Pete put on his coat and struck out for home, turning to shake his fist toward the pond as he departed.

The next morning Pete went up to Johntown, a little trading-post about a mile above his claim, and borrowed a shotgun; then he bought a quantity of powder and shot and returned toward his mine in a vengeful mood. Again and again he said as he strode along: "I'll kill that frog if it's among the possibilities!"

On reaching his claim Pete crawled to a big rock near the pond, and seating himself upon it watched patiently for over an hour, but the frog of Hades was neither to be seen or heard.

"He has run away," said Pete, "but I'll kill him if he's anywhere on the face of the green earth!"

He then moved cautiously along down the canyon. Although frogs were quite common on the Carson river, they were seldom seen in Gold Canyon. At last, however, Pete saw what he thought might be his tormentor. He blazed away with his gun and stretched the creature lifeless on the margin of the rill. He was beginning to rejoice over the victory he had gained, when up from the spot leaped another frog, the very picture of that he had killed. Pete looked at this new apparition, then turned and gazed on the slaughtered animal to be sure it was dead. Finding it still stretched on the ground, he went after the second frog, which he finally succeeded in killing. All that day he hunted frogs up and down the canyon, blazing away at everything that moved. He slaughtered many toads and lizards, but only one other frog.

The next day he was again out with his gun, and every day for about a week, extending his hunt as far as the Carson river, and firing away many pounds of shot to little effect. He talked of little but frogs and the miners along the canyon, who always found great sport in his eccentricities and in his superstitious notions, "stuffed" him with many stories of the baleful influences of frogs and toads.

One morning, to the surprise of the jocular miners of the camp, for whom his insane warfare on the frogs had afforded great sport, instead of starting out with his gun, Pete took his pan and crevicing-spoon, and departed down the canyon in the direction of his claim. An hour later Pete came tearing up the canyon to the camp wild-eyed. "I'll niver sthrike pick intil this canyon again!" cried he. "That imp o' the divil is still there on me claim! I was but jist liftin' me second pan of dirt whin he raised his head from the water and says; 'Pete, have ye sthruck it?' sez he. 'May the divil bless me,' says I, 'if ye can't have the whole bloody canyon; I'll niver sthrike pick intil it again.' No more I will. That frog is no human frog—it's a child o' hell!"

Pete O'Reilly kept his word; he at once "pulled up stakes" in Gold Canyon. He struck out for Six-Mile Canyon, five miles to the northward. Taking Pat McLaughlin for a partner, the two began mining at the head of the canyon, where Virginia City now stands, and there the pair presently "struck it"—struck the great Comstock silver lode, the hidden treasure-house of the gnomes and the wonder of the whole mining world. But for the "goblin frog" O'Reilly would probably have continued mining in Gold Canyon and to this day the Comstock and the "Big Bonanza" might have remained undiscovered. But for the frog the names of Mackay, Fair and a score of other mining millionaires would not now be known throughout the world.

San Francisco Examiner, April 22, 1888

Elam Storm

THE MAN OF THE MOUNTAINS
AND HIS MILLIONS

A fortnight ago I found myself at Lake Tahoe. I had not been at the lake an hour before I had the good fortune to fall in with my old California friend, Ned Meredeth.

"Just in time," said Ned, after we had exchanged greetings. "I had planned a trip to Emerald bay for to-morrow and was just casting about in my mind for a fellow voyager when you hove in sight. We will make the trip together and go prepared to have a regular old-fashioned lunch ashore. We are sure to have a good time."

"All right; count me in," said I.

We took an early start and had a glorious sail up the lake and across the bay. With a spoon-hook trailing astern of our boat, we caught several fine trout during our sail.

Landing in a little cove we went ashore for the purpose of roasting a trout and having a good substantial lunch.

The roast trout was a success and we made a hearty meal. Having appeased our hunger we lighted our cigars and stretched ourselves upon the ground to smoke, to listen to the wind whispering in the tops of the pines and to gaze listlessly upon the waves dancing and flashing far out on the lake.

I might here say something about the grand scenery in the midst of which we found ourselves, but scores of both pen and pencil pictures, better than I could hope to paint, have already made most of those who are likely to read this little sketch familiar with the more prominent points of interest about the lake; beside, my present object is to tell the story of a curious character it was our good fortune to encounter.

We had almost finished our cigars when the crackling of a dry stick just at our backs caused us to start up and face about. Approaching was a tall, gaunt, middle-aged man. He wore heavy cowhide boots, into which were thrust about half the length of a pair of stout corduroy pantaloons, and in place of coat and vest appeared no less than three woolen shirts, the two outer ones very heavy and worn open at the breast. His beard was long and yellow and a shock of yellow hair thatched his head, almost rendering superfluous the tattered slouched hat he wore. On his right shoulder he carried a long Kentucky rifle and an "Arkansaw toothpick" hung from his leathern waistbelt.

Striding up to where we were standing, our visitor said: "Good day, boys," and dropping to the ground, even as he so greeted us, laid his rifle by his side and, crossing his legs a la Turk, looked out at us from beneath the wide brim of his hat for a moment, then abruptly said: "I am a man of the mountains."

"So I should judge," said Ned.

"The voice of the wind in the trees is more familiar to me than the voice of man."

"Been long in the mountains?" asked Ned.

"I am Elam Storm and I have been in the mountains a long time—so long that they seem to have worn down a good deal since I first began traveling over them."

"Every pebble kicked from the top of a ridge rolls toward the bottom," remarked Ned.

"And every drop of rain sends some grains of sand in the same direction," pursued Elam.

"And the winds spread the dust of the mountain top over the valleys," said Ned.

"And the rills from the melting snow," suggested I.

"And the land slides and the avalanches," ventured Ned.

"They are a power," said I.

"Great God!" cried Elam, "they *are* a power!" and he drew the brim of his hat down over his eyes as though to shut out some troublesome vision.

"Do you live in this region?" asked Ned, arousing Elam from a fit of musing that had lasted some minutes.

"Sometimes. I am a man of the mountains. My home is wherever I make my camp. When winter comes I move down the mountains in advance of the snow and with the return of warm weather ascend to the upper valleys and peaks with the deer."

"Is your present camp here on the lake?" I asked.

"I have some traps and provisions stowed away in a hole in the rocks—a sort of cavern—over behind yonder mountain," and Elam pointed in the direction of a high granite ridge to the southwest.

"You are a hunter, are you not?" queried Ned.

"Yes, I am a hunter of gold—a hunter of gold. Boys," and Elam spoke in a low and impressive tone, "there is gold in these mountains; yes, millions on millions of gold!"

"Doubtless," said I, "but the trouble is to find it."

"It was found once and I'll find it again. Yes, I'll find it. I've looked for it years and years, but at last I shall find it. I know the place and I have seen the gold. Too much snow up there—always too much snow!" and thus concluding the wild glitter died out of Elam's eyes, he sighed deeply and his thoughts seemed far away.

"As but little snow fell last winter you should be able to find the gold this summer?" suggested Ned.

"Yes; this summer I shall find it—this summer or never!" and Elam grasped his gun and unfolded his legs as though about to arise.

"You are sure it is there?" queried I.

"As sure as that I am here. Some hint that I am not right here," touching his forehead, "but they do not know my story. I may tell it now—may tell it here, but not everywhere. Listen, and you, too, will know that the gold is there:

"Many years ago a man who was out hunting lost his way in these mountains. In his wanderings he came to a small stream—a mere rill—and lay down at it to drink. While drinking he saw gold on the bed-rock—beautiful nuggets of gold glittering under the water!

"He remained until he had gathered not less than five pounds of nuggets, then—being out of provisions and almost starved—he was obliged to renew his efforts to find his way out of the mountains.

"He traveled down the rill till it entered a brook, down the brook till it was lost in a large stream, then down this last to a still larger, and so on, marking as he descended the mouth of each creek as he left it behind.

"This man lived not far from the town of Genoa, and was my nearest neighbor. He was much excited when he first reached home and showed me specimens of the gold, at the same time giving some account of the way in which he found it, but he soon after became so close-mouthed that he would tell me nothing more; he pretended that his first story was nothing but a joke, and invented a new story to account for his being in possession of the gold he had shown me.

"I was not deceived. I knew the first story was the true one, and sure that he would soon go back to his mine for more gold, so I watched his cabin and shadowed him day and night. I hardly allowed myself time to eat or sleep, and had always on hand, near his cabin, a hidden store of provisions sufficient to last several days, for I did not know what day or night he might start for the mountains.

"At last, after I had watched nearly a week, I saw my man steal forth in the dusk of the evening with a blanket, tools and provisions on his back. I hastily secured my outfit and cautiously followed him.

"All that night I was his shadow, and all the next day I kept him in view. When night came he camped and, after cooking his supper, rolled himself in his blankets and stretched out on the ground by his fire.

"I was cold, and my teeth chattered, but I was afraid to make a fire. I did not once close my eyes that night, for there was gold ahead—thousands on thousands of gold!

"In the morning, after breakfast, my man again moved on, and I stealthily followed. He toiled up a deep, rocky ravine, and I skulked behind from rock to rock and from bend to bend.

"About noon he stopped and lunched, then went on two or three miles, till well up toward the summit of the main range, when he halted and, stowing away his blankets and other traps, soon began the work of picking up and panning out gold.

"He was at work on the south side of a deep ravine, at the foot of a great mountain, the face of which was covered with snow—all one sheet of snow—God knows how deep!

"Having discovered the golden secret, and being greatly in need of rest and sleep, I crept out of the ravine and made my way across the first ridge to the northward, where I might safely make a camp and build a fire.

"As I lay by my fire that night and thought that we two were the only human beings among all the great silent peaks standing about, and then considered the business we were on, there seemed something awful in it—the deep silence was absolutely painful. At last, however, I slept, and slept well, till morning; indeed, till after sunrise.

"Leaving my traps in camp I recrossed the ridge, and crawling from rock to rock and tree to tree at last gained a position about fifty yards above the bottom of the ravine and just opposite where my man was at work. Peering round the end of a block of granite behind which I lay, I could see him picking the nuggets out from among the finer gold after he had washed a pan of dirt. How I longed for the day of his departure in order that I might take his place and dig my share of those golden nuggets! Thinking of this I determined to put myself on a short allowance of provision in order that I might remain in the mountains as long as possible.

"It then occurred to me that he would be likely to hit upon the same plan for prolonging his stay and that I should be starved out by the time he left the spot.

"At one time I thought of boldly discovering myself and claiming a partnership in the mine; then it came into my head to steal upon my man at night as he lay by his fire, kill him and take both his mine and the gold he had gathered, but I said: 'Git thee behind me, Satan!' Yet it was torture to see him heaping up gold that I could not touch. The conclusion I finally arrived at, however, was to husband my provisions and bide my time.

"I had kept my position and watch until nearly noon, and was thinking of making my way over the ridge to my camp, when a faint murmuring sound attracted my attention. I glanced rapidly about but could see nothing to which I could trace the strange noise. It seemed to fill the air overhead and on all sides, and was not unlike the hum of a large swarm of bees in full flight. Soon what began as a mere murmur became a decided roar and, looking across the ravine, I saw a huge avalanche descending the face of the opposite mountain. All that was on the vast slope before me was in motion. Trees were uprooted and swept along with the descending masses of snow, and great rocks were torn from their beds. The roar of the avalanche, combined with the crashing and grinding together of rocks and the splintering of trees, produced a noise the like of which I never heard before nor since. It could only be compared to prolonged and deafening peals of thunder, rising through and heard above the steady roar of a tremendous waterfall.

"Dropping my eyes to my neighbor in the ravine I saw him running, pan in hand, toward the place where he had deposited the gold he had taken out. He had proceeded but a few steps, however, before a great bowlder came bounding down the mountain and, hopping into the ravine, landed full upon him. Almost instantly there followed a rushing hill of snow that filled the ravine and pushed its way nearly up to where I was standing; then all was silent as the grave. It was as though nothing had occurred, for in a moment the old calm and hush of centuries was again on the mountains and in the air. It was only when I looked at the denuded face of the mountain before me and the blockaded ravine at my feet that I could fully realize what had happened.

"The ravine was filled to the height of nearly 100 feet with snow and rubbish, and at the bottom of this lay the crushed remains of the man I had so envied scarce two minutes before—under it also lay all the gold I so coveted!

"For many minutes I stood gazing on the scene before me, utterly astounded and stupefied. All was so unexpected, so terrific and overwhelming, that it appeared to be the sudden interposition of some supernatural power, either of heaven or the regions below.

"Months of labor could not now reach the gold. I must wait until the sun and rains had worn away the mighty mass of snow that filled the ravine. This I saw at a glance, yet for an hour or more I lingered about the place, then turned sadly away and took my course across the ridge to my camp, where I stretched myself upon the ground and seriously considered the situation.

"As my neighbor and myself disappeared from the settlement at the same time, it would be thought that we went away together, and should I return alone it would be looked upon as a suspicious circumstance and in all probability I should be arrested as his murderer. True, I might conduct the officers of the law to the spot where the avalanche descended and there explain the whole affair; but then the gold—I could not give up the gold!

"After duly considering the strange affair in all its aspects, I crossed over to California, pitched my camp in the foothills and taking the name I now bear became a man of the mountains—a wanderer.

"In California I accidentally learned that the sudden disappearance of myself and neighbor was accounted for in the settlement on the supposition that we had been mixed up in some of the cattle-stealing affairs then of such common occurrence on that side of the mountains. This, though not very complimentary, was very satisfactory.

"Every summer and fall I have visited the spot where my fortune lies buried, but have always found the snow lying deep above it—ever too much snow. Heretofore I have always seen the remains of that old avalanche—so much new snow has fallen every year—but this summer it is almost gone. I have been on the ground, and in less than a month shall reap the reward of my long years of watching. Nearly all the rocks and broken trees lie well up on the north bank of the ravine, therefore I shall easily reach the gold—the great shining nuggets that I have so often seen in my dreams, by day and by night. Millions lie there, high up in the silent mountains, and they are all my own. No man can ever find the spot—no man who is not wandering, lost and half crazed would ever go there. To find my gold you must first be lost.

"Now that you have heard my story, I'll thank you for a little smoking tobacco."

Ned passed his pouch.

"I presume you have a pipe?" said Elam.

Ned handed over his pipe.

Elam filled the pipe and then said: "All I now lack is a match."

Having received a whole bunch of matches Elam used one, pocketed the others and then settled himself for a good square smoke. He sat in silence, often blowing the smoke out through his nostrils, like a Mexican or an Indian.

When he had finished the pipe he picked up his gun, arose to his feet and gravely and earnestly said: "You two have heard what I have never before breathed to living man, and what I would not tell everywhere, but my reward is now near, and I felt that I could afford to tell you my story—that after so many years of silence it would be a relief to tell it. I don't ask you to believe it."

"We hope your most sanguine expectations may be realized," said Ned.

"Thank you," said Elam. "And now," continued he, "now that I am going, I'll just take two or three of those trout and what remains of your lunch, that is, if it is all the same to you. I am a man of the mountains, and I stand on no ceremony with those I meet in the mountains."

We both apologized for not thinking to ask Elam to partake of our lunch, saying that the interest we had taken in his strange story must be our excuse for our apparent lack of hospitality. He replied that he had lunched just before sighting our camp, or he should have asked for food.

Having received all he asked for, Elam muttered: "I am now begging broken victuals, but soon I shall have millions, millions!"

Without any leave-taking and still muttering something about "gold," he strode away in the direction of the mountain he had pointed out as that behind which lay his camp.

Looking after Elam, Ned said: "He seems to talk straight enough once he is fairly under way, but do you think he is right up here?" tapping his forehead.

"I hardly know what to make of him. Did I not now see him marching away with those trout dangling from the barrel of his gun I should be in doubt as to whether any such man had been here. Let us up sail and away before some other 'man of the mountains' comes this way and finds us."

Territorial Enterprise, July 29, 1877

Peter Crow among
the Witches

"That beats the Old Scratch!"

"What de trouble now, sah?"

"My bait is gone again, and I haven't felt so much as a nibble. If there was any such thing in the world as a witch, I would think there was one down at the bottom of the river in this reach playing tricks with my hook."

"An' why not, sah?"

"Well, simply because there is no such thing as a witch."

"Doan you be too shore 'bout dat dare ain't no mo' witches, sah. Dar's witches in de wu'ld now, jes' same as dar allus wur. Yes, sah, an' in dis yere 'Debbil's Reach' is jist de place for 'em bekase witches an' de debbil allus runs togedder—dey's birds of de same fedder and tarred wid de same stick. Now de time when I wur a cat, I done got——"

"The time when you were a cat, Uncle Pete! What do you mean by such nonsense?"

"Nonsense! Nary a bit o' nonsense 'bout it, sah. Jist as shore as dat we two is settin' hyar in dis canoe on de Sackermento Ribber, I was onct a cat for a whole night. Yes, sah, an' I yowled an' fit wid de best of 'em! Dat wur back in ole Kaintucky, when I——"

"When you went to bed stuffed with roast 'possum and were troubled with nightmare, Uncle Pete."

"No, sah, nuffin' of de kine, sah. I wan't in bed, an' dar wur no dreamin' 'bout de business. I had a spell wucked on me bekase I was found peekin' in at a witch meeting—I wur hoodooed, sah. Yes, sah, dey done turn me inter a big black tomcat."

"Well, Uncle Pete, if you went yowling about as a tomcat for a whole night, all I can say is, you ought to know the fact."

"Now, sah, you's talkin'! Course I knows de fac'—I've got mighty good reason to know de fac', sah. See whar dat piece is gone out'n de top my right year?"

"Yes—look's like a 'swallow-fork' in the ear of a Texas steer."

"Well, sah, dat piece wur tuck out'n dat air year de time when I wur a cat."

Peter Crow
Among the Witches

BY DAN DE QUILLE.

"Well, Uncle Pete, tell me the whole story, then I'll be better able to judge as to whether you were transformed—turned into a cat."

"All right, sah—guess it's safe enough talkin' 'bout de mattah out hyar in Californy, but back yander, I wouldn't like to chance it even now. Well, when dis thing happen was long befo' de wah, sah. Dem times I wur tol'able young and frisky. It wur in de ole slabery times, an' I belong to ole man Paxton—ole Joe Paxton. He had er big plantation dar in Kaintucky, in Mason County, on Limestone Creek, 'bout ten mile back from Maysville. He raise heap terbacker an' hemp, and keep lots o' fine stock; but I don't wuck in de fields, kase I ain't one de field hands. I wur a stable boy—wuck all de time 'bout de stables takin' keer o' de hosses. Lordy, Lordy, how well I 'member dem times an' ole massa Paxton! De jumpin' Moses, but he wur a case—de ole massa! He uster have a little pony what he allus rode dat he called 'Possum.' He'd go down to Maysville 'bout tree times a week an' he nearly allus come home full as a goose, an' jest a-flyin'. When he'd git in 'bout half a mile o' home, he'd begin shoutin' wid dat voice o' his like de whistle of one of de big ribber boats: 'Hello, Pete! Hello Pete! Come an' take keer of Possum, Pete!' When I heerd dat yell a-comin' nigher an' nigher, I'd run out an' open de big gate of de banyard, an' he'd come a-sailin' in on de keen lope; de fat little Possum a-snortin' every jump. Den he'd circle roun' to de hoss-block and light off, takin' off'n de saddle bags, wid de papers an' letters in one eend and his little stone jug of ole rye in de odder; den he'd sing out: 'Pete, take good keer of Possum!' an' den he'd fence-row it along up to de big house."

"So I sets down with my back to a big poplah tree"

"But, Uncle Pete, what has all this to do with the witches?"

"Beg you' pardin' sah, I'se comin' to dem. Well, you see 'bout once a month or so de ole massa uster take a trip down to Cincinnati an' be gone two, tree days, maybe a week. Den I uster 'joy myself a little, goin' to frolics an' de like. Down de road toard Maysville, 'bout tree mile, wur a little cross-roads town, an' I uster scoot down dare arter brekfas' an' stay all day, takin' in de scrub hoss races, de shootin' matches, de wrastlin's, de fightin's an' all de odder fun. Well, dis time when I have my quare 'sperience, I stay at de 'Corners' till moas' night. Den I start home, an' as I see the sun 'bout down, I 'clude to take de near cut up 'cross de big bend of Limestone Creek. In one eend of a three-bushel bag I had a piece caliker for one de house gals, pair shoes for anodder, some ribbon for 'nodder, some dog-leg terbacker an' a lot of little traps; in de odder eend of de bag I had a gallon jug of old rye dat wus like de oil of gladness, an' dat wus for myself, ole George, Tom an' de rest de stable boys.

"When I start on de trail froo de woods I find it is gittin' dark. It bein' de fall of de yeah de leaves from de trees cover de groun' 'bout four inches thick, an' I soon lose de track; but I don't keer much, kase I think I kin keep on de course. Well, fust I know, I'm lost in de big woods, I'm all turned round. So I sets down with my back to a big poplah tree to considdah de course home.

"As I sets dar at de roots of de tree I pulls de co'ncob out'n de jug an' takes a swig or two to git de pints of de compass. But I kain't seem to ketch 'em. De win' otter blow from de wes', but it blow from de eas'; de Big Dipper got his pinters a-pintin' to de souf, an' de sebben stars an' Job's coffin all twisted roun'—all wrong.

"Well, sah, while I wur settin' dare a wonderin' what had happen to mix up de hebbenly bodies dat a-way, all to once I hears de soun' of fiddlin'. It wur a dance tune dat were a-playin'—a reg'lar 'Rake 'r Down Sall' of a tune. Ses I to myself: 'Dar's a cabin close by, an' a frolic goin' on. Guess I'll jes' marvel along to de house an' shake a leg myself.' So, takin' anodder dram to give me courage, I put de jug in de grain bag and flingin' it across my shoulders started to'ards de fiddlin'.

"De woods was awful thick, an' it bein' only starlight I kain't see very well 'mong de logs an' bushes, but I kin hear de fiddle goin' it like mad an' so kin keep de course. On and on—on and on I goes, froo brush and briars an' over logs an' into holes. I kin hear de fiddle plain as ever, but it seems like it go roun' and roun' and move off furder as I go to'ards it.

"At last I sees a light. 'Bress de Lord! I'm comin' out'n de woods at last,' ses I. But de light radder dim an' seem long way off; 'sides I don't seem to be comin' to no fence or clearin'. I go on and on—de fiddle a-rippin' away an' de light a-twinklum—but still I kaint see no house nor 'provements, an' I am gittin' inter underbrush as thick as de wool on a sheep.

"All at once I runs my nose squar agin a cliff o' rocks high as de tree tops. 'De holy pokah!' ses I—'What is dis?' De light is right afore me—an' in sebberal places—and de fiddlin' is plain as day, but I kain't see no house, no nuffin, but de rocks what I've got my hands on; 'sides I kain't hear de least sound of de feet of de dancers. I stans kinder dazed for a spell, but at last I creeps up to one of de places whar de light streams out. I peeps in froo a hole in de rocks an' I sees a sight dat freezes de marrer in my backbone. Dar in a big cave in de rocks I sees 'bout forty couple of cats up on dare hind legs dancin' fit to kill, while settin' on a shelf of rock above 'em is a cat 'bout as big as a billy goat dat is playin' de fiddle. All de walls of de cave shine like fox-fire an' make de cave as light as any ball-room.

"As I am gazin' in at de dancin', with mouf open and eyes as big as silber dollars, all of a sudden I feels myself grabbed. A thing tall as I am has me in its arms. It has got me from behind. I twis' my head round an' den by de light dat comes out'n de little winder in de rocks I kin see dat

Uncle Pete is "kinder dazed"

de thing looks in de face like a big gray cat. I am so skeert dat I jes let go all holts an' squat—my legs ain't no more use'n two skeins o' yarn. De thing it squats, too, an' wif its two paws on my shoulders looks me in de eyes. As it looks at me dat a-way I sees de face of a woman start and come in de place of de cat face. De thing den twis' my head roun' an' whisper in my year: 'Pete Crow, keep yer mouf shet an' listen. What de debbil brought you to dis place?'

"'De debbil, I guess,' ses I.

"'Well, you's mighty near him dis minit, chile, if yer hear me. Dat's him inside playin' de fiddle. Now, chile, you's 'bout as good as dead dis minit. You's seed things as no one but them as has tuck the promise has a right to see, but if yer 'bey me I kin save yer. I'm de big cat dat keeps roun' de Paxton stables—de one you calls Mollie and feeds and pets—an' I've got a likin' for you on dat kount. Now, quick, eat dis and dey can't find you out.'

"'What is it?' I axed, feelin' suthin' like leaves put in my hands.

"'Witch hazel,' ses she—'nuthin' wus. It'll make you invisible.'

"I eat the leaves and axed: 'Am I invisible now?'

"'Yes, as a man,' ses she. Then she riz up.

"I riz up at the same time, and as I did so, I felt suthin' danglin' agin my legs behind. I reached behind and got hold of a long tail dat I found to be part of me. Den I see dat I wur a big black cat. I wur so 'stonished dat I open my mouf an' let out de biggest kind of er tomcat yowl.

"'Shut yer mouth!' ses Mollie, but it wur too late; I'd been heerd inside and a big yaller cat come to de door of de cave an' says: 'Dance is ober, all good witches now come in an' report!'

"I wur s'prized to see dat I could understan' de cat talk jest same like my own. Mollie den say to me: 'Come in an' keep you's mouf shet. I'll make de report for de Paxton place; so you keep shady. You see we 'uns are all witches dat lives in de families all 'bout here—on Limestone Creek, Lee's

"Up on dare hind legs dancin' fit to kill"

Creek an' Lickin' Ribber—in de shape ob cats; we finds out de weak pints
of all de people for our marster de big fiddler—understand?'

"When we go inter de cave I find dat de big cat done laid down de fiddle
an' is settin' up on his tail wif a pen behind his years an' a big book on
his knees. He is turnin' ober de leaves of de book. When he finds de place
he calls out; 'Marier Mornin',' den a big brindle cat reports on de 'fairs of
de Mornin' family, an' so it go for a long time. De cats report all de mean,
thievin' doin's of de men, an' all de frolics of de married women an' gals,
an' I hear so much rascality, meanness and slippery an' sinful doin's dat
I feel like I want to hide my head. I was completely 'stounded wid hearin'
of de capers of de wimmin folks of some families what I knowed. When
Mollie come to report on the Paxton family, I 'clar' to goodness if de eyes
o' me didn't moas' pop out. Good Lord! what a settin' up dem Paxton gals
did git! An' ole Massa Paxton—his doin's make de berry air smell ob brim-
stone. But all dis kine of doin's tickle de debbil; he grin an' his eyes
trinkle as he look ober de top de book.

"All to once de debbil fro down de book an' look sirious. He say he omit
de rest ob de roll-call for dat night, kase he find dat dar's pressin' business down to Maysville. He den splain dat dar's a mighty big rich man
down to Maysville dat's 'bout to make a will leavin' all his property to his
chil'un an' pore relations, an' say he goten be on han' an' put it inter his

head to give ebberyting to build some kine of public instertoutions. 'Dat a way,' he say 'dat prop'ty be some use ter me—den, 'sides, I got'er do suffin' for my frien's, de lawyers.'

"Den de debbil take up his fiddle an' says: 'All take pardners for de 'cludin' dance.' Mollie grabs me an' I'm jes as wild as any ob de cats for dancin'. Sich wicked fiddlin' I never heerd. It jist lifted me an' I could see de fire fly at ebery rake ob de bow acrost de fiddle strings.

"When de dance is ober de debbil says: 'All dat want special powers for de comin' week will kiss de snake as usual.' At dis a mon'sus big snake let himself down by de tail from de roof ob de cave an' hung wid his head among de dancers. Sebberal go an' kiss de mouf of de ugly ole sarpint, an' Mollie 'mong de rest. Den de sarpint say: 'Now, my good child'n, scatter for mischief, till de break o' day!' An' by de woice I know dat de snake is de debbil himself.   \

"Mollie froze onto me for her pardner for de night's work an' we sot out for de nearest settlement. 'Fore long we come to a cabin, an' Mollie tole me to watch outside for dogs an' she'd slip in an' tend to a bit o' business. After she'd been in some time I heerd a fearful scream from a woman inside. Jist then Mollie come flyin' out an' we tuck to de tops of the fences across de fields, wif a great barkin' of dogs and yellin' behind us. Soon as we was safe, Mollie tole me she had sucked the bref of a chile in de cabin and left it dead. When I hear dat I feel like I want'er suck the bref of a chile, too, an' I ax if it wur good. She say: 'It's good for dis—now I myself git for my life all de years dat chile would have live if let alone.' Den I say I want to do de nex' one, but Mollie say dat if I'm goin' inter de business of bein' a witch, I got'er begin wid makin' cows give bloody milk, tyin' knots in hosses' tails an' de like. Den she tell me I otter kissed de snake and made a wish, for den I'd git de power to take any shape I please an' do all kine of things.

"Nex' we come to de double log cabin of Jim Sipples, and dar wur a light burnin' in one part. Mollie left me outside sayin' dat dis time she wur goin' to do different business. She wur so long inside dat I jumped up to de winder of de room dat had de light in it and looked in. Dar I seed a young woman layin' dead in a coffin, wif an ole woman settin' asleep in a cheer in de nex' room. As I look I sees Mollie climb onto de coffin an' begin bitin' at de face of de corpse. Dis make me feel like I want to do de same, and de fust I knowed I give an awful yowl. In half a second a real cat, an' a mighty big one, jumped off'n a shed an' lit onto my back. We had it rough and tumble for a time, den come de dogs for boff of us.

"I flew up a tree to git away from de dogs, but no sooner was I out of dare reach before Sipples come tearin' out of de house wif a gun. He blaze away at me, an' for half a second it 'peared like my whole head was shot off. Runnin' out onto a limb of de tree I jumped to de roof of de smoke-house an' from dar got on de top of a big rail fence, an' soon got out de way of de dogs.

"In de nex' field Mollie came to me. I up an' ax her 'bout her doins in de house, an' she 'splain to me dat by tastin' de flesh of de corpse she kin take de same 'pearance an' look no older dan de young woman was when she died. 'Already,' says she, 'I feel young an' strong. I wur pretty ole las' ebenin', but now I've got 'er young body again; 'sides I've got all de years of dat chile, an' dey may be a good many, but dat I kain't tell.' Den she notice dat de whole top my right year bin shot off. 'De debbil!' say she, 'dat ar Jim Sipples is a man we goter look out for—dat wur a silber bullet jes as shore as I'm a witch! If de bullet bin lead it wouldn't hurt you bit more dan so much smoke.'

"By dis time it wur gittin' long to'ards de break o' day, so we strike out fo' de cave whar my sack of things wur left when I wur turned inter a cat. When we got dar Mollie went to a bush an' got some leaves. Tellin' me it wur 'wahoo,' she made me eat some, an' dat minit I was back to my nat'ral shape.

"The fust thing I did wur to take de jug out'n de sack an' take a big swig. By dis time Mollie had tuck on de shape of a woman, an' was as nice lookin' a yaller gal as I ever sot eyes on. She wouldn't 'hit de jug,' but seein' a piece of blue ribbon dat I'd bought for one of de gals, she tuck a notion to it; so I tied it roun' her neck in a double bow-knot and stuck inter it a brass breast-pin dat had in it a green glass diamond. Den I give her some taffy 'bout her good looks dat she tuck mighty well; so I says: 'Now, gal, why in de name of de Lord'—

"No sooner do I mention de name of de Lord, dan de gal give an awful scream an' jump inter de cave. All wur dark in de cave, but I kin hear in dare some ter'ble screamin's. Nex' come a whisper from de cave in a voice dat I knowed wur de gal's sayin' to me: 'Run, Peter Crow! Run for you life, Peter Crow!'

"I slung de sack on my back an' charge froo de brush like a bull in a cane brake. I run till I kain't run no mo' an' fall down in a dead faint.

"How long I lay dat a-way I don't know, but when I come to it is daylight, and I am sittin' at de root of de big poplah. De jug is settin' 'longside me wif de co'ncob stopper out, an' beside it is layin' de sack of notions. How I come to steer my way back to de berry tree whar I wur de ebenin' befo' when I fust heerd dat fiddle, de Lord only knows, but dar I wur at de foot of de big poplah.

"Well, sah, takin' a light swig at de jug, I shoulders de sack an' gittin' my bearin's strikes for home, whar I has de luck to slip inter de stables 'for dar is anybody a-stirrin'. Now, sah, arter hearin' dat 'spearience you gwine for to tell me dar ain't no sich thing in de world as witches?"

"I think, Uncle Pete, that all the witches were in that jug."

"Dat's all berry fine, but hear to some mo'. At breakfas' time I tuck de sack up to de quartahs to 'stribute the tings I had bought. When all was done, a gal puts out her lip an' says: 'Pete, whar's dat blue neck-ribbon ob mine?' 'Shore nuff,' ses I, an' I looks in de sack an' turns it inside out, den says: 'It's done got loss somewhar'—but I knowed well nuff whar.

"Arter breakfas' I goes out to de stables an' de fust thing I hears is a 'miow.' I turns an' dar stan's de big cat what I calls Mollie. She looks at me in a smilin' way and gives anodder pleasant 'miow,' an' may de debbil ketch me dis minit ef dar roun' her neck wasn't de double bow-knot blue ribbon wif de brass pin stuck in de front ob it. Now, sah?"

"Well, Uncle Pete, I suppose the old cat had been prowling about hunting birds and squirrels, and finding you at the tree had stopped long enough for you to decorate her; then—being pretty full—you dreamed all the witch business, mixing Mollie up in it."

"Dat's all berry fine, but hear to some mo'. When I sees de ribbon an' de pin, and knows what for critter de cat is, I kain't stan' de notion of havin' her 'bout de place, so I gives her a kick an' says: 'Clar out from dese stables, you child-killin', corpse-eatin' ole witch!'

"De cat look at me wid green eyes, make a sabage face, squalls at me like a painter, an' den turns an' goes away wif all de har on her tail an' back stickin' straight up. I don't see her no mo, an' for sebral days I am in hot water, kase I'm shore she's gwine to git even some bad way.

"One day one de field han's dat had bin down to de 'Corners' comes home in de ebenin' an' says dar's a big 'citement down dar 'bout a murder. Dey's got a black boy name Bill Teeters 'rested for shootin' an ole nigger woman. It seemed dat it wur a clar case agin de Teeters boy. People comin' an' goin' 'long de road had seen him raise his gun and fire; dey had heerd a woman scream, and hurryin' up had foun' an ole woman layin' in a fence corner shot froo de heart. Bill Teeters wur still stanin' in de middle of de road wid a smokin' gun in his han'. He deny shootin' de woman an' say he see cat on de fence an' shoot at dat. Den he hear a woman holler an' see her tumble down, an' dat's de fust he know dar wur a woman in a mile of him. De people dat see Bill shoot won't believe his story, so dey take him 'long down to de 'Corners.'

"Airly de nex' mornin' Massa Paxton send me down to de 'Corners' to git more news of de affair. I find dare is still a big hurrah 'bout de murder. Dey say de ole woman dat was killed was a stranger in de settlement—

nobody 'pears to know her. Some said she look like an ole woman dat once uster live alone in a little cabin up at de head ob Lee's Creek, an' some reckoned dey'd seed her in odder places.

"I went inter de cooper shop whar de dead woman layed, to have a look at her. Dar I seed a black woman dat 'peared to be 'bout sixty year old. Seemed like I'd seen de face somewhar befo', and havin' some 'spicions, I raised de chin an' dar I seed on her neck de blue ribbon wid de brass pin an' glass diamon' in it. It make de cold shivers crawl up my back. De face was de one I'd seed come in place of de cat face when I wur squatted befo' de cave.

"Jim Sipples was dar, havin' been sent for. He said he loaned Bill Teeters de gun to go huntin' wif, an' ef he shot at a cat an' killed a woman she wur a witch, for de gun wur loaded wid a silber bullet, a sarkumstance he forgot about when he let Bill take de gun.

"When Jim Sipples tell dat my han' go up to my right year afore I know what I'm 'bout, but I ses nuffin, 'kase I'd bin 'tarred wif de same stick' as de ole woman. Well, when dey hold de 'zamination dey let de boy Bill Teeters off on de groun' dat de shootin' was an accident, but I wur sure dey all were satisfied in dare hearts dat de ole woman wur a witch. I tell de squire to ax de boy if he seed anything on the neck of de cat he shot at. He say yes, he seed suffin; dat look like a blue ribbon. Den I say: 'Now, go look on de neck of dat ole woman.' Dey tuck a look an' all dar eyes bugged out at what dey seed. De squire say—'De pris'ner is dishcharged.' Now, sah—what now, sah?"

"Uncle Pete, I give it up. There certainly are witches in the world; and listening to your story, with your right ear before me, I'm ready to believe that you are one of them yourself—a big buck witch."

"Tank you, sah. Now lif' up you hook an' see what de witch down in de bottom de ribber bin doin' wid it. Maybe she's put a fish on it dis time."

"Yes, there does seem to be a fish on my hook. Hello! Why, as I'm a living sinner, I've got a big snapping turtle on my hook!"

"Yah, yah! Dat's de ole witch dat's been stealin' you's bait, sah. She's done come up jist for to show you dat for de las' half hour you's been 'sputin' agin reason, sah!"

"I suppose you wouldn't have been at all surprised, Uncle Pete, if she'd come up with your blue ribbon and brass pin on her neck?"

"Not de least grain, sah. De fac' is I feel it in my bones some times o' nights dat I got'er see dat critter agin in some shape. I 'magines some nights dat I hears 'bout my shanty a woice callin' dat's a mighty sight like Mollie's. When she comes an' squats on me, dat gwine ter be my las' night."

Californian Illustrated Magazine, April 3, 1893

V
STORIES

To be an author of literature was
one of De Quille's main goals. He enjoyed journalism and was very
good at it, but he loved literature and always hoped that he would earn
some measure of fame through the stories that he began to write even
before he joined the Territorial Enterprise. His fictions were highly
praised on the Comstock and by 1875 he felt he had accumulated
enough of them for an anthology. When that did not materialize because he was sidetracked into writing The Big Bonanza, he continued
to write new stories and revise old ones and to pursue what amounted
to a second career as a literary figure. He had a surprisingly large
range, and it grew larger and deeper as he grew older. By the end of
his life he had a national reputation, and evidence suggests that the
main activity of his last few years was setting to paper the narratives
that came to him in a final creative surge. These stories ripened within
him so rapidly that he wrote them faster than he could market them,
and what little journalism he practiced merely served to support his
intense literary activity.

"The Fighting Horse of the Stanislaus" is one of De Quille's early, very
popular classics. Although he acknowledged to his sister in an 1874
letter that "I could never see much in the 'Jumping Frog,' yet that yarn
was the one that first brought Mark into notice," De Quille did somewhat the same thing in "The Fighting Horse" that Twain did in "The
Notorious Jumping Frog of Calaveras County." De Quille's tale is also a
story within a story featuring animal fights staged for betting purposes
and is deeply involved with hoaxes. It appears to be an entertaining
reminiscence of a Comstock hoax arranged by John P. Jones, U.S.
senator from Nevada, but beneath its surface story line about a fight
between animals owned by Joggles and Jones, the tale is a subtle but
sharp criticism of human brutality. Jones was a wealthy and powerful
individual and a political ally whom De Quille could not afford to of-
fend. Jones had risen to eminence partly out of native shrewdness and
partly out of unscrupulousness. Ostensibly friendly to Jones, the story
actually casts him in the somewhat dubious role of Joggles's over-
match in a ruthless sport in which the humans are more vicious than

the animals which represent them. A daringly unflattering character portrait of the public figure Jones is thus implicit in this adroitly equivocal narrative.

The battle of the sexes has always been a favorite theme in literature, and two entertaining stories represent this category. Both depict women as having the upper hand in contests of wit. "Marier's Room" is an early favorite describing a bait-and-switch operation that many Comstock lodgers must have appreciated. "Bendix Biargo and His Three Sisters" is a witty and delightfully lighthearted tale. Although all the men in it are vanquished—for their own good—De Quille observes in its conclusion that women are in league with each other only up to a certain point. Beyond that there are certain formalities in the game that the victorious women observe among themselves.

The next three stories all date from De Quille's late period and show that his skill at narration continued to develop as he entered the last decade of his life. They also document his growing reputation. Earlier in his career he would have placed his stories in local newspapers or magazines; the Overland Monthly and Cosmopolitan, both national magazines with large readerships, represented an important advance for him.

In addition to the moral satire implicit in "The Seven Nimrods of the Sierras" there can be found a gentle and good-natured admonition to spirited young men who have more book learning than good judgment. "The Eagles' Nest" is undoubtedly one of De Quille's best stories. Its treatment of "fright of space" is gripping as well as psychologically acute. Although it appears to be a mature man's criticism of himself when he was younger and more foolish, more than most of De Quille's tales it tends to brood upon the disharmony between human nature and the larger domain of Nature, especially in the former's perverse tendencies to avarice and wanton destruction. The narrator, even at the end still wrapped up in himself, remains insensitive to the deaths he witnessed or caused and to the unflattering contrast between animal and human behavior implicit in his own story.

"An Indian Story of the Sierra Madre" is De Quille's elegiac contribution to the classic western story. The last organized Apache resistance to American settlement ended in 1886, and the last major battle fought with Indians was the Battle of Wounded Knee in December 1890. Thus, the exciting recollection of the elemental combats that had occurred between the two races still hung in the air when this story was penned. Captain Ben and his two companions are the last of the race of frontiersmen who learned to think and fight like Indians. They exemplified the qualities of bravery, calm resolution, and resourcefulness that

Theodore Roosevelt was popularizing. The story was almost made to order for an artist like Frederick Remington, and his service as its illustrator speaks both of its character and of De Quille's reputation.

De Quille deeply loved what we now call the Old West. To him, the frontiersman—including the prospector—had been a heroic figure living in a heroic age. De Quille believed the best qualities of America were found in these men, and he was profoundly saddened by the realization that the age of the frontier was at its end. This realization had made him increasingly sympathetic to Indians, whose plight he came to realize was tied up with that of the frontiersmen.

"An Indian Story of the Sierra Madre," one of De Quille's last published tales, is therefore less a story of a victory than it might seem. Although Nordine and Colrick appear to have been assigned a happy ending, they may also be seen as having been awarded somewhat of a consolation prize. They are "cured of all desire for further adventure in the wilds" (emphasis mine); their youthful love of adventure is over, they have stopped being frontiersmen, and they have been put out to pasture in California ranches: retreats of safety, comfort, and profit. Captain Ben is not "cured" of his adventurousness but ironically helps bring to an inglorious end at Wounded Knee that culture he had become "at home" with. By implication, therefore, De Quille appears to bear out James Fenimore Cooper's pessimistic forecast of the inevitable fate of the noble frontier: Indians being supplanted by frontiersmen, frontiersmen being supplanted by settlers, and a magnificent untouched country with its high-spirited way of life being supplanted by tame "progress" and materialistic rewards.

The Fighting Horse of
the Stanislaus

A REMINISCENCE OF THE EARLY MINING LIFE
OF SENATOR JONES OF NEVADA

In the early days, many years ago, Senator Jones was engaged in mining on the Stanislaus River, California, at a place called Cherokee Flat. It was a small camp, containing scarcely more than a dozen habitations, all told. The most imposing structure in the camp was a boarding-house, owned by a Mr. Joggles, a Missourian. This Joggles was a man of sporting proclivities. He owned a vicious-looking old bull-dog, with but one eye, whose nose was covered with scars and whose front teeth were always visible, even when in most friendly mood. This dog he was ready to back against any dog on the river for a fight. He also had two or three game roosters of whose prowess he was boastful. But his especial glory and pride was his fighting horse, a large, powerfully muscled and exceedingly vicious "broncho," which he called "Old Pizen." And "pizen" he was to all four-footed creatures in that region; indeed was so "mean" that he was almost poison to himself.

This fierce and unsocial beast had taken possession of a large grassy flat about half a mile above the camp and would allow no other animal to come upon what he viewed as his private domain; nor, for the matter of that, to come anywhere near the camp. At Cherokee Flat, the old broncho was monarch of all he surveyed. He had whipped and run off every animal that had ever been brought to the camp. The miners several times swore vengeance against "Old Pizen" and would have shot him, but that they liked Joggles, and the soul of Joggles delighted in Old Pizen, therefore they let him live.

Not content with conquering intruders the old broncho would chase them for miles, running them clear out of the country. The moment he saw the strange animal he laid back his ears and went for him, using both heels and teeth.

About all this Joggles didn't care a cent. When told of one of the exploits of the animal he would laugh in spite of himself and would swear that Old Pizen was the "biggest fightin' hoss on the Stanislaus," and that he would "back him agin any critter that ever wore har." He would tell how a big American horse chased away by Old Pizen was found forty miles

163

distant with his tail gnawed off to a mere stump. When he thought of the comical appearance the maimed horse must have presented with his little stump of tail, Joggles would laugh till tears ran down his cheeks.

The fame of the "fighting horse" extended for miles around the camp. Prospectors passing that way with pack animals were warned against him. "Beware of the fighting horse!" was the word through all that section of country.

Sonora, the county seat of Tuolumne County, was the source whence the miners at Cherokee Flat drew their supplies of "grub" and other necessaries. The town was fifteen or twenty miles distant, and the miners would occasionally go up there, order what they wanted and have it "packed" down to their cabins.

One day J. P. Jones and one of his partners went up to Sonora to procure supplies for their company, known as the "Buckeye." They remained over night in town, intending to return the next day. In the morning, soon after they arose, they heard a

Terrible Commotion in a Livery Stable

Just across the street from their hotel. Running over to ascertain the cause, they found that a big Spanish jackass had found his way into the stable through a rear door and was on the warpath among the horses. He had cleaned out several stalls almost at a dash, and had then reached that occupied by a powerful black stallion. Here he found work to do. As Jones and partner entered a furious battle was raging, the horse using his heels and the jack his teeth. The horse being confined by a strong halter the jack had rather the best of it. After tearing and mangling the flanks of the horse frightfully, the furious jack, unmindful of the blows the stable men were raining upon his back, suddenly crowded himself forward in the stall and seized the horse by the under-lip. Here he held on like a bull-dog, the poor horse quivering in every muscle and moaning in agony.

One of the proprietors of the stable drew his revolver and was about to shoot the savage ass, when his owner arrived and a fierce wrangle ensued. The owner of the fighting jack drew his pistol and for a time it looked as though there was likely to be "a man for breakfast."

Finally, however, the owner of the jack succeeded in getting him away from the trembling and mangled horse, and drove him out of the stable.

It occurred to Mr. Jones that here was an animal that would make Old Pizen sick at the stomach. A word of this thought to his partner, and they agreed, if possible, to secure

The Fighting Jackass.

Following the owner of the jack, they soon came to an understanding with him. They were told that the jack was a good pack animal and as quiet as a lamb when no horses were about. When he came where there were horses his whole nature changed and he went for them with the fury of a tiger. The jack being an unusually powerful animal, the owner asked $75 for him. Jones and partner agreed to run him a trip on trial and gave the owner $75, which he was to keep in case the jack was not returned within a certain time.

Having secured the fighting jack, Jones and partner packed him and started home in high feather. As soon as he was out of town, the jack became as docile and sleepy as any other old "burro" that ever trotted a trail. Before getting home the beast became absolutely lazy and Jones & Co. began to fear that off his own dunghill their jack was of no account as a fighter.

It was about sundown when the men reached Cherokee Flat and drove up to the door of the "Buckeye Company's cabin." Their partners had quit work and come up from the bar. They were getting supper, but for a time discontinued the work of frying bacon and baking slapjacks to come out and ask "J. P." and companion how they came by the big donkey.

In as few words as possible Jones made them acquainted with the character of the beast. When he had finished his account of the scene at the livery stable, every man of the Buckeye Company was firmly convinced that the big jack could "walk the log" of Old Nick himself; but mum was the word. No hint of the fighting qualities of the animal was to go out of the cabin.

Joggles Hunts a Game

Presently Joggles, whose boarding house was just across the street, espied the jackass and came over to where he was being unpacked.

A smile struggled about the corners of his mouth as he came.

Walking up to the beast and eyeing him from stem to stern for a time, Joggles said:

"Purty good chunk of jackass. Bin buyin' him?"

"Well," said Jones. "I don't know. We have him on trial. We may buy him. He is big and strong and seems nice and quiet—maybe a trifle lazy."

Joggles, who seemed to be calculating about how many mouthfuls he would make for Old Pizen, at last said:

"Well, yes, he seems rather quiet."

Having unpacked the jack, one of the "boys" gave him a slap with a strap, as much as to say: "You are now at liberty, old fellow; go off and enjoy yourself as you please."

"What!" cried Joggles, opening his eyes in amazement, "you ain't going to turn that jack loose here? The first thing you know he'll poke off up to the flat where Old Pizen is. Then he'll be a dead jack as sure as you live! Why, he wouldn't make a mouthful for Pizen!"

"Well, I don't know," said Jones, "the jack is a very quiet old fellow, and I guess Old Pizen won't think him worth bothering with. Besides, the chances are that he will stay and pick about camp: won't find his way up to the flat at all."

"Well, just as you please," said Joggles, pretending some concern, "but you know what Old Pizen is!"

"Yes, I know," said Jones, "but Pizen is getting old. I guess he don't thirst for the fray as in his younger days. I shouldn't wonder now, if the old jack were to whip him—in case they should get together," added Jones, laughing.

"What!" cried Joggles, turning red, "that blamed old jackass whip Pizen!—Not much! I'll bet you $100—yes—I'll bet you $200 he can't whip one side of him—come now!"

"The trouble is," said Jones, "that the jack is in a strange place. He might not fight. However, he looks as though there might be some fight in him. If the two ever do get together, I rather think he'll make it warm for the broncho."

"You do, eh?" said Joggles. "Well, I don't. Here, here, now—back up your opinion or take water. Here's $200! I'm willin' to jist let the animals alone—let them find their way to each other—and I bet this $200 that when they do meet, Old Pizen whips—that he eats your jack up alive! Come, now, Pixley, here, shall hold the stakes. See me, see me! come down! Two hundred goes that Pizen whips!"

Thus urged, "J. P." covered the coin in Pixley's hand, and once it was done a better pleased man than Joggles was never seen on the Stanislaus. He thought he had the deadest thing in the world.

The bet made, away ran Joggles to tell all the "boys" in the camp what a dead thing he had on Jones; always winding up with—"Old Pizen'll chaw him up—chaw him up alive!" The last thing he said to his lodgers that night, before he went to bed was: "Knowin' Pizen as he does, Jones must be goin' crazy. That jack'll be chawed up—chawed up alive!"

All the evening the jack remained browsing about the camp and the next morning was still there—standing with head down and eyes closed, dreamily moving his ears and lazily switching his scanty tail.

Joggles smiled contemptuously every time he looked at the old jack. Standing on his porch, as the miners of the camp passed on their way down to their claims on the river, Joggles facetiously inquired whether any of them would like to back "That thar ferocious beast against Old Pizen for another $200?"

At last all the men of the camp were down on the river at work. About 9 o'clock in the morning, one of the men of the Buckeye Company happened to go from the bar up to the bank of the river for something. A moment after, grinning gleefully, he called out to those below:

"The Impatient Joggles

Is going to bring on the game. There'll be some fun before long, I see him startin' the old jack along up the valley toward the flat. He's on the sly and is getting rather keen to see that fight!"

Watching Joggles, he was seen in the edge of the timber, throwing rocks to urge the jack to move up a streak of open ground that led to the flat between two groves of pines. Presently he came back and seated himself on his porch—getting up once in a while and stretching his neck to see if the jack was going in the right direction. He was dying to have the animals get together.

At last a man who had climbed upon the bank reported that the jack was not to be seen and that he had no doubt gone over the ridge into the flat.

All was now excitement among the men, and two or three of them were constantly on the riverbank listening for sounds of the fray. Presently they cried out that the battle had begun. All hands hastened to the top of the open ground leading up to the ridge beyond which lay the flat where roamed the fighting horse. Although half a mile distant,

A Terrible Squealing and Braying

Could be distinctly heard—cries of rage and pain from the contending animals. A great cloud of red dust could be seen rising above the ridge. This cloud, that told of the battle, moved to and fro; sometimes appearing to approach quite near to the crest of the ridge, then again to recede. All this time there was heard the most fearful squealing and braying imaginable—sometimes very distinctly, again more faintly, as the varying breeze wafted the sounds, or as the scene of the battle shifted.

Looking toward the camp, Joggles was seen jumping up and down and running frantically about, evidently intensely excited. Soon, he was observed to get a ladder and mount upon the roof of his porch, and thence to climb to the top of his house, vainly stretching his neck to obtain a view of the fight.

Now the cloud of dust was seen to rapidly approach the crest of the ridge and soon it came whirling over it. Then were seen

Two Dense Clouds of Dust,

Both rolling rapidly in the direction of the camp. Wild snorts and hoarse brays were heard. Swiftly the red clouds rolled on and soon in the foremost the form of an animal could be seen. A puff of wind showed this to be the broncho—Old Pizen. At the distance of three or four hundred yards behind, rolled a rapidly following cloud; as we have sometimes seen, two small whirlwinds, in playful mood. What was in this last cloud could not be seen, but the "Buckeye boys" felt that their jackass was *thar*!

Down into the camp charged the terrified broncho, snorting with fear at every jump and occasionally half-turning his head in order to see if the terrible jack was still in pursuit. As the frantic horse tore through the camp with nostrils distended, mane flying in the wind and tail sticking out straight behind, Joggles was heard shouting wildly from the roof of his house:

"Whoa, Pizen! Whoa, Pizen!"

But just at that moment there was no "whoa" in Old Pizen. Down through the little town he came—making directly for the bar, as though in search of human assistance.

Straight on he came till he reached the bank of the river, here fully twenty feet in perpendicular height. At the brink he halted, hesitating to take the fearful leap, and with eyes starting from their sockets took one long despairing look behind.

There came the venomous and indomitable jackass, never breaking his steady, rolling gallop.

With outstretched neck, ears laid back and scant tail whipping up and down with each bound, on he came. The old broncho erected his tail, took one more glance at his approaching foe, gave a snort of terror, and leaped from the bank down into the river. Luckily for him the water was deep. Rising to the surface he swam to the opposite shore and came out all right on a bar that put out from the bank on that side. Here he halted, evidently feeling himself safe.

The jack thundered on, and came near plunging into the river before aware of its presence. But by bracing all aback till his haunches almost touched the ground, he came to a halt. But it was only for a moment. Seeing the old broncho on the other shore, he stretched out his neck and giving

A Diabolical "Yee-haw!"

Unhesitatingly plunged into the river and diligently struck out for the horse.

This reckless and energetic persistence on the part of the enemy was evidently unexpected to the broncho. He gazed for a few moments at the jack, as he rose to the surface and began swimming—gazed as though thunderstruck at the fearful energy displayed by the little beast—then tossing his tail aloft and giving a tremendous snort, he dashed away down the river at the top of his speed.

The jack was soon over the narrow stream. On landing he snuffed the ground a moment, then raising his head and catching a glimpse of the fleeing horse, away he plunged in keen pursuit.

A bend in the river soon hid the animals from view. As the men were still standing gazing after them, a great crash was heard. More than one voice then cried:

"The Gulch! The Gulch!

By heaven! they have both gone into Devil's Gulch!"

What was referred to as "Devil's Gulch" was a narrow ravine, with rocky, perpendicular walls which put into the river about fifty yards below the bend.

"Something fell into the gulch, sure," cried the man, "and it must have been either the horse or jack, or both."

All now started for a crossing, some distance up the river, in order to go down the other shore and see what had happened. Joggles, who had before this descended from the roof of his house, now came pulling and blowing across lots and joined the party from the river—fifteen or twenty men in all, as they came from several claims.

"D——n a jackass, anyhow!" was all that Joggles said, as he came up with the crowd. As all knew his feelings, no one said a word.

"D——n a jackass!" he several times muttered, as they moved down the river, after having crossed over.

Rounding the bend they came in full view of the gulch. There, upon its rocky brink, stood the jack. With outstretched neck he was gazing intently into the chasm below. His ears were lopped forward, as though to shade his eyes and give him a clearer view of what lay at the bottom of the gulch. The sound of approaching footsteps at length attracted his attention. Turning his head and seeing the party drawing near he moved back from the brink of the precipice, gave his tail a flourish and uttered a series of triumphal "yee-haws!"

Looking down into the chasm the men beheld lying at the bottom—motionless in death—Old Pizen, the fighting horse of the Stanislaus. His head was doubled under him—his neck was broken.

When he came up out of the gulch, after having ascertained this fact, Joggles was deadly pale.

Drawing and Cocking His Six-Shooter,

He advanced toward the party and said:

"John P. Jones, *you* knowed what that jackass was. Don't speak! Let no man here speak a word."

With this he turned suddenly to where the jack stood with head down, moping sleepily, and sent a bullet through his brain. The beast fell without a moan, when Joggles advanced and deliberately emptied the contents of his revolver into its carcass. He then seized it by the ears, dragged it to the brink of the precipice and tumbled it down upon the body of the old broncho, saying:

"As you are the only thing that ever whipped him, d——n me, you shall lie and rot with Old Pizen—Old Pizen, the Fitin' Hoss of the Stanislaus!"

Territorial Enterprise, June 28, 1874

Marier's Room

A WASHOE LODGING-HOUSE EXPERIENCE

Among the keepers of lodging-houses in this argentiferous land one occasionally finds a landlady who far excels the "heathen Chinee" in ways
that are dark and "tricks that are vain." She is, to all outward appearance, "serene as a summer's day," and, seemingly, "her ways are ways of
pleasantness, and all her paths are peace"; but in reality she is at war
with all mankind, and in artifices she is simply Luciferian.

When you sally forth in search of lodgings the smiling landlady no
sooner learns your business than her voice mellows and she stands before you one of the most kind-hearted and motherly middle-aged female
personages it has ever been your good fortune to meet.

MRS. TABITHA SMILEY

Thus, when I called at Mrs. Smiley's, Mrs. Smiley, a most robust inveigler
of the "weary and heavy laden," put on her receiving face and said: "My
child, I have just what will suit you. You don't look strong. Have you been
sick, my poor boy? Just step this way, please. Here we are. Ah! the door
is locked. I must always keep my doors locked—there is so many sneak
thieves about nowadays, you know, sir. Now, you must always keep your
door locked, sir—the sneak thieves are so bad. Ah! yes; the door is
locked; the Chinaman has the key—but I'll call him. Wing Lee! you good-
for-nothing, where are you?"

The Chinaman, a shrewd-looking, pig-eyed rascal, who was chamber-
maid and also man-of-all-work, finally made his appearance with the
key, and the door of the room in front of which we stood was unlocked.
When the door swung open Mrs. Smiley struck an attitude at the en-
trance, crying: "There, sir! ain't it lovely? There is a bed, sir, fit for a
prince! Double-spring mattress, with genuine curled hair—no pulu
there, sir!—and all the kivers of the best! Chairs, wash-stand, readin'-
stand—to put at the head of your bed if you are fond of readin' o' nights,
sir, as some is—towel-rack, beautiful lamp, and everything heart could
desire!

"You see, sir," continued she, "all of them alabastered vases, them bronge statutes, the purcelain fixtures, the chromoed picturs and them air imidges in terra-incognita—lovely! ain't they?"

Beginning to warm to her work, she cried, with great enthusiasm: "This, sir, is 'Little Mary and her Lamb,' and this is a pictur of the 'Crucifixtion!'—shows how our Savior suffered on Cavalry. This here, in bronge, is Don Quickset, a powerful knight who went and fit with the Crewsajers, in werry ancient times."

"SAINTED MARIER!"

"Ah, poor fellow!" said I: "poor fellow!"—for I was thinking of the Don.

"You may well say so," remarked Mrs. Smiley; "you may well say so, for I believe he was killed by the bustin' of a windmill. Also, sir, you may be supprised at seein' of everything so tasty: but sir, it was my dear darter's room," and Mrs. Smiley lifted a corner of her apron to her left eye.

"Ah!" sighed I, looking solemnly heavenward.

"She's not dead! oh, no, sir!" cried Mrs. Smiley.

"Ha!" cried I; "she lives?"

"She does, sir," said Mrs. Smiley, "and I believe she's quite hearty—thank you, sir. She is over to school in California—over to the High School, at Bernicia, where I hear she is makin' great progress in the Frentch tung! I hate offully to rent her room, but in these ere times, sir—what with the licenses, taxes and all that—why, we must do a many things as we don't like."

Turning suddenly toward a window, she said: "Beautiful view you'll observe, sir, from this ere south winder? From this winder, you'll obsarve, you can see the top of Mount Davinson—you can even see the flagstafft up at the top! Marier—the name of my dear child, now over to Bernicia, sir—Marier she us't to admire to look up there at that air landscape. You'll have the use of the bal-*cony*, too, sir. From the bal-*cony* the view off east is perfectly charming, as the sweet child very frekently would remark. You can see clean out to the Twenty-two-mile Desert!"

MAKING THE BARGAIN

"But the rent, madam! What rent do you ask?" cried I.

"The price of the room, my dear child? I hardly know what to say. The fact is, I've not bin rentin' this ere room. Bein' as it were formerly my darter's boodwo-*ra*, I've in a manner kept it sakerd."

"Well," said I, "the price?"

"O, yes; the price!" cried Mrs. Smiley. "Well, sir, I'm sure you won't think $45 a month out o' the way for sich a room—with any little thing I can do for you in case of sickness, and a bed fit for a prince, and busts and picturs, and bronges and terrra incog——.''

"Thirty dollars is all I can give," was my answer, firmly spoken.

"What! *Thirty dollars* for this room? O, no, sir! Why, my dear child, wherever could you a bin stoppin' at previously. See the home comforts!" cried Mrs. Smiley, growing red in the face with enthusiasm; "see the works of art! But, hows'ever, as I like your looks, we'll say $40. Dear me! what would Marier say to this: Her own room, too!—the dear child's boodwo-*ra*! There, now, it is over!—the room is yours at $40! Will you send your trunks and things this afternoon? You, Wing Lee! That Chinaman has gone again, and you will want the key to the room. O, but you will be snug here, sir!—What! you can't pay $40?"

Thus we fight it down—$5, and finally, $2.50, a round—till at last Mrs. Smiley, very red in the face and apparently completely exhausted, says: "It would break the heart of that poor child if she knowed it, but somehow I've taken sich a likin' to you—jist as I may say while we have bin a-talkin' together—that to help you—as I see that you're not in any big payin' business—to help you, my child, I'm willin' to sakerfize my own intrusts. Well, then, if I must I must! and you can have it for the $30—$30 in advance, understand!"

MYSTERIOUS DISAPPEARANCES

To make a long story short, I took the room—the room, "Mary and her Lamb," Don "Quickset," and all the rest of the "bronges" and "terra incognitas."

For about four days all went well. The fifth night, when I came home, I observed that I had a broken-nosed pitcher; also my easy chair had disappeared. "Doubtless the Chinaman's mistake," I said.

In a day or two I missed "Mary and her Lamb" and the "Crucifixtion" on "Cavalry"; next went a few of the vases and some of the more startling "terra incognita imidges"; after these departed the warlike old Don and all of his fellows in "bronge."

"Rather strange!" say I, but I arrive at the conclusion that Mrs. Smiley thinks that I do not appreciate these works of art as I should; or, that she has concluded that they—they being the "goods and gods" of her "sweet Marier"—should not be profaned by the daily gaze of sacrilegious eyes.

Soon my reading-stand, towel-rack, my lamp, and even the lace curtains from the windows disappeared—also my last chair goes.

The "sneak thieves," so dreaded by Mrs. Smiley, now came into my head—they were gradually stripping the room!

I now, for the first time, remembered that I had not seen Mrs. Smiley since taking the room. I also recollected that in that last interview, when she said, "Thirty dollars in advance, understand!" she forgot her dulcet, motherly tone, and her voice had a harsh, metallic ring—the chink of hard gold!

I resolved to see her and tell her how things were going, but every day the Chinaman, Wing Lee, met me with: "Madam gone out; she gone down town. Yes; *sure* she go down town!"

The end of my first month was now approaching, and "one fine night" I went home and found my fine bed—"fit for a prince"—gone, while in its place stood a little rickety "three-quarter" concern.

TABITHA WAS EQUAL TO THE EMERGENCY

This was the feather too much, and I besieged the house in season and out of season, rushing in whenever I could snatch a moment from my business. Finally I pounced down upon the old lady and turned loose upon her all the batteries of my wrath. Bless me! she was as serene as a Mayday morning. She had known all along how things had been going. She didn't blame me for the loss of the "bronges" and other fine things—"no; poor child! he wasn't to blame!" She had had the "perlice to work constantly for three weeks." "It's the nasty sneak thieves!" said she.

"But," said I, "how about that fine bed?—the sneak thieves didn't take that and bring in a little, old, rickety three-quarter—"

"O, my, no! but the bed—you must have noticed it, sir?—the bed was sadly out of repair. The little spirous springs was all smashed down and I've sent it to the upholster man to have it fixed. It will be home to-morrer; then you can have it again."

About the broken-nosed pitcher she gave Wing Lee all the blame; also, about the chairs and many other things—but all should be "tended to." The curtains "were taken down to be washed," except that there was not a decent article of furniture of any kind left in my room, and for over a fortnight I had been reduced to a tallow candle.

The next day, and the next, and the next, I saw no Mrs. Tabitha, but I finally saw her, and she abused the "upholster man" at a great rate.

PETARD TAKES "MARIER'S ROOM"

A day or two after, as I was leaving my denuded room, I met in the hall my friend Petard, Secretary of the Hoist Gold and Silver Mining Company.

"Hello!" said he, and "Hello!" said I. Petard informed me that he was rooming in the house, and invited me into his room to take a cigar.

"Been lodging here nearly a week," says Petard, as we enter his room.

No sooner have I entered than my eyes begin to expand, as they roam about the room. There, before me on the mantel, stands that masterpiece of modern art, "Little Mary and her Lamb"; nearby is Don "Quickset," the warlike, and all the other "bronges," while on the wall flames the "Crucifixtion," and other familiar "picturs." Looking farther, I see my lamp, lace curtains, reading-stand, and, last but not least, my bed! That bed, "fit for a prince!" and nearly all lost from my room, I here see snug and safe in the room of my friend Petard.

I vigorously puff the cigar, which by this time I have lighted, and neither by word nor by look give Petard any hint of the discovery I have made. Finally, I venture the remark: "Petard, this is a very snug room in which I find you quartered."

"Yes," complacently assents Petard.

"Good many works of art?" said I.

"Well," said Petard, "the room is good enough, but as for the 'works of art,' as you are pleased to call them—bah! horrible things, most of them! It is a room," continued Petard, "that the landlady has never before let. It was formerly occupied by her daughter Maria, a young lady who is now at school at Benicia, California. She must be an exceedingly romantic young lady! Why, Mrs. Smiley tells me that she should sit for hours at that north window, gazing out there at that old pile of rotten granite called Cedar Hill—that she thought that dirty old wart on the face of creation 'perfectly magnificent!' Queer taste, I must say!" sneers Petard.

"MARIER'S ROOM" AGAIN BECOMING RESTIVE

All this time Petard is seated on the side of "that bed," while I occupy the only chair in the room. Presently he says: "I did have a nice easy chair in the room when I first came, but it disappeared a day or two since. Some of the Chinaman's blundering, I presume; and—blast his almond eyes!—I see that he has given me an old cracked wash-bowl! also, is throwing off on some other little things."

I see that the game has been commenced with my friend Petard; but I only ask what rent he is paying. He tells me $40 per month, and thinks it rather high; but says he could do no better at the time he took it—"didn't have time to look about much."

I take my departure, leaving Petard smoking his cigar and musingly studying the "Crucifixtion."

In going down town I made inquiries of two or three friends in regard to furnished rooms. One of them carelessly asked my present "camping-place." When I mentioned Mrs. Smiley's, a gleam of light, showing suddenly awakened interest, flashed across his broad, good-humored countenance. "What!" cried he, "are you housed in 'Marier's room?'—her 'boodwo-ra?'—and is the 'sweet child' still at 'Bernicia' studying the 'Frentch tung?'"

I fear that I blushed slightly as I made answer that, for a time, the boodwo-ra was mine; but I lost no time in explaining that our mutual friend, Petard, was now the happy possessor of that mythical apartment—the "Crucifixtion," the knightly Don, and all the movables.

"SAINTED MARIER" BUT A "BEAUTIFUL DREAM"

My friend laughed long and heartily before proceeding to explain that he, too, at one time, reveled in the possession of "Marier's room." He then went on to tell me that "Maria" was a myth; at least as painted by Mrs. Smiley. "The only daughter she ever had," said my friend, "was a grass-widow when she first struck the Comstock range, and she was not here a month before she ran away to Montana with a faro-dealer. Mrs. Smiley," proceeded he, "has but about three sets of decent furniture in her whole house and these, or the component parts thereof, she is constantly moving from room to room, in order to catch anywhere from $25 to $45 in the shape of rent in advance. Her other rooms—those not 'Marier's'— only bring her in from $12 to $15 per month. I have known her to get $40 three times in one month for 'Marier's room,' just by parties raising a row and leaving when the work of stripping began. Few persons have ever stuck to the old lady as faithfully as you have done. She must have been fearfully disgusted with your powers of endurance, your forbearance and your infernal good nature!"

I saw it all. That very day I found new quarters. A fortnight after, I met Petard and asked him how he liked "Marier's room."

"D——n 'Marier's room!'" cried he, "do you know that ———."

But I knew it all. * * * * * My friend Abijah Clayton now has "Marier's room"; he moved in only two days ago and is very happy among all those "bronges" and "terra incognitas."

Territorial Enterprise, November 7, 1874

Bendix Biargo and His Three Sisters

**A STORY OF EARLY DAYS AMONG THE
ROUGH DIAMONDS OF CALIFORNIA**

CHAPTER I
BROTHER BENDIX

"Well, if I am in for it, I may as well begin," said the old '49er, thoughtfully, stroking the long white beard that flowed down over his breast and reached nearly to his broad leathern pistol belt, "but the only story I can tell you is a true one. It is all about things that I saw in the early days of California and affairs in which I was myself to some extent concerned when I was engaged in mining on Fall Creek, a tributary of the South Yuba, Nevada county. As true stories are almost always considered to be either very tame or altogether improbable, I hope you will bear with me on this occasion; for, as you all know, I would rather work a week in a wet drift than to try to sing a song."

"Let us have the story!" cried all the prospectors who were assembled about the campfire. "There are always too many who prefer singing a song to telling a story."

The old man knocked the ashes out of his pipe, looked up toward where the wind was harping amid the tops of the tall pines, gazed away eastward with dreamy eyes to where the rising moon was silvering the granite peaks of the Sierra Nevada mountains, and, having finally collected his thoughts, proceeded to tell the following story:

Bendix Biargo mined at Fall Creek in the early days of which I have spoken, and had one of the best paying mines in the camp. Well up toward the head of the creek he struck a streak of very rich gravel, and followed it into a big flat. In that flat he got hydraulic diggings of the biggest kind. He made from half an ounce to an ounce a day, week in and week out. He had secured so much ground on the flat that he felt fixed for life.

Bendix had about the best cabin in the camp, but one spring he built an addition to it that made it more than twice as big as it was before. While we were helping Bendix to raise this addition the boys began joking him about getting married. "We shall soon have a Mrs. Biargo in the camp," said they.

"Not so," said Bendix. "But I do expect soon to have a housekeeper."

The boys stared at one another, as much as to say: "Oh-oh!—oh! Bendix Biargo!"

"Yes," continued Bendix, unconscious of the glances some of his friends had exchanged. "Yes, I am going to have a housekeeper. I've sent home to Hartford, Connecticut, for my youngest sister, and she'll be here on this creek and in this house before two months have passed. She's of a somewhat romantic disposition, and is determined to come out here and keep house for me. Some weeks ago I wrote home that it would take three or four years to work out my claim, touching nothing but the richest ground. My sister at once announced that she was coming out to me to take care of my house and hurry me home. I thought the girl was joking until I received a letter from her father and mother. The old folks explained that some neighbors of theirs were about to sail for San Francisco, and Fannie would accompany them to that city."

"Is not this rather a wild notion to be taken up by a young lady?" said a long-faced old chap who was trying to prove a success as the chief representative of the moral and religious rectitude of the community.

"Not at all, not at all!" cried in chorus half a dozen marriageable and susceptible young men.

"I will tell you," said Bendix Biargo, his face flushing and his eyes flashing; "I will tell you," and he held up his right hand to silence the young men. "Let me talk! The girl wants to see something of the world, and she particularly desires to see California. Through my letters and the newspapers I have sent home her head has been filled with these grand old mountains, the great pines, the bright skies and the beautiful flowers. The old folks are now well advanced in years, are comfortably settled, and it is not at all likely that they'll ever come to this country, so, as I thought it would seem good to have some member of the family with me, I have sent the girl money to bring her out here. That is all there is of it, and it's all my own business."

In those early days even married women were "few and far between," and the arrival of a woman—married or single—in a camp was to the forlorn as the visit of an "angel." Ah! I well remember when the first woman arrived in Downieville, Sierra county. When the boys saw her, a mile away, coming down the mountain trail with her child in her arms before her, they left the bars in the river and swarmed into the town. As she came riding in along the principal street the men fired off their revolvers, and when she halted before the one hotel of the place they took the child from her arms and passed it about from man to man. Tears rolled down the cheeks of many a father as he took the little one in his arms. The poor woman was almost frightened out of her senses at the to her strange conduct of the rough-bearded and wild-looking men who surged about her. Before the little one was returned to its mother's arms the miners had taken off its shoes and filled them with gold dust, coin and nuggets.

As soon as it became known in our camp that Bendix Biargo had a sister coming out to him, the boys mining up and down the creek began to take a good deal of interest in him. They found him very companionable. Every Sunday afternoon Bendix had a regular "matinee." Even during weekdays one and another would drop in and turn to and help him for an hour or two at polishing up the new cabin, or about the fence he was putting up round his place.

Bendix was then a man about 35 years of age, was sober and steady—a man who never went into any kind of nonsense. We all thought well of him before we heard that he had sent for his sister, but that news gained him new interest in the eyes of almost every one in the place.

When Bendix had finished his new house, he set to work to fit it up and furnish it in good style. Although it was but a log house, Bendix vowed that it should be a palace within. He purchased the finest of furniture, carpets and bric-a-brac of every kind, and then he called in Mrs. Clancey, the wife of a particular friend, to arrange everything. Mrs. Clancey and her old colored woman, Aunt Susan—Mrs. Clancey was a highflier from Memphis, Tennessee—were at Bendix Biargo's place off and on for about two weeks, rigging up a bedroom for the girl, a parlor and a sitting-room, or, as she called it, a "boodwar."

As soon as it became known that the "Tennessee madam" was "bossing" this business several of the boys got mighty "sweet on her." One of them made her a present of a gold specimen shaped like a moth that he had refused to sell for five ounces. What this young man wanted was that Mrs. Clancey should find out if Bendix had a picture of the sister that was coming out, and if so, wished her to try and get to see it, and report to him upon it.

Mrs. Clancey ascertained that there was a photograph, saw it, and not only reported to the knight of the "Golden Moth," but to everybody in the camp as well.

"She's an angel!" cried Mrs. Clancey, radiant in her enthusiasm. "Such eyes! such hair! such beautiful features and Oh, such a sweet expression! Without exception, the girl is the loveliest creature I have ever seen!"

Then she was called on to describe the features—the shape of the nose, of the chin and forehead—and of the form as to fat or lean, as well as might be judged from a photograph, and to enter into all manner of details.

"The hair is jet black and hangs over her neck and shoulders in the most beautiful curls," Mrs. Clancey would say, and would then proceed with wonderful volubility to give many other particulars; so many in all directions that we all concluded that the photograph must be a "full-length." All that Mrs. Clancey said was seed that fell into fertile ground everywhere up and down the creek and she found herself obliged to accept not a few rings, pins and gold specimens, that were forced upon her by young fellows who all at once found her the most interesting and entertaining woman in the camp.

CHAPTER II
SISTER FANNIE

When the steamer was due that was to land the sister in San Francisco, Bendix went down to that city to meet her and conduct her to her mountain home.

When the return stage, which carried Bendix and his sister, reached Nevada City, Bendix was much surprised at seeing in that town so many Fall Creek boys. Most of them were so rigged out in "purple and fine linen" that he hardly recognized them.

Shyly and slyly they came about the coach and hotel, saying: "Ah, why, Mr. Biargo (usually they called him Bendix), who would have thought of seeing you here!" and—"Why, hello, Mr. Biargo, glad to meet you! How do you do?" then their eyes stole in the direction of the sister.

Miss Biargo was introduced to the boys, who bowed and blushed. Not a few, after a backward scrape of the foot, after the manner of a Shanghai rooster, ran away without saying a word, then went to their rooms and butted their heads against the walls for being so stupid. The resounding blows in the several rooms of the hotel, and the cries of "Take that, you donkey!" or "Oh, miserable ass that I am!" might have induced a stranger to believe himself in the midst of a society of Flagellants engaged in doing penance for their sins. However, several of the young men had the nerve to speak to Miss Biargo, and to kindly inquire how she "stood the trip"; also to inform her that she "found herself in a very wild country, a country very different in appearance from her Connecticut home."

Miss Biargo smiled sweetly and thanked every one. She had "enjoyed the voyage greatly," except for a day or two "off Hatteras," where they had a big storm.

All the Fall Creek boys were so charmed that they soon began to glower on one another like so many Bengal tigers. Not one among them thought of asking another to take a drink; old friendships seemed as though they never had been. All had suddenly become sullen and selfish, and in going home the majority stole out of town and struck out alone for the South Yuba and Fall Creek.

Bendix secured a fine saddle-horse for his sister, and another for himself, when the pair took the trail for Washington, thence to the camp on Fall Creek. As they rode away they were followed by the wistful glances of such of the boys as had lingered to the last. That night at Washington Bendix found, about the hotel at which he and his sister stopped, an unusual number of Fall Creek friends.

The next day, as they neared home, Bendix noted with some surprise, as they advanced up the creek, that quite a number of the miners who were usually hard at work in the claims at that hour of the day, were loitering about the trail in white shirts and "Sunday duds," all as gay as peacocks.

It struck Bendix that there must be a funeral or a holiday of some kind in the camp. So many white shirts had never before been seen in the place. It made Bendix uneasy and nervous, so when he met the next white-shirted man he asked if there was a funeral in camp. "No; no funeral." "Was there some kind of a holiday raging in the camp?" "No; there was nothing festive in progress."

Bendix rode on, ruminating upon the phenomenal breaking forth of linen and garments of unusual gloss and texture. Finally he thought he had reached the bottom of the business, and said to his sister: "Well, it is really very kind of the boys to make the camp look as civilized as possible. I hope they will keep it up during the two or three years we must remain here before our return to the States."

"I see nothing unusual in the dress of the people," said Miss Fannie.

"Of course not; but I do, and it is really quite astonishing," said Bendix.

"Bless me!" cried Miss Fannie, "you take on at such a rate that I am almost forced to conclude that the men usually go about looking like a set of tatterdemalions or savages!"

Bendix Biargo made no reply, but mused deeply as he rode along. He felt that great respect was being shown him, and glimpses of a seat in the State Legislature, that came and went like fire-fly flashes, were not absent from his prophetic vision.

Mrs. Clancey called at once to welcome Miss Biargo to the camp, as also did the half-dozen other women living in and about the place. Also, as excuses offered, most of the young men of the diggings "came to the scratch"—the bolder ones within two or three days, and the others straggling along for a fortnight, two or three of the "Flagellants" making their first call under the shelter of the skirts of the "Tennessee madam."

Mrs. Clancey sent Aunt Susan to assist Miss Fannie for a week or two, until she should "get the hang of housekeeping in the mountains," and it was but a few days before things were made so snug and comfortable that Bendix declared again and again that it almost seemed as if he were living in his old Connecticut home.

Just here, however, I must pause to say that for a day or two after the arrival in camp of Miss Fannie Biargo, there was quite a flurry when it was seen by all the women that she had "blazing red hair," and by all the the men that her "tresses" were of a "golden-auburn hue." Mrs. Clancey was asked how it was possible she could have been so much at fault as to report that her hair was black. That lady frankly acknowledged that she ought to have known better; and said that had she once thought of the auburn locks of Bendix Biargo, she would not have made the mistake, as it is a well-known fact that in a photograph red hair always appears as being jet-black. But this little breeze was soon over, as all the men declared themselves best pleased with "auburn" and "golden" hair; and it was not long before the younger women of the camp were hard at work bleaching out their locks to a blonde hue.

Having the field all to herself among the unmarried men of the place— being the only marriageable young woman on Fall Creek—Miss Fannie very shortly began to show herself quite a coquette. She had half the young men of the camp at her feet before the end of her first month's residence in it, much to the astonishment and dissatisfaction of her good brother Bendix; who began to fear being left alone in his fine house, just when he was beginning to thoroughly realize and heartily relish the home comforts by which he was surrounded.

Miss Fannie scouted the idea of marrying and leaving "brother Bendix" to keep "bachelor's hall." Had she not, at great "pains and peril," crossed two oceans and journeyed all the way to California to be his stay and comfort. Indeed she had, and she would remain with "brother Bendix" and keep his house. O, yes, she might flirt a little—a very little—with some of the young gentlemen, but they expected her to show some life and spirit—and it was all fun. There was not one of the young gentlemen that did not understand that it was all fun.

Thus rattled on the gay young girl—thus she prattled it off! Little did she know of men watching one another from behind trees with shotguns, of the bloody deeds that almost took place, and of green-eyed men prospecting their coffee-pots for poison.

After brother Bendix had several times been "thoroughly reassured" by

Miss Fannie, he was not a little surprised, the second day after the most protracted and elaborate reassurance of all, to be waited upon by Mr. Frank Densmore, a handsome young fellow, and a general favorite in the camp (in time of peace), who asked his sister in marriage.

It came to Bendix Biargo as a bolt of Jove from a cerulean vault. The shock staggered, but did not wholly prostrate him. Young Densmore was not only a most estimable man, but was the owner of very rich diggings in the camp; also of a fine ranch in Sacramento Valley. Brother Bendix could make no objection to the match, as a match. He tried, however, to stave off the wedding, and suggested that it would be time enough to think of that in the course of eight or ten months.

Frank Densmore rose in his stirrups. He would hear of no such delay. He would not have a longer delay than one month—then declared he saw no good reason why the wedding might not take place at once.

As young Densmore grew pale and firm, "brother Bendix" also acquired some degree of pallor and firmness. He said he should insist on that part of the business being referred to Fannie. He was quite sure she would not hear of such a thing as leaving him under five or six months.

At this Mr. Densmore smiled in a way that Bendix Biargo did not half like. Had Bendix put his thoughts into words, that smile would have gone upon record as a "sneaking, insinuating smile."

Bendix took an early opportunity of broaching the matter to his sister, making it very apparent that in his opinion six months was about the length of time that ought to elapse before the wedding took place.

Miss Fannie fixed her guileless gaze upon the ceiling, and said six months was the time she had herself thought of naming; then artlessly added that she was in a terrible quandary, and hardly knew what to do, as Mrs. Clancey had just bought and made up a new silk dress, which she had "solemnly sworn" not to appear in until it was put on for the purpose of attending her wedding; therefore, to oblige Mrs. Clancy, she had finally told Mr. Densmore that—here Miss Fannie gave a little gasp— that she could be ready in about two weeks.

Hearing this, that smile of Mr. Frank's again presented itself to the gaze of Bendix Biargo. He mused a moment, then said: "Suit yourself, Fannie—suit yourself, girl!" and marched away to his mine.

Within a fortnight Mrs. Clancey was arrayed in her new silk, and Frank and Fannie were made man and wife. The young couple took a trip to the "Bay" and to the Sacramento ranch, leaving Bendix alone in his fine quarters.

Fannie was so well pleased with the ranch that she insisted upon making it their place of permanent residence, saying—in her letter to Bendix—that it reminded her of the valley of the Connecticut. Also, she had an eye to the "main chance," and the ranch appeared to her as a thing more tangible and enduring than any patch of mining ground.

Bendix stripped his house of all the fine things it contained, and sent them to Fannie to be utilized in fitting up her home on the ranch. "Of what use are they to me now?" said he, as he surveyed them.

CHAPTER III
SISTER KATE

After the house had been thus cleared of furniture and fixtures, it began to appear immensely large to Bendix—"Vast, lonely, and uncomfortable!" was his comment as he surveyed it. Again, he was back to his bake-kettle and frying-pan, and both Bendix and his table groaned under slap-jacks and "Cape Horn bacon." He now had both the house and his time to himself. The rising young men of the camp no longer dropped in to pass an hour in the discussion of the political questions of the day. His flashing visions of the Legislature paled, and finally wholly faded away.

Bendix worried and fretted and fumed along a month or two, when a bright idea struck him. He had at home an unmarried sister, two years older than Fannie, whose name was Kate. He would send for Kate.

He wrote home at once to this sister, sending her money, and requesting her to come to him at once. He made it almost discouragingly plain to Miss Kate that he should expect her to stand by him, and not marry the first man that might offer himself. He did not desire to be again deserted just as soon as fixed to live in comfort.

Finally in a postscript—so much did the matter burden his mind—Bendix warned Kate that she would be terribly beset by lovers. These she was to steel her heart against. She was to come prepared to fight these fellows off for at least two or three years. Great firmness would be expected of her.

Now the placing of this lively battleplace before the eyes of Miss Kate was almost idiotically injudicious; but Bendix Biargo only thought of binding her down firmly to the bargain he proposed.

In due time came a letter from Kate. She thought her sister Fannie had acted very selfishly. She had always given her credit for "more heart." Fannie ought to have stood by him for a year or two, at least, particularly as he had sent money to take her to California, and had been at such great expense in fitting up for housekeeping. Miss Kate had never thought of coming to California, but in view of the singularly thoughtless manner in which Fannie had acted she would come. Brother Bendix might send the money, and she would start as soon as it reached her. She would keep "brother's house" for him as long as she lived; marriage was a thing that had never yet entered her head.

Again Bendix Biargo fitted up his house in palatial style. He said again and again, while this new furnishing was in progress, "Kate comes to stay; she shall find everything as fine as was provided for Fannie; indeed all shall be just a little finer, as Kate will be with me all her life." In this mood he sent to San Francisco and purchased a fine piano, many books and several costly paintings—"old masters" by "Young America."

Of course, as soon as these grand preparations began, it at once became known far and wide that Bendix Biargo had sent to Connecticut for another sister. Again the young men of the camp aroused themselves and began to gird on their armor. Mrs. Clancey had been called upon to superintend the refitting of the house, and she and her old colored woman, Aunt Susan, had been at the work, off and on, for many days. Again the "Tennesee madam" was in high favor—was in brisk demand at a high premium. Her information on the present occasion appeared to be equally interesting and reliable. She was able to state positively—she had it from the first sister, now Mrs. Densmore—that Miss Kate Biargo was a very handsome girl. No; her hair was not red—it was a beautiful, glossy brown. Gold specimens, pins and rings were not now so abundant as formerly; still Mrs. Clancey found herself "almost forced" to accept a few such things.

Presently it became known that Bendix Biargo's "new sister" would arrive on the next steamer. Again Bendix observed that the hearts of his many unmarried friends began warming toward him, and he did not at all like it. He now understood them. His visions of legislative honors had faded out, never to return. It was in no good feeling that Bendix observed that several young men began to make improvements about their cabins. One fellow went so far as to build to his cabin an addition almost twice as large as the original structure. Him, Bendix thought of waylaying and shooting. However, he contented himself with scowling upon the offender and snubbing him at every opportunity.

Not a few of these ominous proceedings were pointed out to Bendix by Mrs. Clancey, and were so jubilantly commented upon by that lady that he became quite resentful.

"This sort of thing has got to stop," said Bendix, "or I shan't go down after the girl at all; or, I'll go down to 'Frisco and send her right back to Connecticut—that's what I'll do!"

But Bendix did not long remain in this unwholesome frame of mind.

No schoolboy, or miner on winter vacation with well filled sack, could have started off for San Francisco in a more gleeful mood than that in which he left Fall Creek when it was time to go and meet the incoming steamer.

When Miss Kate arrived everyone said she was much handsomer thàn her sister, Fannie. The "high-flier from Memphis" declared that she was a "regular stunner."

Very few of the Fall Creek boys, who had made it their business to be loitering about Nevada City in their "store clothes" when the looked-for stage from Sacramento arrived, had the courage to advance and greet their friend Bendix—such a peerless beauty seemed the sister that alighted from the vehicle and stood by his side. The majority fell back abashed. They gave up the fight when they lifted their eyes and saw before them the full force and nodding plumes of the enemy. And it was much the same when Bendix and his sister reached their home at Fall Creek; there was no charge of the bachelor brigade.

Miss Kate made herself very agreeable, and treated all who approached her very kindly and respectfully. Bendix was delighted, and frequently said to himself with a chuckle; "No flirting with Kate! No nonsense of any kind about Kate!"

Kate was very sedate, indeed, and her brother was charmed with her bearing and conduct. She frequently assured him, when he ventured to slightly prospect her feelings and aims, that she desired no better home than his house; in it she could live all her life quite contentedly.

All this was very reassuring to Bendix, but at the end of about four weeks Mr. Hudson, a big ditch owner and one of the leading merchants of Nevada City, a man with whom Bendix had many business transactions, desired a private interview. Plump and plain, Mr. Hudson told Bendix that he was about to do himself the honor to become his brother-in-law.

The iron that now entered the soul of poor Bendix transfixed him as effectually as though it had been a harpoon hurled by the sinewy arm of a Nantucket whaler. He gasped like a speared dogfish; but what could he do? Mr. Hudson was a man of irreproachable character—a man in whose record could be found no blot. He was a widower of three years standing, with one child, a little boy.

Bendix was forced to accept the inevitable. While he had been watching and fighting off the young fellows he had left to the widower a clear field. This was now so plain to Bendix that at the moment, he would gladly have exchanged his stock of worldly wisdom for that possessed by an ordinary Digger Indian. Not only had Kate and Mr. Hudson come to a thorough understanding, but the latter had concluded his talk with Bendix by telling him that the wedding was to take place the very next week.

When Bendix next met his sister he had only sufficient heart left to sigh forth: "Oh, Kate! how could you so deceive me?"

Kate blushed scarlet, burst into tears and between sobs said: "I am two years older than sister Fannie, and, and you cou-couldn't expect me to wa-wait as long as she did?"

Bendix gave it up. It occurred to him that nothing he could say would cover the whole ground; therefore he held his peace, except that he said: "Well, dry your tears, sister, by the time I return—I'll go out and take a look at the men in the mine."

Had any one been looking in at the window, the light of which fell on Kate's back, he would have observed that she turned a little aside and smiled behind her handkerchief as her good brother Bendix, with heavy heart, marched out the door.

Miss Kate Biargo became Mrs. Hudson the next week, and Bendix was again monarch of all he surveyed in his log house. Kate went at once to Nevada City to take charge of the house (and little boy) of her husband. As this house was already elegantly furnished in every particular, Bendix did not again part with the contents of his home.

CHAPTER IV
SISTER MARTHA

Bendix Biargo moped about his house and his mine for about a week, when, to the surprise of all his friends, he suddenly brightened up and became not alone cheerful, but really decidedly jolly. His daily brooding upon his finely-furnished house had hatched an idea—an idea upon which he at once proceeded to act. It soon became known through that diligent and enthusiastic disseminator of delectable and useful knowledge, variously known as the "high-flier from Memphis," "Tennessee madam" and Mrs. Clancey, that Bendix had sent for another—the third—sister, and again expectation rose upon tip-toe. The boys all up and down Fall Creek—and even away up at Diamond Creek and Poor Man's Creek—began to "put their houses in order," for Mrs. Clancey did not stop at telling it in Gath, but rested not until she had plentifully published it in the streets of Askelon (and San Juan).

There was a merry twinkle in the eye of Bendix Biargo when next he set out for San Francisco to meet the in-coming steamer. "I've got 'em this time!" said Bendix to himself as he took his seat in the coach—"got 'em sure!"

Now Bendix had back in the "States" an old maid sister, ten years older than himself, who was living with a younger married sister at Mount Vernon, Ohio. It was for this venerable spinster that he had sent, and he chuckled to himself as he lay back in a corner of the coach and thought of the damper she would bring upon the matrimonial machinations of the "boys" when they made their customary charge upon him, on the arrival of his vehicle at Nevada City.

In vain had Mrs. Clancey tried to sound Bendix in regard to the age, personal appearance and disposition of his sister Martha. All he would say was that she was the "best of the lot." Therefore had Mrs. Clancey declared and everywhere made it publicly known that the coming sister was "younger than Mrs. Densmore, handsomer than Mrs. Hudson, and had more good solid sense than both put together."

Meantime Bendix was rolling along up from the "Bay" with his old maid sister. He was right in regard to the "damper" she would put upon the love-longings of the young men of his camp. Although Martha was a well-preserved and handsome woman, yet she had an air and manner so unmistakeably ancient and motherly that the boys took but one look at her, when their ranks began to waver, then to thin and finally even the boldest threw down their arms and fled.

We may be sure that this sudden abandonment of the field, without a blow having been struck, afforded Bendix infinite amusement, backed and braced up by much inward satisfaction.

"Now," said Bendix, as he installed his ancient sister in his snug home—"now, at least, I've got a housekeeper that will remain with me; one with no nonsense about her. Nobody is going to run away with Martha in a hurry!"

Alas, poor Bendix! There was in the mountains, up at Bear Valley, a "cattle-king," Isaac Richardson by name, and a man of herds upon many hills and vales, who was Martha's old lover. The story of the old time unsmoothness of the course of their true love, I need not repeat. Let it suffice to say that no sooner had this old lover—now a man 50 years of age, and as rugged as a grizzly bear—heard of the arrival of his sweetheart of other days than he discovered that he still had a heart that warmed up and was capable of tolerably strong palpitations. Like an old bald-eagle he swooped down from his mountain height and pounced upon Martha as though she had been but a spring chicken, carrying her away before she had time to utter more than one faint little squeak of remonstrance.

CHAPTER V
"TENNESSEE MADAM"

Poor Bendix Biargo! He became morose and melancholy. Some feared that the lonely man would commit suicide. He was so irritable that no one dared to say a word to him about his sister, nor dared ask if a further supply existed anywhere in the "States."

A month or two after the carrying away of Martha—whose stay had been the shortest made by any of the sisters—Jack Clancey, the husband of the "high-flier from Memphis," whose existence I have only found it necessary to mention when he ceased to exist, was killed in his claim by a cave.

The funeral was a successful one in every respect. All Fall Creek attended—and the "boys" came down from Diamond Creek and up from Washington, from Alpha and from Omega—and we buried him in good shape.

No sooner was poor Jack Clancey comfortably settled in his grave than it was semi-officially announced that Bendix Biargo and the widow were to be married. The news fell upon the camp like a landslide. It overwhelmed and flattened out everybody; mentally, morally and almost physically. When at length one among us had sufficiently recovered consciousness to rise up and question Bendix in regard to the correctness of the report, that gentleman said that for once Madam Rumor was a lady. He would marry the "high-flier from Memphis," even if at the muzzle of a revolver.

"You may talk about indecent taste, and all that kind of thing," cried Bendix, "and be hanged to you! I don't care a fig what is said. I make no secret of my intention. I have long enough been made the sport of the gods of love, marriage and mischief—of Cupid, Hymen and other sons of Bacchus and sons of Belial, both aerial and terrestrial, and I will be bedeviled no longer! Consider how I have been routed and discomfitted in all my housekeeping enterprises and arrangements! I say it right here, and say it boldly and above board that I went for the widow on the way home from the funeral. I am generally a quiet man—am patient and long-suffering—but once the lion within me is aroused there is thunder in the woods! Yes, I made my first approach to Mrs. Clancey at the early date mentioned, and, hang me if I had found that any one was ahead of me if I had not at once gone for her nigger woman—old Aunt Susan!"

Thus did the "murder out." Between her sobs the "Tennessee Madam" said to her neighbor, Mrs. Hoyt, "What could I do, my dear? There was my poor, dear Jack killed, and no one left to work the claim. I could not stay here and starve! I can cherish the memory of poor Jack just as well under the protection of Mr. Biargo and in his house, as I could alone and in my own shanty, my dear!

"I am sure that poor Jack will never be out of my heart," said the "Tennessee Madam," sliding her handkerchief further down her nose in order to critically inspect the changed expression of Mrs. Hoyt's features.

"That he will not, dear," said Mrs. Hoyt in a tone of the deepest conviction.

"Mr. Biargo (formerly she spoke of him as Bendix Biargo, often merely said Bendix), Mr. Biargo, who loved Jack as a brother, insisted upon my continuing to cherish his memory," sighed the widow.

Mrs. Hoyt opened her eyes somewhat just here, and applied her handkerchief to the end of her nose in order to conceal any queer twitching that might appear about the corners of her mouth.

"He says," continued the widow, "that I am merely to look upon him as a brother—to come to him, and in the peace and quiet of his home mourn the loss of poor, dear Jack."

"Very thoughtful and kind of him indeed, my dear," said Mrs. Hoyt, and she took her handkerchief from her face and looked Mrs. Clancey squarely in the eyes.

Turning her face aside for a moment to pick up from the carpet a stray end of thread, Mrs. Clancey said in an altered and persuasive tone: "It is not, Mrs. Hoyt, as if I had never known Mr. Biargo. When I was fixing up his house for Fannie and for Kate I saw so much of his kindness that I almost felt towards him as a sister toward an elder brother—you know I am only 23, my dear, and he is at least 32."

Mrs. Hoyt, the non-committal, nodded her head sidewise, half-affirmatively.

"Yes. Just as I would feel toward an elder brother," repeated the widow, eyeing Mrs. Hoyt over; "and now I am to go to him in my affliction."

"It will be a great comfort, my dear," said Mrs. Hoyt, and she patted the "Tennessee madam" on the knee.

The latter did not much relish the tone in which Mrs. Hoyt had spoken, and to give the conversation a more solemn and impressive tone, she said: "Do you know, Mrs. Hoyt, that I sometimes think I see the hand of the Lord in what has occurred—in this raising up of a friend and protector when and where least expected?"

Mrs. Hoyt had never before heard Mrs. Clancey mention the Lord, hand nor foot, and she was now so puzzled on hearing her proclaim her reliance upon an overruling Providence that she knew not what reply to make.

The widow thought she saw that she had gained some advantage, and determined to follow up the vein.

"Yes," said she, "the Lord stretches out his wing ("Queer notions she has of the Lord," thought Mrs. Hoyt), he stretches out his wing for the protection of the poor, lone wid—widow." Here Mrs. Clancey raised her handkerchief to her face and sobbed gently, keeping, however, an eye uncovered with which to catch any flitting shades of thought that might pass over the countenance of her neighbor.

In less than a month after this "trying" scene between the neighbors Mrs. Clancey was Mrs. Bendix Biargo. At once she was put in full charge of her new husband's house, where she found so much to do, from the rising to the setting of the sun, that she lacked daylight leisure to weep for "poor Jack"; but, as she confidentially informed Mrs. Hoyt, she "sobbed herself to sleep every night."

By his bold stroke Bendix Biargo now had not one but two housekeepers, for with the widow came Aunt Susan, the old colored woman, who was in herself a host at all kinds of work. As that friend to whom Bendix had first communicated his early attack on the widow was wont to say, "It was just as good as if he had in reality 'married the nigger.'"

To Mrs. Biargo came children—half a dozen boys and girls—a care and joy she had not known as Mrs. Clancey. No longer was she styled in the camp the "Tennessee madam," nor the "high-flier from Memphis." At last accounts, however—once in a year or so, when Mrs. Hoyt came to spend half a day with her—she did not neglect to take out her handkerchief and shed in a corner of it one or two tears to the memory of "poor Jack," for she had not yet forgotten the conversation that took place with her neighbor during the time of her semi-widowhood. So highly does she value her reputation for truthfulness and consistency, that she will persist in this little exhibition of feeling down to her dying day.

For about three years Bendix Biargo's sisters did not darken his doors, so little did they appreciate his dash, his daring and his grand achievement as a knight on the scalp-strewn battleground of Cupid, but when they did come they arrived with welcome reinforcements in the shape of a pair of girls and boys each, as to Fannie and Kate, and even the old war eagle of the heights came down with a "chip of the old block" in the shape of a promising young eaglet, and "Aunt Martha" looked rosy, and spoke well of the climate up in the mountains.

Here the story of the '49er ended, and he stroked his long white beard and sighed. "Ah," said he, "I shall never forget that first sister, Miss Fannie!"

"Then you were one of the ravening pack that beset her?" sternly said our old mountain guide.

"In me you behold the knight of the 'Golden Moth,'" and musingly the venerable Argonaut plucked a straggling hair from his beard.

Sacramento Daily Bee, December 24, 1885

The Seven Nimrods
of the Sierras

On a pleasant September morning a party of seven lusty young Comstockers boarded a wagon, chartered for a month's cruise, and set out for a ramble in the Sierras. The party numbered just seven. This fact was noted and commented upon by our Comstockers as they set forth. Seven being a mystical and symbolical number in the world's history, both sacred and profane, it was considered a good omen that the party consisted of just seven men.

The Seven   In their exuberance of spirits, and the inflamed state of
Nimrods   their fancy at setting forth upon an expedition of so
Take Names   much importance as a four weeks' ramble in the mountains, the happy fellows determined to rechristen themselves,—to take *noms de guerre*, after the fashion of adventurers of the olden times. In regard to the names there was much discussion. No set of names could be hit upon that was satisfactory to all. When a man found a name that satisfied himself, his friends objected to it as one they would be unable to remember, or as being too long and unwieldly.

At last one of the young men repeated the following scrap of doggerel:

"Matthew, Mark, Luke and John,
Acts o' 'Postles, Dick and Tom."

"Here," cried he, "are names for all of us, and easily remembered, too. This is a roll-call ready made."

"But, hold on," objected another; "Matthew, Mark, Luke, John, Dick, and Tom are but six names."

"That is easily arranged," said the first speaker; "we have only to call one man Acts o' 'Postles and there are names enough."

"Excellent!" cried a big, good-natured fellow—"just the thing! I'll be Acts o' 'Postles."

The other names were distributed satisfactorily and the party went forward as—Matthew, Mark, Luke, and John, Acts o' 'Postles, Dick, and Tom.

"It is rather curious, is it not," said Matthew, "that in that bit of doggerel there should be found exactly the number of names required for our party?"

"Not at all," said Mark. "This is a most important expedition; it is followed by the eyes of the gods from Olympian heights—then bear in mind that seven is a magic number. It is composed of the first two perfect numbers, equal and unequal, three and four, (for the number two, consisting of repeated unity, which is no number, is not perfect,) it comprehends the primary numerical triangle, or trine, and square, or quartile conjunction, considered by the favorers of planetary influence as of the most benign aspect. In the Bible, everything that is good goes by sevens, from the creation of the world down to the seven eyes and seven horns of the Lamb. We are predestined to be fortunate in all we undertake on any one of the seven days of the week, in any of the seven phases of the moon, or under the light of the seven stars, sifting down through the seven heavens."

"Then," said John, "the Persians, Egyptians, Indians, Greeks, Romans, and all the nations of antiquity believed in the virtues of the number. The Pythagoreans—"

"Yes," broke in Luke, "then there are the Seven Wise Men of Greece."

"And the Seven Wise Masters," said Mark.

"And the Seven Sleepers of Ephesus," said Dick.

"And the Seven Wonders of the World," said Tom.

"Jacob served seven years for Rachel, and seven additional before all was settled," said Matthew.

"And Pharaoh's dream of the fat and the lean beasts, and of the years of famine, was all in sevens," put in Luke.

"Hippocrates says: 'The septenary number, by its occult virtues tends to the accomplishment of all things, to be the dispenser of life, and fountain of all its changes,' " said Mark. "But why pursue the subject further, for as the moon changes her phases every seven days, so this number influences all sublunary beings. Yes, all things move by sevens, and we are seven who will move all things," and the young man gave a comprehensive wave of the right hand, as though sweeping the whole world back into chaos.

"If we are not the 'Seven Wise Men' of the world we will at least let the world see that we are not 'Seven Sleepers' nor the 'Seven Fools' to be like old Nebuchadnezzar turned out for seven years to grass," cried Acts o' 'Postles, slapping his hand vigorously on his thigh. "We are the Seven Nimrods of the Sierras! That's what we are."

All day the "Seven Nimrods of the Sierras" traveled on, and in the evening pitched their tent near a ranch at the edge of the forests of the foothills of the Sierra Nevada mountains and at no great distance from the town of Genoa, situated some miles below Carson City.

The seven heartily enjoyed the novelty of cooking their own supper, and ate it with wolfish appetite after it was cooked. Pipes and cigars followed. Reposing about their camp fire the Seven Nimrods were for a time supremely happy. All the wonders of the mountains, at the foot of which they reclined, lay before them. These wonders they were about to explore. Filled with a fervor fierce as that of old Don Quixote, they had sallied forth in search of adventure, and they itched to begin their exploits forth with.

The Nimrods   To break ground in a small way, they concluded that a
Decide to   good thing to do would be to make a raid on the nearest
Raid the   ranch and secure a stock of potatoes. The night was pro-
Ranchers   pitious. There was no moon and the only light was that
                 shed by the stars. This, however, was the light best
suited to a plundering expedition.

Being provided with a pack of cards, the seven brought them forth and performed an operation called cutting, for the purpose of deciding which of the party should go out against the potato field.

The lot fell upon Acts o' 'Postles, whose name by this time had been cut down to "Acts." A worse selection could not have been made by the Fates. Acts was the poorest mountaineer of the party. Outside of a town he was as helpless as a child. He knew nothing of the craft of the hunter or the art of the angler. Notwithstanding this ignorance, he had brought with him a great stock of hunting and fishing implements. "I shall learn the whole business in an hour," said he.

Acts had also insisted upon retaining his city attire, even to his white shirt and diamond studs. "If I die," said he, "I shall die like Nicanor, in my harness." He was a six-footer, a Hercules in build, good-natured, and as easily governed as a child. He was strong enough to have carried six bushels of potatoes, had they been dug and placed upon his shoulders; which was about what was necessary to be done in order to make him a success at potato stealing.

However, Acts had not the slightest suspicion that he did not possess every qualification necessary to insure the success of the enterprise on which he was about to issue forth; and when supplied with an empty barley sack, he carelessly flung it over his left shoulder and set out in the direction of the ranch he was to raid, quite confident of the success of this his first predatory expedition.

It was about eight o'clock in the evening when Acts thus set out. Nine, then ten o'clock passed, and he had not returned. Along about nine o'clock, Matthew, Mark, Luke, John, Dick, and Tom had put forth not a few jokes in regard to the success of the remainder of the couplet, Acts o' 'Postles.

Some said he would come into camp loaded down with unripe squashes and melons, as they had forgotten to tell him that potatoes grew under the ground; others asserted that he would not find the ranch, to say nothing of the potato field, though they had passed it but half an hour before making camp.

At ten o'clock, all in the camp had grown really uneasy about the "Potato Fiend," as they had begun to dub their absent friend. They talked over every evil that could by any imaginable chance have befallen him.

He could not have been detected and shot, as they had heard no report of a gun. This was about their only consolation. Several were of the opinion that Acts had become bewildered and was perhaps, even at the moment they were speaking of him, wandering away from the camp, far into the hills.

It was finally decided that Luke and John should go down to the ranch and search for the lost Acts; that Dick and Tom should go up the road beyond the camp; and that Matthew and Mark should remain at home to keep house. Matthew and Mark were to keep the camp fire blazing, as a beacon, and all arrangements had been made for setting out, when Luke held up his hand and cried:

"Hark!"

"What is it?" asked the others.

"I thought I heard a noise as of the snapping of a dry stick, off down there," said Luke, pointing in the direction of the road.

"One of the horses," said Dick.

"No, they were both grazing back here five minutes ago," said Luke, nodding his head toward a dark region behind the camp.

"A stray cow or sheep—" began Matthew, but he concluded with:

"No, by Jove! I see some one coming! See, down there toward the road!"

"Sure enough!" exclaimed Luke. "Why, it's a bloody, begging Washoe Indian. They're camped all about here."

"It does look like an Indian," said Matthew, "for his head is done up in a rag."

Acts Returns   At this moment up stalked the subject of the foregoing
Defeated,   wondering remarks, marching into the full light of the
Inglorious   camp fire.

                   "Acts o' 'Postles himself, by the two-headed Janus!" cried Tom.

Acts had also been at once recognized by the others, but all were too greatly astonished for the moment at the woeful figure he cut to utter a single syllable.

Well might they be astonished. Poor Acts was in a pitiable plight. Little remained of that "harness" in which he had resolved to die, in imitation of Nicanor. All that was left was his pantaloons. He was stark naked from the waist up. A handkerchief was tied about his head, and his feet were wrapped up in rags.

It seemed almost impossible that this abject being could be the same Acts o' 'Postles that two hours before sallied forth gayly, and so finely arrayed, to win the plaudits of his comrades in arms by bringing into camp a three-bushel sack of potatoes. He was a dilapidated-looking foraging expedition.

"Are you hurt?"—"Are you wounded?" was soon the general cry.

"Haven't got so much as a scratch—wish I had!" was the puzzling answer of Acts.

"Glad of it, my boy," said Dick, "but by the blazing Jupiter you look as if you had been run through a threshing machine!"

"Never you mind about that!" was the gruff reply of Acts, and taking up a blanket he wrapped it about his stalwart form and gloomily squatted himself down before the fire, as stolid in face as an Indian.

Acts the   Great was the wonder of the remainder of the Apostolic
Saddest of   crew at the restrained manner and woeful countenance
Mortals   of Acts o' 'Postles. For a time they respected his grief; but
curiosity was tearing at their vitals. It was not in the nature of Acts long to bury in his bosom any trouble he might have, therefore when Matthew, his most valued friend, said: "For Heaven's sake tell us what has happened!" Acts turned his eyes sadly upon the speaker and said, "I've had a fearful time of it!"

"That is plain," said Matthew. "To have been reduced to your present condition you must have passed through a terrible struggle."

"The mere physical struggle," moaned Acts, "was nothing—amounted to nothing at all. Really there was no struggle in that sense; but my mental sufferings have been extreme, I assure you. It was the keenest of torture to be made to suffer the indignities that have been put upon me—inflicted tonight while I was unarmed and utterly helpless. I pledge you my word I would have preferred being grievously wounded—shot through and through—to being so infernally mistreated as I have been. But you cannot understand this till I tell you all that happened."

"Surely not! We are all in the dark! Tell us all about it!" cried the assembled Apostles.

"Well," began Acts, "you all know how promptly and cheerfully I set out to do the bidding of the Fates. Good fortune attended me at first. I found the potato field at once and soon had filled and shouldered my sack. In passing out of the field, I even had the luck to stumble upon a melon patch. So I halted, poured out a portion of the potatoes and put into the bag a big watermelon, thinking, as I made the exchange, what surprise it would be to you fellows in the camp.

How Acts Fell "Full of happy thoughts, I shouldered my sack, left the
into the field, and struck into the road. I was going along mus-
Hands of ingly with my head down, thinking how delicious the
Robbers potatoes would be, when nicely roasted in the ashes,
and was in the very act of smacking my lips when a smack of another kind aroused me—a smack across the back.

"'Put down that sack and hold up your hands!' cried a gruff voice. I lost no time in obeying the command. When I had lowered the sack, and had pushed my hat back from over my eyes, I saw standing on each side of me a man with a leveled shotgun. Near at hand stood a third man. He also had a shotgun. However, it was on his shoulder, not leveled upon me. As I looked toward this man, he laid his gun on the ground and approached. I was now placed in the center of a triangle of footpads.

"'What is your name, my child?' said the taller of the two ruffians that were holding me under their guns.

"'Acts o' 'Postles,' said I almost before thinking.

"'Acts of the Apostles,' said the fellow, in a tone of surprise, then added, 'Indeed,' and turning to the man who had laid down his gun said, 'Go through him gently, Thomas.'

"'Gently as a young mother would handle her first baby, Captain,' replied the man.

"I own that at first I was somewhat startled at the appearance of the men, but their mild talk so far reassured me that I said, 'Unarmed as I am you'd find me no baby if you came for me one at a time, or even two; but as you are three to one I submit myself to your tender mercies, confident that—though you do come three at a time—you are men of courage and gentlemen.'

"'Spoken like an angel!' said the tall one. Then turning to the short villain he said: 'Handle him as though he were a kitten, Thomas, we must respect the Acts of the Apostles.'

"As the man addressed as Thomas began fumbling in my pockets, I felt some satisfaction when I remembered that I had on my person, all told, but about fifteen dollars."

"Just fourteen dollars and seventy-five cents," said Matthew, who was taking great interest in the story.

"Thank you," said Acts, "but it is all the same now. Well, when the undersized villain had prospected all my pockets and announced the result of his labors, the Captain gave vent to a fearful growl.

"'You infernal fraud,' roared he, 'what do you mean by deceiving us in this manner and giving us all this trouble for a paltry fifteen dollars?' "

"Fourteen dollars and seventy-five cents," corrected Matthew.

"Well, well," said Acts, "let us not bother about the odd cents. 'I've a good mind to blow out your brains,' yelled the tall robber—the Captain—shoving the cold muzzle of his gun into my right ear. 'Do you know, you Biblical cuss, that through your fancy toggery and affluent appearance in general, you've made us follow and dog you all the way from Carson? It's a mercy we got you out alone, otherwise you might have been the cause of our cutting the throats of your whole camp, and all for the trifle of fifteen dollars.' "

"Just fourteen dollars and seventy-five cents," quietly murmured Matthew.

Acts turned upon Matthew a look of protest, but said nothing.

"'Shall we allow such a fraud as this to go up and down through the country, deceiving honest and industrious men?' asked the robber chief.

"'Death to the fraud!' shouted the others, and I felt my hair rise and my blood run cold to my heart.

"'No,' said the brigand in command, 'no, he is unworthy of your steel, my brave lads. You fly at higher game than a pitiful potato thief—a potato thief! Bah! only to think of our having followed the dandy chap all the way down here to find him out stealing potatoes, and digging them up with his paws at that—with his paws like a d—— coyote.'

"This was truly my humiliating position, and I made no attempt at retort.

"'What defence can you make? What have you to say for yourself!' thundered the robber chief.

"'Why you should not be shot?' said the short man, who by this time had picked up his gun, and seemed to be thirsting to use it.

"'No, not shot,' said the chief, 'but why sentence should not be passed upon you?'

"'Sentence for what?' asked I beginning to grow angry.

"'Blazes of h——l!' roared the brigand chief, 'have I not told you? For being a thief and a fraud, and for going about deceiving your betters! But I'll give you a lesson you'll not forget till the last day of your life. Bring him out this way, my men.'

"The chief left the road and stalked away some two hundred yards across the open country, the two men marching me after him at the muzzles of their guns; indeed the short rascal took a fiendish delight in keeping the muzzle of his gun pressed between my shoulder blades."

"It's a mercy his gun did not go off," said Luke.

"I wish to God it had!" cried Acts, "for what was to come was worst of all.

"Well, at last the chief halted, and as we came up he faced about and sternly said: 'Take off your coat, sir.'

"I hesitated a moment, but up came two guns, and I took off my coat and threw it on the ground.

"'Take off your vest, sir.'

"I took off my vest.

"'Take off your shirt, sir.'

"Instead of obeying, I said: 'This is a little too much! Do you mean to strip me naked?'

"'Not quite. Do what I tell you—off with that shirt!' yelled the chief, stamping the ground in his fury.

"The muzzles of the two guns arose, and I hauled off my shirt and added it to the pile of discarded garments.

"'Now your undershirt and boots,' cried the chief, and I was obliged to obey.

"'I shall leave him his pantaloons,' said the chief.

"'Captain, I believe his pantaloons would about fit me,' said the short fiend. The wretch! it would have been like Tom Thumb in the breeches of the Chinese Giant.

"'I have said he keeps his pantaloons,' was all the answer the robber chief deigned.

"'And, sir,' said I, 'pray be good enough to leave my boots also. The sharp stones will cut my feet cruelly.'

"'His boots will just fit me,' puts in the short devil. 'Wait a moment and I'll run and get his barley sack; I'll tie his feet up in that. I'll be as good to him as if he were a sucking babe,' and away the fellow ran, the captain chuckling heartily at the idea of tying up my feet.

"Soon the rascal was back, and seating me on a stone the two under robbers tore up the sack and bandaged my feet with it.

"'His hat! O, I want his hat,' cried that pestilent short thief. 'It is just a fit,' said he, trying on my hat, which came down below his ears. 'He will do nicely and will not take cold in his lungs if I tie his head up in his handkerchief,' and soon I was rigged out as you see me.

"Then they escorted me back to the road and started me up it, telling me neither to halt, cry out, nor look behind me till I reached camp, on pain of being shot. I obeyed to the letter—the more strictly as I heard, or fancied I heard, footsteps behind me for a considerable distance—and here I am, a sadder and a wiser man than ever before in my life."

All had listened to this long and circumstantial account of Acts's disagreeable adventure with much patience and interest, seldom disturbing the flow of his story with interruptions. Now, however, his companions in arms began to ask questions on various points, all swearing it was the "greatest outrage" ever heard of,—there seemed something malicious about it.

"Were the robbers masked?" asked Tom.

"No," said Acts, "but at the same time their faces were stained or painted. As well as I could see, all their faces were of a dirty red; much the same as if one were to take some of the burnt clay of this camp fire, wet it, and rub it on his face."

"Indeed," said Matthew, "I should think that would be a rather thin disguise."

"On the contrary," said Acts, "it was a very good one and very perplexing."

"But you could see their features?" queried Luke.

"Not at all," answered Acts, "the dim light and the dirty red, made all their faces look as flat as a board. All I could make out was their height and build; I could not even distinguish the color of their clothing."

"About their build, now," said Dick, "about what was their stature and bulk?"

"Well," began Acts, stroking his chin and musingly looking about him, "the captain of the gang was a man very nearly of the height and build of Matthew; the mean little devil as about your height, Dick, while the other rapscallion was much of the size and build of John."

"Oho!" exclaimed Matthew, "sits the wind in that quarter? I see by the way in which you are sorting us out that you are beginning to suspect that we played you this trick. I can honestly assure you that not one of us thought of such a thing—that not a man of us was away from this camp during your absence."

"No, no!" protested Acts, "do not do me that injustice. I merely selected you and Dick and John because you came handy,—I mean because you are about the size and build of the fellows I was trying to describe. No, I should have recognized your voices. The robbers seemed to speak in their natural tones and theirs were voices I never before heard."

"Well, it was an outrage that must not go unpunished," said Matthew. "We will turn our hunt for game, winged and antlered, into a hunt for the robbers, and we will make it very disagreeable for them when we find them."

Incomprehensible Conduct on the Part of Acts

"It will be of no use to bother with them," said Acts. "We shall never find them; besides, if found, they might kill half our number,—they are cool and desperate villians, I can assure you."

"They can never kill *half* our number," said Mark, "for are we not seven, that indivisible and magical number?"

"Still they might kill three and half kill another," said Acts, mournfully regarding his companions. "I care nothing for my loss—let it pass—let it go. I forgive you all if you put up the cards on me. It's only fifteen dollars and some old duds!"

"Fourteen dollars and seventy-five cents," said Matthew, the correct and practical.

"But," said Mark, "his diamond studs! Do they count for nothing? They were worth every cent of three hundred dollars."

"The devil!" exclaimed Acts, bounding to his feet so hastily that his blanket was left behind—"the devil! I never once thought of the diamonds! It was no mean haul after all. By the head of St. Anthony I *have* paid dearly for my whistle! It is bad enough to have to pay the piper, but much worse when there is also the devil to pay!"

"But we shall catch them—we shall get the rascals yet," cried Matthew. "At the first peep of day we will go to Genoa and put the affair into the hands of the authorities. We will all be deputized and will assist the officers. Now I think of it, we should go tonight—at once. Let us lose no time!"

"No, no; not tonight," protested Acts, "I must have time for thought—time to reflect."

"It appears to me to be a plain thing enough," said Matthew. "You are stopped by three highwaymen, who strip and rob you. I can't see why you should wish to reflect upon such an affair?"

"Well, there is more in this than you know," said Acts. "It is a thing to be well looked into and considered."

"What!" cried Matthew, "have you kept something back? Have you not told us all that occurred—the whole truth?"

"O yes; yes, all. I have told you everything I could think of, but—"

"But what?" asked Matthew. "Let us have no 'buts'—let us be off to Genoa tonight—at once. Boys, some of you catch up the horses."

"No, no!" cried Acts, "don't do it. I can't go tonight, and I will not go! I must think it over. I am too nervous—am exhausted. My nervous system is completely shattered by what I have passed through."

"It strikes me that you are getting bad all at once," said Matthew. "You said nothing about nervous exhaustion when you came into camp."

"I beg your pardon!" cried Acts, "but did I not dwell particularly upon the mental strain?—did I not say that my mental sufferings had been 'extreme,' or words to that effect?"

"I believe you did, but you did not look it," said Matthew.

"Look it or not, I felt it, and feel it yet," persisted Acts.

"I did not observe any indication of mental torture," returned Matthew, "until mention was made of your diamond studs."

"Ah, the devil! Yes, the studs—my poor studs! Why will you bring them up to torture me?" groaned Acts.

"Then why will you persist in refusing to go and give the affair into the hands of the authorities?" flung back Matthew, sharply.

"That is what he should do, and at once," cried the united apostolic crew.

"I tell you, gentlemen," said Acts in a serious tone, "there are things to be considered. There are points against me. For instance, with what sort of face can I go and make complaint of being robbed, while myself out on a thieving raid,—while stealing potatoes? Think of that, gentlemen! 'What were you doing out on the road at that hour of the night?' asks the justice. 'Stealing a few potatoes, your Honor.' Now, what kind of reply is that for a gentlemen to make?"

"Nonsense!" shouted the apostolic band. "We will explain that it was only a bit of a lark,—a bet,—a little job we put up on you. Besides, what are a few beggarly potatoes? Pooh!"

"And a melon, too," groaned Acts, "bear in mind the melon."

"Well, potatoes—probably a peck of them—and—"

"No, at least two bushels," interrupted Acts—"at least two bushels. I had at first all of three bushels in the sack and I didn't pour out more than a bushel to make room for the melon. Gentlemen, I will not have even the smallest lie about this whole miserable business. Let the truth, the whole truth, and nothing but the truth, be told."

"So help us God!" fervently exlaimed Dick.

"Well, telling the whole truth," said Matthew, "what are two bushels of potatoes—?"

"And a melon," sighed Acts.

"And a melon," said Matthew, "to a suit of clothes, fourteen dollars and seventy-five cents, and diamond shirt studs worth three hundred dollars, to say nothing of a most outrageous highway robbery?"

"O those studs!" groaned Acts. "Why did I not think of them and hold on to my shirt? The robbers might have taken all else and welcome, but d—— it, the studs!"

"This affair must go before the authorities," said Matthew in a tone that showed he meant what he said. "It is now so late that we will give it up for tonight, but before sunrise tomorrow morning we set out. It is less than two miles to the town; we can soon be there and start the officers on the track of the robbers."

"It will do no good," said Acts, "besides there is the affair of the potatoes and the melon."

"Nothing need be said about that matter," put in Dick.

"But the officers will find the potatoes lying in the road when they go to look for the tracks of the robbers," cried Acts.

"Bother the potatoes and devil take the melon!" cried Matthew, "they are trifles. Besides, we can see the owner of the ranch and explain all to him. He will see it as a good joke, will laugh at the matter and so it will end. But for the robbers it will be different; we'll make things hot for them."

"No, no!" protested Acts, "no, let the rancher go. I will go and tell my story to the justice, but we will not go near the rancher. He is an outsider, he is in no way concerned in the business and need not be told of it. Respect my feelings. How can I face him?"

"Acts" Is
Compelled
to Act

"You are silly in your fear of this ranchman,—a jolly good fellow I'll be bound,—but let it be as you say," said Matthew, who, as a sincere friend of Acts, was taking the lead in the affair, advised all hands to turn in at once for the night. Bright and early next morning, Matthew aroused the camp. Breakfast was hastily cooked and eaten, the horses were caught up, and all was soon ready for a start to Genoa.

It was decided that Dick and Tom should remain to keep camp; Matthew and Acts would ride the horses, while Mark, Luke, and John would take their guns and go on foot, it being but a short walk and there being some hope of getting a rabbit or a few quail.

At the last moment, and even after he was mounted, Acts fell into a lugubrious mood and refused to proceed. He said it would all be of no use and would end in the disgrace and confusion of all concerned. "Let the studs go," said he, "let all go, and let us proceed on our pleasure trip the same as if nothing had happened."

But Matthew would not hear of it. An outrageous highway robbery had been committed and the perpetrators should be punished.

Finally, Acts was again brought to the sticking point, but all that was to be required of him was to allow him to make a single statement of the facts to the justice, when they would leave him to act as he might think best.

The justice was soon found by Matthew, and when all were seated in his office—Mark, Luke, and John having arrived—Acts was requested to tell his story.

Acts Makes
a Statement
That
Astounds
the Apostolic
Crew

"Well," began Acts, "there is very little to tell. I was passing along the road in a contemplative mood, having left the camp for a little walk. I was gazing up at the starry heavens, thinking of the millions on millions of worlds revolving far away in the eternity of space, millions and millions of miles beyond the reach of all telescopes yet mounted on this visible diurnal sphere, when suddenly two men stepped out from behind a large rock and confronted me with leveled shotguns. I turned to retreat and behind me found two more men with leveled guns."

Matthew, Mark, Luke, and John looked at each other in astonishment.

"I told the judge," said Matthew, "in giving him a slight sketch of the robbery, that there were but three highwaymen. I certainly understood you last night to say three."

"Last night," said Acts, "I was a good deal excited, but now I am calm and collected. You see I was only thinking of the three that at first came in front of me with leveled guns and ordered me to halt."

"But that," said the judge, "with the two men behind you, would make five men, and but now you said there were only four."

"That was all," said Acts; "three men in front, and one behind—four in all."

"I understood you a moment ago to say there were two men behind you with leveled guns when you faced about?" said the judge.

"O yes, so there were, but you must know," said Acts, "that I did not at first see the short villain. He was sitting down on the ground, and was the leader of the gang, the greatest rascal of the lot. It was he that at first slapped me on the back and cried out: 'Put down that sack!'"

"What sack was he speaking of?" asked the judge.

"Did I say anything about a sack?" questioned Acts, gazing innocently into the face of the judge.

"You certainly did," answered the judge, eyeing Acts in some surprise.

"If I did it was a mere figure of speech," said Acts. "What the tall fellow, who was captain, did say was, 'Hold up your hands!'"

"But," cried the judge, "just now you said the short man was the leader of the gang."

"Beg your pardon, judge," said Acts, "but I said it was the short one that slapped me on the back, but it was the tall one that cried out: 'Put down those potatoes!'"

"Potatoes!" shouted the judge, growing red in the face; "what do you mean, sir, by talking of potatoes?"

"Did I mention potatoes, your honor?" coolly asked Acts.

"You certainly did," roared the judge.

"If I did I was only speaking figuratively, meaning 'Come out with your coin, your kale seed,' or something of the kind."

Matthew and all the other apostolic friends of Acts were so astounded at hearing him giving utterance to such a jumble of nonsense that for a time they were rendered speechless. At this moment the door of the court-room opened, and in came a strapping six-footer, bearing under his left arm a large bundle.

Acts glanced at this man, turned deathly pale, and darting quickly to a window, threw it up and attempted to get out of the room.

This he found no easy matter when obliged to hold the sash of the window up with one hand. Before he had succeeded in doing more than to get one leg outside, he was hauled back into the room by a man who had accompanied the justice and Matthew to the office, and who proved to be a constable.

"What is the meaning of all this?" roared the justice, glancing from face to face. "Mr. Lewis," said he, addressing the big man that had come in with the bundle. "Mr. Lewis, what is up? Do you know this man?" pointing to Acts, who stood near in the clutches of the constable, and who was now blushing like a school-girl.

"I do not know the gentleman's name—having never had the pleasure of an introduction—but I know his face. We have met before—once before. I see that he remembers me. He probably has no good opinion of me, seeing that I made him peel off these here duds, but I'm not a bad sort of man after all. You know that, judge?"

"As to that, neighbor Lewis," answered the judge, "as to that, I will go further and say that no better man lives in this section. What I cannot understand is how you could have headed a gang of cut-throats and robbed this gentleman," pointing to the blushing Acts.

"What does he say about the affair?" asked "neighbor Lewis."

The judge gave the story as told by Matthew and as gathered from Acts, then appealed to Matthew and the others to know if he had correctly stated the case.

Matthew said that in the main circumstances it was right.

"Ha, ha, ha!" laughed Mr. Lewis. "A strange story indeed. It shows that the young man is full of inventions."

"Can you throw any light on the matter, Mr. Lewis?" asked the judge.

"Can I?" cried "neighbor Lewis," "well, I guess I can give you the whole business."

"You will oblige me very much by doing so," said the justice.

"Neighbor Lewis" deposited his bundle on the judge's desk, Acts dropped limp into a chair, while Matthew and the others of the apostolic band stared about them without well knowing what to think or do.

The Ranchman Gives a True Account of the Acts of Acts "Well," began ranchman Lewis, "last night, after I got my supper, I was sitting reading my paper and smoking my pipe when my wife says to me, 'George ain't there somebody a-hollerin'?'

"I listened and said: 'I guess not.'

"'There it is again!' says my wife.

"This time I heard it myself. I went out onto the porch and listened. 'Whoo-oo-ee!' yelled some one. 'Whoo-oo-ee!' yelled I.

"'Whoo-oo-ee! Hell-o-o!' yells the other feller.

"I went back into the house and says to my wife: 'Jane, I guess somebody's in trouble somewhere. I'll go and see what's up.'

"'Take your gun, George,' says my wife.

"'Of course, Jane,' says I.

"So I took down my own double-barrel and struck out.

"'Whoop-ee!' yelled the feller.

"'Whoop-ee!' answered I.

"'Whoo-roo-oo!' yells the critter.

"The hollerin' seemed only two or three hundred yards away, just off in my pasture lot. I answered the yellin' and went straight toward where it seemed to come from. In the lot are a good many trees, and in places some thickets of brush, so for a time I could see nothing; besides, you know, it was only starlight.

"Pretty soon, findin' I was gettin' near the yells, I says: 'Hello!' rather low. 'Hello!' says the feller, quite near.

"I had just got through a patch of brush into an open space. I looked all about but could see no one, though the voice seemed close by.

"'Hello!' says I again and the voice answered, 'Hello!'

"I could still see nobody, so I sings out, 'Where are you? What do you want?'

"Then the voice says: 'For God's sake come here, whoever you are; I'm treed by a bear!'

"Looking up, I could then see against the sky a big black lump, stickin' against the side of a considerable sized pine tree, about thirty feet up and about fifty yards away.

"'Is the bear there now?' says I.

"'Yes,' says the feller, 'he's here at the lower end of the tree.'

"'Sure of it?' says I.

"'Yes, sure,' says the man up the tree, 'I can see him now.'

"'What is he doin' of?' says I, for I didn't want to make any rash breaks with a bear around.

"'He's eatin' of a watermelon,' says the voice.

"This was a puzzler and I began to think someone was playin' a trick on me. However, there was the man up the tree, no doubt of that.

"'How did the bear get the watermelon?' says I.

"Says the voice: 'I was goin' across lots, toward the light of my camp fire, with some potatoes and a watermelon in a sack, when the bear made for me out of the brush and I throwed the sack on the ground and took to this tree.'

"'And the bear is there now eatin' of the watermelon, is he?'

"'Yes,' says the feller, 'I s'pose the melon busted when I chucked it down and he's eating of it—I can hear him a-chompin' of it.'

"'Hold your halt,' says I, 'and I'll see about him.' You see I didn't know but a bear might be packin' round there after my pigs, so I cocked my gun and moved up very cautious—just a step at a time.

"At last I could see a black object—some animal—near the foot of the tree. I could also hear him chompin' away at the melon. I squatted down so as to try and bring the critter against the sky, but the brush behind him was too high. I leveled my gun and was about to let drive, pretty much at random, when the animal spoke to me."

"Spoke to you! What do you mean, Mr. Lewis?" cried the judge.

"I mean just what I say, judge. The critter spoke to me, and I knowed his voice in a minute. It was my big old Berkshire boar, and I knowed his voice the first grunt he made.

"I laughed right out when I heard Blossom—that's what I call the old fellow—when I heard old Blossom grunt his wheezy grunt. I went up to old Blossom, sent him away with a kick, and said to the gentleman up the tree: 'come down, the bear's dead!'

"Judge, I dropped on the whole situation at once. I saw that the gentleman had been making a little free with my potater and melon patches and that, in trying to take a near cut across lots, he had mistook the light of my winder for his camp fire and was a-steering for it when old Blossom sauntered out toward him, probably from seein' the sack or smellin' the melon, for he is a great pet on the ranch.

"As for the strippin' of the gentleman, judge, I did make him peel. I thought I'd larn him a bit of a lesson. I asked him how much money he had about his clothes, and he said fifteen dollars."

"Just fourteen dollars and seventy-five cents," put in Matthew.

"So it proved," said the ranchman, giving Matthew a nod. "Well, I told my man that was not enough; that it would not pay half his fine if I marched him away to the justice of the peace. In short, I gave him his choice, to peel his duds as I directed, or be marched off to jail at the muzzle of my gun. Well, my gentleman peeled, even to his boots, and would have given me his pantaloons had I asked for them. Then I made him tie up his feet in the sack, marched him out into the road, and ordered him to strike out for his camp, which the gentleman did.

"Havin' had my joke, judge,—you just oughter heard Jane laugh when I showed her the duds and told her what I'd done,—havin' had my joke, bright and airly this morning I took all the gentleman's things, money and all, and went out to the camp to turn them over to him.

"Well, at the camp I found a couple of chaps that told me the gentleman and his friends had come over here to town to lay complaint of an outrageous robbery. They told me some of the particulars, when I up and gave 'em the facts, opening my bundle and showin' the gentleman's duds to prove what I said. Then you should just have seen them two fellers roll and laugh.

"When we'd all had a good laugh, I struck out over here with the gentleman's things, which he is heartily welcome to. That's all there is about it, except that when you boys get down to camp you can come to my ranch and get all the pertaters and melon you can eat, and if you come to the house you can have all the milk and buttermilk you want. Jane would be pleased to see you all, and particularly the gentleman who was up the tree."

During all the time the ranchman had been talking, Acts had not said a word, though he had turned half a dozen colors, and once or twice had faintly smiled.

When all had been told and the laughter had subsided, Acts said: "All is true, just as the gentleman relates it. I acknowledge the corn,— acknowledge the potatoes, the bear or boar, and all else. Now, I ask you all, what could I do but invent the story of the robbers, after having allowed myself to be stripped as I did? Had not things turned out as they have, I would have lost five times as much rather than have told you fellows the true story. Now that the truth is out, I throw myself on your mercy. All I ask is that you never tell this story on the Comstock."

All promised faithfully, as Acts led the way to the nearest saloon, with his apostolic tail, the judge, the constable, and several of the townspeople trailing at his heels. It is hard, however, to completely suppress such a matter, and, save the true names, the reader now has the whole story.

Not quite the whole story of this eventful trip, however, for there is still a sort of sequel, an occurrence that probably operated to prevent the remainder of the apostles from bearing too hard upon poor Acts.

Matthew, Mark, Luke, John, and Acts left Genoa a little after nine o'clock in the morning, and toward ten o'clock were nearing their camp. Only a small hill intervened between them and the camp. Suddenly they were startled by hearing several reports in rapid succession, like a string of firecrackers exploding. These light reports were followed by two heavy explosions. Looking toward their camp they saw a smoke rising above the trees.

Grand Blow up of the Seven Nimrods of the Sierras   All hastened forward as rapidly as possible. Acts and Matthew, being on horseback, were first on the ground. They found their wagon a mass of flames, with fire underneath and all about it. Cartridges or pistols were still occasionally exploding, making it unsafe to go near.

It was a considerable distance to water; besides the buckets and other vessels were being consumed in the fire. Therefore there was nothing to do but look on while their whole outfit was being destroyed.

Where, all this time, were Dick and Tom? They presently arrived, having heard the exploding of the cannisters of powder. It turned out that after the ranchman left they had concluded to go fishing, as it was not likely that any one would disturb the camp. A rising breeze had scattered sparks from their campfire and these had fired the woods. The pine boughs and bedding under the wagon, with the tent alongside, had taken fire and the result was before them.

This accident ended the exploits of the apostolic band and brought to a close the "great expectation." On horseback and on foot—"riding and tying"—all managed to get back to the Comstock; but it was long before a word could be got from any one of the party in regard to what had caused their sudden return, and they never once alluded to themselves as the "Seven Nimrods of the Sierras."

Overland Monthly, January 1888

The Eagles' Nest

In the upper part of its course the South Yuba River dashes and boils down through a tremendous cañon for a distance of many miles. Everywhere from the town of Washington upward the mountains on both sides of the river, north and south, rise to such a height that one must "look twice" to see their tops. But down near Washington the inclosing mountains are not vertical, as are the walls of rock up where the river breaks down from the main range of the high Sierras. Up there the waters of the river thunder along between perpendicular walls hundreds of feet in height.

It is above this mighty cañon that the waters of the river were, in the early days, turned into what was then known as Kidd's Ditch,—I suppose the same that is now called the South Yuba Canal. In constructing this ditch it was necessary to carry through the cañon a large flume. This flume had to be carried along the vertical south wall of the cañon for a great distance, at a height, in places, of from three hundred to five hundred feet above the bed of the river, and from two hundred to three hundred feet below the top of the wall, from which at several points lumber and timber were lowered by means of ropes.

The flume was supported on iron brackets, holes for which were drilled in the face of the cliff by men suspended on platforms like those used by housepainters. These platforms were lowered from above by means of a strongly anchored windlass. To construct a flume thus in mid-air was a costly and perilous work, but for gold men will venture all things,—even life.

The men working on the flume in time became accustomed to the dizzy height, and indifferent to the dangers that beset them. In the whole work only two or three lives were lost. Though the men employed upon the flume seemed to move fearlessly about in their work, one not hardened to such business could with difficulty nerve himself to venture near enough to the awful chasm to look down to where the river boiled along its bottom.

Owing to the swiftness of the current through the cañon, and to the many jutting ledges of rock, bowlders, rapids, whirls, swirls, and swashes, the water was everywhere churned into foam. Seen from the top of the cliff, the water in the channel of the river looked as white as milk.

One experienced very peculiar sensations while looking down upon the boiling and foaming waters,—a very creepy, unpleasant feeling. In look-ing into space above one feels all right, but on gazing into space below all is wrong; one's head seems turning upside down.

Besides this there was in the scene something weird and unnatural. But what was it? Presently it occurred to one that what made the scene uncanny was the silence,—the absence of the roar that should accom-pany waters visibly so tumultuously tossed and agitated. Instead of the deafening roar and swash natural to such a scene, we only caught now and again, as brought near or wafted afar by the shifting winds, a faint and monotonous murmur,—the one note into which was merged and blended all the pouring, plunging, splashing, and dashing, so far away below.

To stand on the brink of the chasm and look down upon the wild whirl of waters at its bottom gave a man about the same uncanny feeling he would experience were he to see walls and buildings falling on all sides of him, without producing more sound than if they were walls and build-ings of air,—the structures of dreamland.

It required great nerve to move to the brink of the precipice, and look down upon the white line that marked the windings of the river. No be-ginner could endure to stand so for many moments. Then came on a feeling that his legs were preparing for a leap into the abyss, and in spite of all the resistance his head could make, would soon plunge his body into the chasm, unless he at once turned away. This feeling begins with a sort of lifting and throbbing motion in the ground, apparently, and a tickling sensation in the soles of the feet that is very unpleasant.

One Sunday while the work of carrying the big flume through the ca-ñon was in progress, I went with a party of half a dozen miners and oth-ers from the town of Omega to see it. We had heard so many wonderful stories about the great undertaking, the difficulties that were being over-come, and so on, that we were all anxious to see with our own eyes what was being done.

Some of us obtained on the trip such a surcharge of the peculiar sort of sensations which I have tried to describe above, that we have never since had any hankering after a repetition of them.

In going to the point where the flume-building was in progress, we procured horses and took to the main ridge above the town, where we had for nearly the whole distance a wagon road,—the Bear Valley road, I believe it was called. When opposite where the flume was going in we left the road, and taking to the forest, zigzagged down the face of the moun-tain to the camp of the workmen. There was not another dwelling of any kind within ten miles of the spot.

Being all young and full of fun we charged down upon the quiet camp like a band of wild Indians, and soon had the place in a considerable state of commotion, for we were received in about the same spirit as we exhibited by all who were visible about the camp. Then an irruption of visitors was not an every day occurrence.

With our party went a Mr. Van Vranken, the hotel-keeper of the town of Omega. He was the hero of our first adventure, as he came near being plunged head first into the abyss. On our arrival at the camp we had dismounted and tied our horses to some trees near the boarding-house; that is, all except Van Vranken, who being older than any other of the party, and more careful of his bones, had lagged behind executing numerous elaborate zigzags on the face of the mountain.

When Van arrived we were all out near the verge of the chasm. Seeing with us a carpenter who was an old acquaintance, Van rode directly up to our party. Shaking hands with his friend he dismounted, and stood talking with his bridle on his arm.

Van had a shepherd dog he highly prized, and this dog had come with him on the trip, as he and the horse Van rode were inseparable companions. Had the dog been left at home, he would have cried his heart out.

Now, it so happened that there were two or three cows kept at the camp, and one of these had a calf that was kept in a pen near the lodging-house. As soon as Van halted and dismounted, his dog began prospecting the camp. About the first thing that attracted his attention was the calf, and he went to the pen to see it.

No sooner, however, had he reached the pen than he was discovered by the mother of the calf. The cow charged with a snort of wrath, and the dog turned tail and fled toward his friend the horse.

Seeing the yelping dog coming with the cow in full chase, the horse was startled, and throwing his head up began backing directly toward the brink of the precipice. The more Van pulled the higher the horse threw his head and the faster he backed. In running backward the horse pulled Van with him, who with feet braced was sliding along on the carpet of pine needles, quite unaware of the near proximity of the precipice.

"Look out!" "Let go the horse!" "Look out for the cañon!" cried a dozen voices, yet Van held on. Having been engaged in conversation from the moment of his arrival, he had not looked about him, and little thought he was so near a vertical precipice over seven hundred feet high.

Not heeding the babel of voices roaring at him, Van still pulled at his horse, which caused the animal to pull back all the more stubbornly, going squarely to the edge of the chasm.

"Let go the horse for Christ's sake!" yelled the carpenter, at the same time making a rush for Van and grabbing him by the coat-tails. At the very instant he did so the horse went over the brow of the cliff, the bridle luckily slipping out of Van's hands.

The horse seemed to cling to the brink a fraction of a second by his fore feet, and then disappeared. No sooner had the horse tumbled into the abyss than the dog ran to the verge and without an instant's hesitation leaped over after him.

All was over so quickly that Van hardly realized what had happened, and would have run to the brink of the chasm to look after his horse and dog had not his friend the carpenter held him, and told him of the danger. Van said afterward he thought all the time the fuss was all about some little gulley.

The next moment after saving Van the carpenter was again all excitement. "My God!" cried he, "My God! the men below! The men on the flume are all killed!" and he ran to the railing by the windlass and looked over. After a glance he turned to us and said, "Thank God, they are all right!"

We afterwards ascertained by calling down to the men that the falling horse had passed only about ten feet in front of the end of the flume where they were at work.

One of the men said: "We thought old Satan was coming with one of his imps after him!" Another said that they all very plainly "felt the wind" of the falling horse.

Looking down from the railing by the windlass we could see a black spot—the horse was black—at the edge of the milky stream. We could see nothing of the dog. We called down to the men, three hundred feet below; they said the horse was motionless, but a speck that was probably the dog seemed to show some motion at times.

As the horse was in a place that could not be reached except by a tramp of five miles up the river to where a descent into the cañon might be made, Van left ten dollars to be given to any one among the workmen who would bring out his bridle and saddle, and send them to Nevada City at the first opportunity. The man was also to bring out the dog, if he were not hurt beyond hope of recovery.

I may say right here that the man who the next day descended into the cañon found the dog with his back and both hind legs broken. The poor brute had dragged himself to the head of the dead horse, beside which he lay. He greeted the workman with glad barks. In order to give the dog a last gratification the man gave him all the water he could drink, and then put a bullet through his head.

The windlass and railing of which I have spoken were on a platform of timbers of large size and about seventy-five feet in length. The ends—there were a dozen logs—had been pushed out five or six feet over the brink of the precipice, while the "inshore" ends were anchored far back from the bank, and weighted with cribs of stone. When we had been shown this place, we could in safety stand and look down into the chasm.

As we were about starting for home, the men at the flume camp told us that about a mile and a half down the river was to be seen the nest of a pair of eagles, in which were two eaglets. They said we might return that way and see the nest, which was on a scrub cedar growing on the verge of the precipice, and projecting over the abyss.

"But," said the man, "we do not feel afraid of your carrying off our pets. The nest is over a part of the cañon that is about one thousand feet deep, and out on the branches of a nearly horizontal tree. Not a man in the State has the nerve to climb out along the trunk of that cedar and bring in the young eagles!"

We concluded to ride by the eagles' nest in returning, as it was not out of our way.

As we rode along down the river all the talk was of the eagles. "Evidently no one working on the flume dare try to get the young eagles," said Van, who had made a bargain with one of our party to go home on foot and let him ride.

So much talk was made about the feat of going after the eagles, that I at last said I was not afraid to go out after them. I had gazed down into the cañon so long from the windlass platform that I imagined I had cured myself of dread of mere depth, and had gained such control of my head that I could trust it; besides, I would not look down into the cañon. I would follow the rule of the rope-dancers, and see nothing but the trunk of the tree and the eaglets.

I was dared, hooted, and scouted. Two or three were ready to put up fifty dollars to fifty cents, and as many more one hundred dollars to one dollar, that I would not dare go out after the young eagles. I said I would consider the bets when I had seen the situation of the nest.

When we came to the nest it was seen at a glance that it could not possibly have been so placed as to be more difficult of access. The cedar grew on the very brink of a precipice, rooted in a large cleft that contained some soil. It was only about eight inches in diameter, and extended almost horizontally from the brow of the precipice, which was vertical. Out about ten feet the tree put forth several branches, which spread out like a fan. The boughs of the tree formed a sort of platform on which was the nest and the young eagles, with naught below for a distance of a thousand feet more substantial than thin air.

The eaglets seemed to be pretty well feathered, and after a critical examination of them and the situation I told my companions I would take all their bets and go out after the birds, but would not agree to bring them in, as they might perhaps fly away.

All held to their offers.

I stripped to shirt and drawers. Then even such as before had been doubters began to believe me in earnest. Bob Paxton, a brother "Buckeye," earnestly labored to dissuade me from the undertaking. He had a real brotherly regard for me, not alone on that occasion, but to the last day of his life. Poor Bob! his bones now lie in the land of the Mormon.

An eagle that had been wheeling about at a height of some hundreds of feet above us—probably the mother bird—began to grow uneasy at sight of our party so near its young. It uttered several shrill shrieks as it circled above our heads. Its cry was presently answered, and we saw coming from the north, as from the top of the great pineclad mountain on the opposite side of the river toward Eureka, the mate that had been called. The two shrieking birds swooped about in a manner so threatening that Bob Paxton said they would surely attack me if I ventured out near their young. He made me belt to my side a long "Arkansaw toothpick," which he always carried, and which he informed me would "cut like a razor."

The belting on of the big knife completed my preparations for the perilous adventure. My determination was to see nothing except the tree and the eaglets. By persisting in that I thought I should easily succeed in the venture. Had the tree been out on level ground, any one of our party could have climbed out to the nest in three minutes. All I had to do was to keep out of my head the awful space below. I might look upward into space, for that I was accustomed to.

I was barefoot and stripped to undershirt and drawers. A silk handkerchief was bound tightly around my head. Amid a silence that was almost breathless I advanced to the verge of the cliff, and dropping to the ground crawled astride the trunk of the little projecting cedar. I fixed my eyes on the young eagles and would see nothing else.

It was only ten feet out to the nest. Soon I was out to where the branches put forth from the trunk, and spreading fan-like formed the platform on which was the nest. I could almost reach it. The old eagles screamed nearer and nearer, and I could hear the whistling of the feathers in their wings as they swooped to and fro above my head.

The young eagles soon became alarmed. They reared up, spread their wings, and opening their great mouths began to make a hissing noise. This appeared to enrage the parent birds, and one of them came so low as to brush my head.

Thus far I had not ventured to look up toward the old birds. Seated astride a pole only eight inches in diameter, I was not in a position to look aloft. Let any one make the experiment in a safe place on level ground, and he will at once discover that it is difficult to retain his balance,—to escape toppling over.

After being touched by one of the old birds I saw that it was absolutely necessary to pay some attention to them, or I should be struck on the head and knocked off my slender perch. Reaching out with my left hand to where the limbs put forth, I grasped one that was about two inches in diameter. Thus anchored I was at liberty to make some use of my right hand. I must finish the fight with the old eagles before touching the young ones.

Drawing my bowie knife, I held it above my head, and when next one of the old birds swooped down at me I struck it somewhere on the body, cutting out a little shower of small feathers.

Either the glitter of the knife or the upward motion of my arm frightened the young eagles. Both hopped out of the nest and went fluttering downward and away. Down, down they went, their wings but half supporting them in a feeble flight that carried them toward the opposite side of the cañon, with the old birds dashing headlong after them.

I turned my eyes to watch the course of the eaglets, and in doing so for the first time caught sight of the milky water of the river and the rock-strewn earth toward which the birds were half falling,—the earth and the stream dimly seen far, far below.

In that downward glance of a moment my eyes had taken in the awful depth that lay below me. In an instant, terror—the terror of the awful space beneath—seized and overwhelmed me. I felt impelled to pitch headlong downward into the chasm, and at once terminate the torture which knowledge of the great gulf below me inflicted upon every nerve and muscle of my frame.

The knife dropped from my hand into the abyss, and the self-command that I still retained was barely sufficient to give me such control of my senses and use of my muscles as to permit of my tightly closing my eyes, and bending forward until my breast rested upon the solid substance of the spreading branches of the tree.

That last half instinctive action was all that saved me. Had I remained upright astride of the tree trunk another moment open-eyed, I should have ended the torture that throbbed through every nerve of my body and brain, by throwing myself at once into the space below that so thrilled me.

With my breast upon the boughs and each hand firmly grasping a thick branch I lay with closed eyes, determined not to make another move until I had become composed, and regained sufficient self-possession to do what remained to be done in order to escape with my life.

The eaglets being gone, it only remained for me to make my way back to the brow of the cliff and to the firm rock. Without moving I mentally glanced over the route. That which immediately occurred to me was that I was faced the wrong way. I could not well go backward and make a safe landing upon the brow of the cliff; I must turn and get my face toward the top of the wall.

I studied over the maneuver that would be necessary to place me in the desired position. I saw that it would involve my having for a short time both legs on one side of the trunk of the tree; that for a moment I should be seated sidewise upon it, as a woman sits upon a horse. It would be no trick at all performed on a pole in a gymnasium. It was wholly in the thousand feet of space below me that the trouble lay. I therefore determined to perform the feat of reversing my position with my eyes shut. The branches which my hands grasped were about two feet apart, which would give me a good deal of purchase.

When I felt myself thoroughly nerved for my maneuver of facing about, I accomplished it almost in an instant, that I might have not time in which to think of the perilous position it involved.

Not until I had again firmly clasped the trunk of the cedar with both hands did I venture to open my eyes; and then I directed them in advance so that they would rest upon the edge of the cliff at the root of the tree.

As I completed my reversal feat I had heard a sort of tumultuous cry from my friends on the cliff,—the first sound I had yet heard from them,—which I took to be a sort of spontaneous outburst of applause, but when I opened my eyes I saw at once that it must have been a cry of horror.

My tree was rapidly sinking,—was giving way at the roots. Now that my attention was directed to what was occurring, I could hear the cracking of small roots as the tree settled down and swung in toward the wall. I could no longer see any one on top of the cliff, for I was already several feet below its brow. I could see the earth crumbling and dropping from the brow of the cliff as the roots of the tree stretched in the ground.

Each moment I expected the tree to tear loose and carry me with it to the bottom of the abyss. Strange as it may seem, I did not in this situation experience any such feeling of terror and horror as that which for a moment overwhelmed me when I looked down after the falling eaglets. The calmness of desperation now took possession of me. There was no more of the horrible tingling and thrilling of the nerves. All would doubtless be over in a few seconds, and I was braced for the shock. I knew the worst and was prepared to endure it. I even looked down to the rocky floor of the cañon a thousand feet below without a tremor. Space gaping beneath no longer had any terrors for me. I was already no better than a dead man.

But the roots of the tree did not tear loose as I had expected to see them do. When the top of the tree had turned directly downward the roots still held, and I clung to it ten feet below the verge of the cliff. I was astride the trunk just at the point where the main boughs, spreading out like the ribs of a fan, supported the whole weight of my body; indeed, the trunk of the tree being about eight inches in diameter, I could not so clasp it except with my arms as to sustain any weight.

The tree did not hang flat against the vertical face of the cliff. There were projecting branches that kept it about three feet away from the wall. In this position it stopped; and as the roots still held, I began to hope that they would continue to hold until I could be rescued; however, with the least motion or agitation it might give way at any moment.

Finding that I was not to be instantly hurled down to death, I presently ventured to lift my eyes to the brow of the cliff. I could see no one, nor could I hear the voices of my late companions. I began to fear that I was deserted. Having seen the tree sink down out of sight, they probably believed it had fallen and carried me with it to the bottom of the cañon. Not one of them would have the nerve, in view of the happenings of the day, to come to the brink and peer over in search of me.

I looked upward along the trunk of the tree, meditating as to whether an attempt to climb it would be likely to prove successful. I saw at once that to escape in that way would be impossible.

Even though I should be able to climb the trunk, I could do nothing when I came to the brow of the precipice. I also feared making even the slightest motion,—the least jar might cause the tree to give way.

My thoughts then again turned to my friends. My soul sickened at the thought that they might have gone away,—gone up to the flume camp to report the latest accident.

I was scanning the line of the cliff as far as my eyes could follow it, in the hope of seeing one of my party out at some curve, when I heard a voice far above me, in the sky, as it sounded to me, "Are you still alive and safe?" it said.

Was I "still safe?" It seemed a cruel joke.

I turned my face upward to answer, but for a short time I hesitated. I feared that my mere exertion in shouting would so agitate the small tree as to tear loose its roots. At last, however, using my voice carefully, I cried, "Can you hear me?"

"Yes, plainly," was the reply.

"Well, then, I am still alive and on the tree, but not safe!"

"Hang on," came back. "Hang on, and we will try to save you!"

I looked up. No one was visible on the verge of the wall. They were afraid to approach it; afraid to stand where I would have given worlds to have been placed. What to them seemed a place of peril would have been to me as the Rock of Ages.

Again I was left to my thoughts and fears. I did not like this seeming desertion. It appeared to me to be very cowardly in them not to show themselves and stand by me. In such a situation, even the sound of the voice of a fellow man is a comfort.

At last another voice—one that seemed almost by my side—called to me. I looked up and saw peering down at me over the brink of the precipice a face that I recognized as that of a young man named Peter Bowers.

"Hold on as you are," said young Bowers. "My brother John has gone back to the flume camp on the best horse for a long rope. He will soon be back."

Good God! "Soon be back!" It was a mile and a half to the camp. I must wait until a man had ridden three miles. Here was a wet blanket for me.

Somehow, when I saw a face within ten feet of mine, I had felt as though I was saved. I would be up on the cliff at once. Now they were going to make me wait until a man could ride three miles before trying to try to save me. It was rascally! Why not help me at once?

"Can't you drop me the end of a lariat?" cried I.

"No. We've only got one lariat. That's tied around me and the men are holding the other end."

"What is all that for?" cried I, in astonishment.

"Why, to keep me from falling over into the cañon."

"To keep you from falling! Good Lord! Why, aren't you safe enough anywhere up there on the solid rock?" sneered I.

"No. I can hardly stay here with the lariat fast to my waist. My head wants to go down and my heels feel like they'd fly right up into the air in spite of all I can do!"

"What a cowardly set!" thought I. "All up there is so solid and safe, yet every man there is afraid to come near enough to give me the end of that lariat!"

But I was in no position to fight any one, therefore I softly said, "Surely they can come near enough to drop me the end of the lariat!"

"Yes, but who is to come to the edge to drop it to you if he is not held fast?—and we've got but one lariat."

I groaned.

After a moment's thought I said: "Where is Bob Paxton?"

Pete turned his head and looked.

"Out holding your horse," said he.

"Ah," said I, "he is always thoughtful. Bob is determined that I shall not go home on foot."

I was so mad that I did not much care whether the tree held or pulled up by the roots.

"Wait a bit and hold fast. Do have patience!" said Pete. "John will soon be here with the rope."

"Well, if I am to wait till then I wish you'd send me down a lunch. I saw Bob Paxton slipping some biscuits and cold meat into his pockets just before we left the flume boarding-house."

Pete's head disappeared. It may to some appear very unlikely that I talked and felt in my situation as I have reported. My situation was in truth so desperate that I also became utterly desperate; and coolly so. The brink of the precipice, which an hour before would have turned my head, was now as nothing. I could have danced along it from end to end. I could now gaze down into the chasm without a qualm. My greater danger, my imminent peril, had killed all the smaller dangers. To paraphrase Pope—

> Small dangers intoxicate the brain,
> But great ones sober us again.

My danger was so great that I was perfectly sobered by it. It was about the same as lost. There was, however, a chance of a rope's coming before the tree gave way, and I would make the best fight I could for that chance.

Again I was left alone, suspended between heaven and earth. To add to the terrors of the situation, gusts of wind began to sweep through the cañon and sway me and my tree. I was still keenly alive to whatever threatened the stability of my tree,—if stability could be said to pertain to such a thing. Occasionally I could hear a root snap, and at times dirt fell from the edge of the cliff; as if the tree were slowly but surely giving way. All these things gave me very keen little starts and pangs, but had no power to overwhelm me,—to upset my brain.

To find all drawing back from me and keeping out of sight disturbed me not a little. I thought they should have appeared to be doing something,—might at least have given me the comfort of their presence. I have since seen how eagerly a man that is about to have the hangman's noose placed about his neck catches at a kind word or even a nod of recognition, and know that the word and nod filled a yearning vacancy.

Finally, after, as it seemed to me, I had been hanging over my grave a month, I heard a great—a mighty cheer.

"John Bowers has come with the rope!" thought I.

Soon Pete Bowers again peered down at me and said: "They have got a long rope. They are going to tie one end of it to a tree, and will then make a noose in the other end and let it down to you. Hold on a little longer and we'll get you."

"I can hold on a month," said I; "I am well enough fixed for holding on, but what is the good of my holding on if the tree gives way? You fellows seem to think all depends upon me and my holding on. This tree is giving way all the time."

Pete withdrew to impart this information.

It seemed an hour before he again crawled to the brink,—for he came by crawling on his belly. "I've got the end of the rope," said he, "but I'm afraid to come square over you to drop it. I'm afraid to go near the roots of the tree. The ground there is all cracked and loose."

"For God's sake, keep away from there!" cried I. Then, "Can't you throw the rope so that the loop will pass beyond the trunk, and slide along down to me as it slacks in drawing back?"

Pete threw the rope, but it fell short. Again and again he tried. Once it came near me and I reached out and clutched at it. As I did so there was an ominous cracking above, and small clods of earth fell and rattled down through the branches of the tree that rested against the wall.

I clutched the tree, afraid to wink or breathe for some moments. Then I said to Pete: "What is the matter of you?—why can't you fling the rope as I told you?"

"I can't throw so hard."

"Why not?"

"If I do my heels will fly up and I'll go head-first into the cañon!"

"What! With a lariat around you and a dozen men holding you?"

"Only four, and they'll let go and run if they see me go over. They say we've lost too many men already today to take any more chances."

"O yes, I see!" said I, again beginning to forget that I was not on terra firma.

I thought a moment, and then said: "Tell the men to cut a long, slender pole; sharpen the upper end of it, then twist the strands of the rope at the noose backward and thrust in between them the point of the pole; then you can pass the noose down into my hands. Do you understand?"

"Yes, I'll have it fixed," and Pete withdrew.

In about ten minutes—it seemed to me as many hours—Pete was back with the pole and rope.

I wrapped my legs tightly about the trunk of the tree in order to have free use of both hands.

Down, down came the noose at the end of the pole. I never saw a thing move more slowly. At last I clutched it, and with a death grip. I soon had the noose over my shoulders and about my waist. I then told Pete to haul up the slack. As soon as the noose tightened I felt that I was safe.

With my left hand I took a vise-like grip on the rope above the noose and prepared to emerge.

"How many men are now holding you?" I asked Pete.

"Only three now."

"Can they hold you while you give orders?"

"I guess so."

"Well, don't let your heels fly up. How many men are holding me?"

"Four or five."

"And is the end of the rope still fast to the tree?"

"Yes, sir, still fast."

"Well, then, I may as well make a move and get out of here. However, now I think of it,—where is Bob Paxton?"

"On the rope, sir."

"My rope or yours?"

"Yours, sir."

"Tell him that I'm hungry, and ask him to please to save for me the lunch he has in his coat pocket."

Pete opened his eyes in astonishment, but turned his head and gave the order. Though I felt almost as safe as if out on the brow of the cliff, I knew that the "space fright" still held Pete in its power, and I did all this talking to try his steadiness before giving him my real business orders.

The first thing was to taut the rope in line; for Pete was still holding it. I told him to let go of it and tell the men to haul gently on it until I cried halt.

Pete did as directed, and repeated my order when I called a halt. The rope did not lie directly in a line with the trunk of the tree, and I made him veer the men by motioning with his hand till it was right.

I had studied out the whole programme while waiting for the rope. I wanted to steady myself by the trunk of the tree in going up, instead of swinging in against the wall and banging about, as the butt and roots of the tree would be of assistance in getting up to the crest of the cliff.

I explained this to Pete after the rope was in line and taut. Then I said to him: "Now, Pete, if you feel quite safe we'll start up."

"I am ready, sir."

"Very well. Now repeat my orders to the men instantly and exactly as I give them."

"Yes, sir."

"Haul away steadily!" cried I.

The order was repeated and acted upon. Up I went, calling out as I went: "Steady, steady!—not so fast!—so—steady, so!"

I made but one halt. That was when my head was on a level with the brink and at the point where I had partly to support my weight upon the butt of the tree in order to mount over the roots. After that a steady haul brought me upon the brink, when I lost no time in making a few rapid steps inland, where I tumbled down all of a heap.

I was weak as an infant.

"Water, water!" I murmured. "I'm so faint!" and I came near fainting in reality.

Water was brought from a rill, and with it was mingled some brandy, which Van Vranken had remaining in his flask. Next I took a shivering fit,—I began to feel the cold,—and was helped into my clothes. I was still too weak to stand alone, so sat on the ground for a time and rested. When helped to my feet, I rose the biggest coward in the crowd. A yoke of oxen could not have drawn me to the brink of the cliff over which Pete Bowers had thrust his head while helping me. Pete went out and got for me a piece of cedar root, to show me that it was almost as tough as a buckskin string. I thought it was very hardy of him to brave so much for so little.

At last I was able to mount my horse with some help, and we started for home, sending the rope back by some men that had come down from the flume camp. In about an hour I was all right, the motion of the horse starting my blood again through all my veins.

It was not until we were almost in sight of Omega that any one ventured to speak of the bets I had won. I said that I wished never again to hear them mentioned,—that I would hold the man to be my enemy that ever again said a word about the bets; and I felt and meant it. Strange as it may seem, while I was hanging in the tree and vexed with my friends for not doing more for me, I said to myself over and over again that if I ever got out alive I would exact from those fellows the last cent of every bet I had made.

My performance was not one that I was proud of, and for years it was not mentioned in my presence by any one who cared to be my friend.

As long as I remained in the town of Omega,—even till the year 1860,— when I saw myself pointed out and eyes following me, I thought it was being said: "There goes the blamed fool that went after the eagles' nest!"

Also, even to this day, the adventure often interferes with my sleep. Just when I am on the point of quietly entering the realms of dreamland I find myself out on the cedar, see the young eagles falling fluttering down, down into the awful abyss, and again I am thrilled in every nerve with the old "fright of space" yawning beneath me. It is true that I have discovered the cure for this fright, but it is "big medicine" and I don't hanker after it.

Overland Monthly, May 1891

An Indian Story of
the Sierra Madre

I
THE TWO RAVENS

"Thank the Lord! At last we're out of the desert. The country ahead is no Garden of Eden, but it's better than that eternal sand back there."

The three prospectors reined in their horses on the crest of a low ridge which marked the beginning of the mesa, and surveyed the ground ahead. It was less sandy and somewhat more broken than that they had just crossed, one of those burning deserts known in that region as a "journey of death" (jornad[a de la muerte]). They had been down in the Sierra del Perro, and even across the edge of Old Mexico, and were coming northward to the Sierra de las Animas by way of the Sierra de San Luis.

The men were all mounted on large and handsome mustangs. By their arms they were plainly aware of the fact that they were traveling in a region teeming with dangers; each, in addition to the invariable Winchester, carried a revolver, and that heavy Mexican knife so like the cutlas in use and appearance.

Halted upon the crest, the red rays of the sun slanting across, they formed a striking and picturesque group—a group representative in dress, arms, equipments, and ruggedness of appearance of the class of hardy and fearless prospectors roving through the Sierra Madre and other ranges of New Mexico and Arizona.

The elevated mesa stretching before the party might have been five miles in length by nearly three in width. It was covered with small stones and cut up by many dry gulches. The only vegetation to be seen was the low-growing cactus, relieved here and there by a fantastic group of yucca. To the westward was a grand ridge of castellated rocks that looked as though it might be the home of cliff dwellers, and behind it rose a high mountain.

While they were yet gazing for a break in the northern hills, a pair of hoarsely croaking ravens flew over the mesa and toward the ridge. The captain followed them with his eyes.

223

Drawn by Frederic Remington.

"Going to roost," he remarked, sententiously. "What we ought to be doing."

The ravens were interesting, insomuch as they were the first living things the party had seen that day. Dick Nordine shaded his eyes with his huge hand, which was, however, in excellent proportion when one considered his height and build, and looked toward the setting sun.

"By George!" he shouted. "Did you see that, Cap?"

"See what?"

"Why, the ravens—how queer they acted?"

"I see them coming back as if Old Nick were after them," said Captain Ben. "They're putting for the east ridge."

"I mean the back somersault they turned when they struck the rocks."

"Back somersault!" Captain Ben queried.

"Yes. They never lit at all. Jist as they were lightin' they begun to tumble over theirselves in their hurry to git away and take the buck track."

"The devil they did!" cried Captain Denton. "Then we've got to look out for our scalps, that's all. We may thank those ravens for telling us what's in store for us. Nothing but a human being could have given the birds such a fright, and if there's a human up among those rocks he's an Apache."

"That's gospel, Captain Ben," said Burt Colrick. He, too, was a strapping six-footer, and, like Nordine, a mountain man in every respect. "The only critters ravens is afeerd of is human critters, and therefore there's a human there."

Captain Ben whipped his field-glasses out of their case and leveled them at the ridge, every detail of which was now strongly outlined by the light diffused over its crest by the sunken sun.

"I thought so," he said, when he had examined it some minutes. "The ravens did not wheel without reason. I see two heads over the rocks, and one is a feather head, sure as I'm alive."

"Proverbly there's a lot more," suggested Nordine.

"Of course, they've seen us?" said Colrick.

"Of course, Burt," said Captain Ben, "saw us the moment we rose this ridge, and dropped behind the rocks to watch us. Well, it was lucky!"

"What was lucky?" Colrick asked.

"Everything, so far. If we'd been ten minutes later rising this ridge, we'd have had some hot work by now, and some of our scalps might have been looser. We'd have struck them about here."

"How so, Cap?"

"Well, here to our right, off east about a mile, I can see the tops of some trees in line with the ridge. There is a grove there and a water-tank. The Indians were heading for that grove to camp when we turned up. Their business now is to find out what we are going to do."

"And what are we goin' to do?" asked Nordine.

"Roost. Strike for the grove and camp there. There is no other camping place in sight; it's the natural thing to do."

"I don't see, Cap, why we've got to camp in the grove," said Colrick.

"That or fight right out here now on the open mesa, and it's pretty sure they're too many for us. Do you see that big arroyo coming down from the ridge? They will follow that, and its banks will hide their ponies until they're right on us. They'll never let us pass that point, and if they have a large party they have men in the arroyo now. If we go into camp at the grove it will give us time to do some head work before the fight comes off and to find out how many they are. Then we will have the choice of the battle-ground, and the first fire."

"I s'pose you're right, Cap, but blame if I can see through the business any further than slippin' away from 'em while they're thinkin' us asleep at the fire."

"That will be a good move," the captain returned, "but what we come across at the grove may alter our plans. Start the pack-mule along, Dick."

"All right, Cap, but I'm afraid he'll be temptin' bait for them Apache rascals. If there's one thing an Apache will risk his life for, it's mule meat. The very sight of a 'John-day-zin,' as he calls a mule, makes his mouth water."

II
THE FLIGHT

Captain Denton took the lead as they drew near the grove.

"Here's a creek, fellows," he shouted. "I thought the grove was beside a big water-hole."

"All the better, Cap," said Nordine.

"Yes, but we've got to be watchful, because they will crawl along the banks above or below us. They must have water. They're already on the move," he added, as he scanned the ridge with the glasses.

Captain Denton's party descended the steep slope to the banks of the little stream. The grove gave no signs of having been recently visited, though the bent poles of half a dozen lodges showed it to be an old Apache hunting-ground.

Denton gave orders for picketing the animals on a patch of meadow by the side of the creek, but some distance from the cooking. Then they began looking about for a position in the grove. They found that the ridge was of such height that it shut off the view down the creek. The captain swathed his head and body in green willow twigs and climbed the tallest cottonwood, taking with him his field-glasses, and leaving the camp-fire and supper to his two subordinates. It was fast growing dark when he descended.

"Well, men," he said, "it's just as I expected. Those fellows have slipped down along the south side of this ridge and are now lodged in a small grove about half a mile below. It isn't such a bad box as it might be, there are only five all told."

"Only five!" cried Nordine and Colrick, deprecatingly.

"I saw none coming down the arroyo, and up the creek there are neither trees nor grass. They would know that."

"What are the fellows below us about?" asked Colrick. "Have they regularly gone into camp?"

"They are picketed on a patch of grass, but there's no smoke that I can see. If they have a fire, they have used coals chipped from burnt logs and stumps."

And so the party sat down to supper. Afterwards Captain Denton crept away into the gloom to reconnoiter, while Nordine and Colrick set about baking enough bread for two days' rations. They had been engaged in their culinary operations but a few minutes, when Nordine's quick ear detected a low, creaking noise.

"S-s-s-t! the captain," he said. And presently the captain appeared.

"Quick!" he exclaimed. "We shall have a visitor here in about ten minutes. Roll up some of those blankets for a dummy. Behave yourselves well before your company."

And with a little laugh Captain Denton again disappeared.

It did not take them long to fix up the dummy; they placed a hat over its face and laid it down with its feet toward the fire; then they went on with their breadmaking. It was two hours before Captain Ben came back again.

"Well, boys," he said, "it's all right. They feel pretty sure of us, and their scheme is to charge on our camp at daybreak. They were so busy spying us out that it never struck them I would follow their man back."

"How long did he stay here?" asked Colrick.

"Only about ten minutes. He was within twenty feet of your fire. Then he crept out to the edge of the grove and took a look at the horses; I would have knifed him if he had started to cut them loose, but that would have spoiled things. We should have had to go right down to their camp and settle up with the others."

"That would have been easy enough," said Nordine.

"Yes, if things had gone our way; but I can tell you they are a strapping lot of fellows—four picked braves, as far as I could see, and the head chief, whose feathers we saw."

About ten o'clock they brought the mustangs from the meadow where they were grazing, and soon all was ready to move out of the grove. They threw a few old logs and stumps on the fire, that the smoke might be seen in the morning, and thus induce the Indians to move slowly and cautiously. Then they took up their course northward across the mesa, now dimly lighted by a small moon and the bright stars of a clear sky. They traveled leisurely, the captain insisting that there was no need of haste. When they drew near to that part crossed by the arroyo, the leader dismounted and scouted carefully. Returning, he reported the arroyo dry, and quiet as a tomb, with an easy crossing ahead. In the same way two smaller arroyos were traversed, and an uneventful march of five miles brought them to the northerly extremity of the mesa.

Here the men were surprised to find a creek coming down from the bordering hills; but Captain Ben explained that it was the same which flowed past the camp at the grove, having traced its course with his glass from the cottonwood. His reasons for leaving camp without a supply of water now became apparent.

"Now we shall take water in more ways than one," he said.

The creek was only about three yards in width, and very shallow. After filling the canteens, they entered it and rode up along the bed for a few yards. Then, doubling on their tracks, they descended with the stream, and finally left it separately at points some fifty yards apart. On its shelving and sandy margin each dismounted and muffled the feet of his animal with pieces of blanket, tied on with strips torn from an empty barley sack. Then, walking backward till the bushy bank was reached, all tracks were obliterated with water sprinkled from the gold-pan. Mounting at the edge of the brush, and maintaining the distances between them, they struck out southward over the open mesa.

They did not take their buck track, but moved several points more to the westward. Down in their hearts the men felt that the captain's dodge would not win; with Apaches it was work thrown away. After about a mile of this open order, Captain Denton gave his signal for the men to close up. In the meantime one or two foot-mufflers had been lost, and Colrick asked the captain what should be done in the event of others coming off.

"Let them go," said the captain. "It is just what I want."

"What you want—after all the trouble of lashin' them on?" queried Nordine.

"Yes, of course. You don't suppose I had the least hope of fooling Indians with that trick, do you?"

"Then what was the good of all that business at the creek?" asked Colrick.

"It was to make them believe that we thought the trick a very cunning one. What I want to do is to give them the impression that they have to deal with a set of cowardly and clumsy greenhorns; that they have a good and easy thing."

After reaching and descending the big arroyo, they turned westward and began moving up its dry bed.

"Why, Cap," cried Nordine, "don'cher know that this 'ere gulch'll take us right square up to the big rocks whar we fust saw the devils?"

"That is just where I wish to go," said Captain Denton.

"Up we go, then," said Nordine; and, turning to Colrick, he added in a lower tone, "a thing with two heads is mighty little account, whether it's an expedition or a young bull-calf."

As they ascended the arroyo its sides became more and more rocky until, within three hundred yards of its head, it was a veritable cañon. Here they halted, and the captain rode alone to the summit. After a considerable interval, he returned on foot and moved his men about fifty yards higher up. He and Colrick then took from the pack-mule their last whole sack of flour,—a fifty pound one,—and, lifting it high over his head, the captain threw it upon the ground with such force as to burst it open.

"Now, come on," he said; "there is bait for our game."

The men gazed on the flour thus sacrificed with long faces and drooping under lips, but they uttered no word of remonstrance, although they could not imagine what their leader was about. At the head of the cañon they again dismounted, and, leading their horses, they followed Captain Ben along a kind of rough trail that wound eastward among the rocks of the north wall of the cañon, until they came to a small lateral ravine. This, after a turn or two, opened out upon a little flat on which were a number of small pine and juniper trees. The captain's horse was fastened to one of them, and alongside of him the men hitched their animals, and the "John-day-zin."

"Now," said Captain Ben, "if any of us has to retreat, we shall have our horses, here back of us. I have been up this ravine, and it leads to a big, flat-topped hill, from which there is a choice of a dozen pretty fair routes in as many directions. I hardly think we shall have to scamper out of the ravine in this way, but before going into a fight it is always best to mark out a good and safe line of retreat."

"This is fine, Cap," said Nordine. "Couldn't have been made better to order."

"It leaves our animals safe from flying bullets, which is allers a good thing in a bit of a scrimmage," added Colrick.

"Nothing like manoeuvering to get the choice of ground," said Captain Ben. "It's everything in a game with these fellows. Now let us take a look at our breastworks."

A fairly direct path was found to a point on the high and rocky wall of the cañon just opposite to the abandoned sack of flour, apparently dropped in the hurry and excitement of retreat. There, at a height of about seventy-five feet above the floor of the cañon, and not a hundred yards distant from the captain's "bait," was a sort of natural breastwork of rocks. They set to work to improve this by placing huge stones on the natural ledge, so as to form loopholes, taking care so to dispose of them that they would not attract attention.

III
THE FIGHT

These arrangements completed, they made a hearty breakfast upon the food prepared the previous night, and before any signs of daylight appeared. Captain Ben was on the alert with the first streaks of dawn. Ascending a high rock near at hand he began to sweep the whole mesa with his field-glass. It was not long before he signaled his men that the five Apaches had come out of the grove and were on their trail, riding northward across the mesa on a gallop. He saw them puzzle at the creek for a short time, two going up and two down the stream. As he expected, the two downstream signaled to the fifth, who had been left standing at the ford, and soon they were all examining the strange trail. Plainly it did not take them long to arrive at a conclusion, for they all moved off together on the trails left by the muffled animals. Presently one of them found a lost hoof muffler, and, after holding it aloft for a moment, tossed it high in the air in derision. Crouching low upon the rock, the captain watched the advancing Indians until they galloped down into the big arroyo. Then he clambered down and found his men stretched lazily upon their backs behind the impromptu breastworks.

"Get up, boys," he said, "and stretch the kinks out of your arms and legs; it's time for business. They are dashing in here like a pack of fools, and won't be satisfied until they get hurt."

Knowing the bad effects of a long suspense, the captain had purposely withheld the news until the moment for action was near. Nordine and Colrick took up their rifles and held themselves in readiness, Captain Ben placing himself at a loophole between the two. They had not long to wait. Shortly the five braves rounded a bend of the cañon and rode carelessly and slowly up its now steep bed; some of them were even talking and laughing. When they came in sight of the sack of flour they pulled up, craning their necks and pointing and jabbering. At last one of them ventured to ride ahead and investigate, and, on reaching the sack, he laughed heartily and shouted out to his companions, "Eccahn!" (flour). At this all hands took up the cry, and were soon bunched around the sack, talking rapidly, each speaker ending with a wave of the hand toward the head of the cañon; this was as much as to say that those who had thrown away their flour had fled over the mountains. Although the Indians presented fair marks, Captain Ben whispered to his men to hold back.

It soon became evident that the Apaches could not leave the flour behind. They took a blanket off one of the horses, and two of them began to roll the bursted sack in it, another throwing them a few feet of small rope.

"Now, Dick," said Captain Ben, "your man ties the rope; Burt, yours is beside him on the ground. Keep them covered, and when I fire, turn loose. My chance is when I get two of them in range."

A moment later Captain Ben fired, and the reports of the guns of his companions instantly followed. The captain's shot killed one Indian and dropped the horse of another. One of the dismounted Indians was also killed, and both loose horses turned and stampeded down the cañon. The three left alive were for a moment bewildered, and looked about in every direction but the right one to discover whence had come the shots.

"Now it is three against three," said Captain Ben. "Give them some more."

Again the three rifles cracked, and another pony fell.

The survivors now caught sight of the barricade, and immediately began to return fire briskly with their Winchesters. The Indian to whom a horse still remained dismounted, and all three sheltered themselves behind it.

"Colrick," cried the captain, "knock over that pony. Dick and I will pepper the fellows behind it if they show their heads."

Colrick accomplished this by a well-directed shot, and thus left the three Indians exposed. But almost in a twinkling they dragged two of the dead ponies, piled them across the body of the third, and were safely ensconced behind the breastworks thus formed, notwithstanding the bullets the captain and Nordine had sent whistling about them while they were at work.

The Apaches now being almost as well sheltered as the whites, the firing on both sides became more cautious and less rapid. It was very soon seen that under proper shelter the Indians were cool, keen-sighted, and very dangerous riflemen. They seemed able to see into the very port-holes of the stone breastworks: a proof of this was the fact that Colrick had soon lost a piece of an ear, and Captain Denton a bunch of hair with a little bit of scalp attached.

"This is all foolishness," said the captain. "This sort of duel just suits those fellows, but we can't afford to gratify them in it. We must put a stop to their fun before one of us gets hurt."

"How can we do it, Cap?" asked Colrick.

"Easily enough," answered Captain Ben; "and we may as well end the business at once. Nordine, slip out of this, circle round the head of the cañon and take shelter among the rocks on the south side, while Colrick and I keep up the fire in front. Make your first shot from the rear count, Nordine, for the crack of your rifle on that side of the cañon will bring the fight to a focus."

In a moment Nordine was worming his way among the rocks on his errand. The firing on neither side was rapid nor regular; it was more of a game of close watching for opportunities than of shooting. Captain Ben recognized this fact, and in a moment or two after Nordine had left the breastwork, he said:

"Colrick, I can keep up appearances and do all the firing here, so you may make your way among the rocks and get into the cañon below. When Nordine shoots, those left alive will make a break down the cañon. After your first shot drop your rifle and use your revolver. I will only use my Winchester once, and then dash down after those fellows with my six-shooter; so you'll not have all the fun to yourself."

"But, Cap, suppose the fellers run up the cañon when Nordine opens fire to the rear?" questioned Colrick.

"They'll not do it. They'll break down the cañon; there are two loose ponies down there, you know."

"You're right, Cap; here goes for it."

"Drop in at the first bend of the cañon, and keep out of sight," whispered Captain Ben as Colrick began creeping away behind the reefs of rock. Then the captain began to fire several shots in rapid succession in order to keep the Indians amused, after which he resumed his former cautious firing, in the expectation, each moment, of hearing the crack of Nordine's rifle.

Presently, the awaited report came, and the three Indians sprang up from behind the dead ponies, one to fall backward upon the ground almost instantly. Taken by surprise, the two remaining turned and cast their eyes up toward the rocky south wall of the cañon. They stood thus exposed for the winking of an eye, but that was sufficient for the captain. There was a puff of smoke from behind the rocky breastwork, and one of them pitched forward and fell with his face to the ground. The other at once bounded away down the cañon.

Captain Denton gave a shrill, peculiar yelp for a signal to Colrick, and, dropping his rifle, jumped to the rocks below and made his way to the bottom. He had run but a few yards when he heard Colrick's shot, and in another minute the Indian came dashing up the cañon with his right arm dangling. Seeing the captain running toward him, his revolver in readiness, the wounded brave took to the rocks. Unfortunately for himself, however, he chose the south wall of the cañon; he scaled the rocks with the agility of a mountain-sheep, making good use of his legs, though crippled in an arm, while both Colrick and the captain peppered him.

"Nordine!" shouted Captain Ben, in a voice to awaken the dead.

The answer was the crack of a rifle well up on the south wall and the fleeing Indian tumbled backward. The fight was over and not a single one of the Apache band remained alive.

IV
TO THE VICTORS BELONG THE SPOILS

Being now masters of the field, our prospectors had time for a critical examination of their fallen foes. They proved to be well-built and powerful men, only one above middle age. The oldest of the party appeared about fifty-five, and was, undoubtedly, a chief, as he wore a buckskin helmet beautifully beaded and surmounted with three eagle feathers. He had been killed at the first fire. Two others also wore buckskin helmets and were probably braves and "medicine-men," as the backs of their helmets were made of the tanned skins of the tails of horses, so sewed in that the long, black hair would quite cover the back and shoulders of the wearer. The chief's helmet, however, had a shorter fringe of this black hair at the back and sides, and was, apparently, the mane of a horse. All wore bracelets of buckskin hung with shells and small gold and silver coins. Their moccasins (inday-bekay), of buckskin handsomely ornamented, were the kind that, in the shape of leggings, reach to the knees, as a protection against cacti and thorns. The shirts of some were of the

same material, fringed and covered with beadwork, small shells, and por-
cupine quills dyed in several bright colors. Everything showed the party
to be men of note. Their clothing and blankets were new and clean. Inside
the shirt of one of those who wore horsetail helmets was found a beautiful "medicine-wand," about two feet long, decorated with colored feathers, shells, and the skins of lizards of brilliant hue. Two of the party also
wore necklaces of bears' claws, puma teeth, and shells.

While these articles of dress and ornament were being examined, Captain Ben suddenly exclaimed:

"I have just thought of a good dodge, boys. Here we have the means of
disguising ourselves as a party of high-up Apaches—a big chief and two
first-class 'medicine-men!' And I know how to work the scheme of our
being out on a 'secret medicine mission' to some distant branch of the
tribe. We are not yet out of the Indian country, and the beauty of a 'medicine mission' is that no Apache dare approach the party composing it
when he is waved back, and the sign of the mission and that of the
branch tribe to which it is going is given. Here we have the dresses, the
'medicine-stick,' and all else required, and at the sign language I am
equal to any Apache in the country. I have practised it among a dozen
different tribes."

"Just the racket!" cried Nordine.

"You take the chief's outfit, and we'll do the medicine fellows. What do you say, Burt?"

"Oh, I'm in for it. I've always had a sorter sneakin' notion for Injun finery, and here's a chance to come out in grand style."

"Well, pick out the best and finest shirts, moccasins, ornaments, and everything else. We'll take all their ammunition, and hide their Winchesters and other weapons," said the captain.

"What! Why, Cap!" cried Nordine, who was stripping a beautiful buckskin shirt off one of the bodies. "Why, by the Lord Harry! If this fellow hain't got a regular money-belt around his waist—see!"

"Take it off," said the captain.

In a second the belt was off and opened, when, to the astonishment of all, it was found to be stuffed with greenbacks—and nearly all one hundred dollar bills.

"Something worth fighting for!" cried Captain Ben.

"Here's another belt on this one!" exclaimed Colrick.

The other bodies were quickly examined, and on all were found either belts or Indian made pouches replete with bills of high denominations. Then Nordine went off to search the Apache he had shot up on the south wall, and soon came back with a fifth well-filled belt. "Well, this beats the devil!" cried the captain. "How do yer account for the Injuns being so loaded with money, Cap?" asked Nordine.

"Robbery and murder," replied the captain. "These fellows were the head men of a big war party on a grand raid. They've probably killed one or two cattle kings, a government paymaster, a big mining operator, and captured a mailcoach or two. These fellows whose accounts we've just settled constituted themselves treasurers of all the money captured on the raid. They were too sharp to let the common bucks fool away that which, if spent judiciously, would buy a vast deal of ammunition and other needed supplies. We've got to clear out of this whole section now as soon as possible, because their war party can't be very far away. They're probably camped not many miles west of this range. If the five braves do not return at the time appointed, the whole party will be over here, red hot."

"What d'ye s'pose brought the five big ones up this way, Cap?" inquired Nordine.

"Well, I think they were on the way to cache their money in some cavern or hole known to them in these cliffs. When we turned up they decided to take us in, and cache all their plunder at one time. It is likely they were to be absent only a night, and so it won't do to settle down here alongside their dead bodies. You fellows go up the ravine and bring down our stock, and be spry about it."

The men were soon back with the animals, and loaded the mule and all the horses with the spoils of war, not forgetting the sack of flour, which was found wrapped in a valuable Navajo blanket. The party then moved down the big arroyo on a brisk walk; it was impossible to go fast, cumbered as they were with the plunder. A hiding-place for the Winchesters and other weapons of the Indians was discovered after about half a mile, and, thus lightened, they were able to proceed at a trot. Presently Nordine ventured to ask:

"Where are we striking for now, Cap?"

"There are a good many reasons for going back to the creek. Not to the grove where our camp was, but to the little one where the Apaches put up—their last on this side of the 'happy hunting-grounds.' We'll find the two loose Indian ponies down there, and we want them now. What we ought to do is to start north at once; in stopping another night on the creek I am letting love of ease take the place of good judgment, but we'll risk it to-night, though we rue it to-morrow."

"We'll go on your judgment, Cap," said Nordine.

"Not my judgment, but my laziness."

"Well," said Colrick, "we'll trust you, Cap, in any shape. Perhaps we ain't worth much at headwork, but when it comes to fighting—that's different."

Captain Denton went to the small grove for better reasons than he gave. He left the larger and more attractive camping place to be occupied by any band of Indians that might happen along toward evening, taking for his camp a patch of brushwood hardly noticeable, and so situated as to be hidden from view, except to one in [the] top of the largest tree in the upper grove.

The two escaped horses proved to be Mexican mustangs, and equal in size and beauty to their own mounts. Evidently, they had been stolen from whites, because, after the other animals were picketed, they came up and allowed themselves to be handled.

A hasty meal was then despatched, and the captain settled down to the task of counting the contents of the five belts. His manner, as he proceeded, first betokened surprise, and then wonder. Finally, he asked the men to guess at the amount. Colrick thought it might be three thousand dollars, and Nordine four thousand five hundred. The captain, in reply, began taking up the belts.

"This," he said, "contains six thousand five hundred dollars; this, nine thousand dollars; this, five thousand dollars; this, four thousand dollars. That makes twenty-nine thousand dollars, boys, doesn't it?"

This seemed to them something fabulous. The captain handed them his notebook, and they went over his figures again and again before they were convinced, and even then they feared he had made a mistake in counting the bills.

"If I had known this before," said the captain, "I would not have come back here; I would have pushed north all night long. So much money makes a man cowardly. I have a presentiment that we are going to have trouble—we have had just a little too much good luck. Now, for fear of accidents, I shall divide this money into three equal lots."

The men wanted to take five thousand dollars each, but Captain Ben would not hear of it, and each received equal portions, one-third of the whole. This matter settled, the other work to be done proceeded rapidly. They were all soon clean-shaven, and, having made a decoction of two or three kinds of bark, they stained their hands and faces a good and durable Apache color. When they had donned their Indian dress, they would have passed in any frontier town as genuine braves. Captain Ben made a noble-looking chief in his eagle-plumed helmet and beaded and fringed skirt, and Colrick was prouder than any Apache dandy in the Sierra Madre. He was now given instructions by the captain upon several points of his new rôle of chief medicine-man.

The clothing they had discarded was made into convenient bundles, and everything put in preparation for an early start in the morning. As the saddles found on the mustangs were of Mexican make, and new, it was decided to retain them, as bundles of clothing and other light articles could be easily packed on top of them, and firmly bound in place by lashing blankets over all. All the necessary work was finished before sunset. The captain closely examined the large grove, and, finding it unoccupied, seemed again at ease in mind; nevertheless, he led his men away in the dark to an insignificant patch of willows standing alone a hundred yards down the creek, where all quietly rolled themselves in their blankets and were soon sound asleep.

V

IN THE HANDS OF MEXICAN SOLDIERS

With the first gray streaks of dawn of the coming day Captain Denton and his companions were astir. After making a hearty breakfast, they packed the mules and the newly acquired mustangs, mounted their horses and set out, just as the sun was peeping over the top of the eastern range. They moved directly up the creek, past the upper grove, and thence struck northward across the mesa toward the ford from which they had turned back two nights before. It was a bright and beautiful morning, and they moved gaily forward, discussing their luck in the capture of so great a sum of money—an amount that would give to each a small fortune.

"But," said Captain Ben, "when we reach the settlement we must make some inquiry to find out the names of those from whom it was taken."

"I s'pose that would be the right thing to do," said Nordine. "Still, after sich a big fight as we've had, it'll be kinder hard to give it up."

"I reckon we'll be allowed decent wages for recoverin' a stack of that size, if them as proves property don't happen to be a set of miserable skinflints," remarked Colrick.

"In regard to that," said Captain Ben, "we must again trust to luck; besides, we are not yet out of the Indian country, and there is many a slip between cup and lip in the Sierra Madre."

The captain turned on his saddle and glanced back toward his companions, who were following in Indian file, and as he sat thus they could see his expression suddenly change.

"By Jove, look yonder!" and he pointed back toward the low ridge on the south border of the mesa, and at that identical ridge on the crest of which they had stood a few days before, watching the ravens.

"Them fellers looks like soldiers of some kind," said Colrick. "They ain't no Injuns, that's sure."

"No, but about as bad," said the captain, who had his field-glass upon the party. "They're a squad of infernal greaser soldiers!"

"They've spotted us, and are a-comin' for us like mad," cried Nordine. "They take us for Injuns."

"Sure enough," exlaimed the captain, "I had almost forgotten our disguise. In this case it is a bad one for us. We'll have to let them know we are Americans, or they will soon be firing at us. Nothing could possibly be worse for us than this rig—it will place us in their power almost completely, and give them a chance to accuse us of being out on a robbing expedition. They have us in a bad box, that's sure."

"Twelve of 'em," said Nordine, ruefully.

"A hundred would be no worse," said the captain. "We must mail them a letter, and then fall back out of range to await developments."

"Mail them a letter!" exclaimed Colrick, in surprise.

In reply, Captain Ben tore a blank leaf from his note-book and wrote: "Nos tres buenos Americanos. Todo mascarada identico Indiano."

This note was pinned to a white handkerchief, and, riding to a bunch of yuccas, Captain Ben fastened it to a branch that extended out like an arm. Then, waving his feathered helmet to the advancing troop of Mexicans, he rejoined his companions, and they all rode on some distance, where they halted and faced about.

"Now," said the captain, "remember that not a man of us understands more than a few very common Spanish words. The note is written in

such mongrel jumble that they will never guess I understand their language. Literally it reads: 'We three good Americans, all masquerade same Indians.'"

"They're goin' for the letter," said Nordine.

"I hope there's a man among them with a sense enough to know what it means," Captain Ben replied.

The troopers appeared to puzzle over the note for a time, and then advanced a few yards. They placed the handkerchief on a musket and held it aloft as a flag of truce. Captain Denton and his companions instantly and fearlessly went forward. The captain shook hands with the lieutenant in charge, crying heartily over and over again, "Buenos días, señor!" slapping himself on the chest, and saying impressively, "Un Amigo."

It seemed, indeed, quite superfluous to ask the captain if he spoke Spanish, but out of politeness the lieutenant did ask, "Habla Español, señor?"

"Un poco bueno no mas sabe," said the captain, smiling serenely.

"De donde viene usted?" inquired the lieutenant.

"Como, señor?" said Captain Ben, looking puzzled, "Que es esto?"

"Clearly he understands nothing," said the lieutenant to a man near him. "We must have an interpreter. Manuel Otero!"

A soldier stepped forward; he spoke English fairly well, and Captain

Ben was asked to give an account of himself and his companions. With the exception of the greenbacks, he told the truth, and explained fully their object in disguising themselves.

The lieutenant was very polite, and lauded their courage in attacking and killing so strong a party of Apache braves. Then he asked the captain to guide him to the spot where the Indians had been killed. The captain replied that he could direct them so that they could not miss the bodies. But the Mexican pointed out that to find a party thus masquerading was a somewhat suspicious circumstance; that it seemed almost incredible that three men should be able to overcome five leading Apache braves, and, therefore, they must excuse him for asking them to go with him.

"You will understand," said he, "that I am obliged to trouble you, because you are strangers to me. I do not doubt your ability to substantiate your story, but I have to perform my duty faithfully toward my government, and, therefore, must make no mistakes. Besides, it will be only a little out of your direct route."

Seeing there was no help for it, Captain Ben said to the interpreter:

"Tell him I will guide him to where the bodies lie, with the greatest of pleasure."

On hearing this, the lieutenant smiled pleasantly, and, turning to one near him, said in Spanish, and in a low tone:

"They really have killed the Indians. Would that we knew whether they had found any of the American money."

The man said, in reply:

"We were on the track; if the money cannot be found on the bodies, then these men have it. Why not ask them at once if they have the money? Manuel can explain how it was lost."

"It would be of little use," replied the lieutenant, "they would deny it. However, Manuel may tell them why we are out in pursuit of the Indians, and meantime we can watch their faces."

Not a word of this was lost to Captain Ben, who was seemingly absorbed in telling Manuel the particulars of the fight of the previous day.

In giving his instructions to Manuel, the lieutenant cautioned him to be careful to use the word "traders" instead of "smugglers." The latter then turned to the captain and said:

"We are searching for a war party of Apaches who have murdered and robbed several traders, on Mexican soil, who were returning from a trip over the border. Besides much valuable property, over thirty thousand dollars of United States money was taken from them."

"Money!" cried Captain Ben. "Who would think of the Apaches having money?"

"I told you they would deny finding it," said the officer to the man to whom he had been talking.

Still, the readiness of Captain Ben to show them the bodies puzzled the lieutenant. He once more became very polite, and assured the captain repeatedly that he need not fear being placed under any restraint, and thanked him again for his kindness in consenting to guide them to the scene of the fight. To each of these protestations the captain answered:

"Gracias, gracias, señor comandante!"

The united parties were soon on their way across the mesa. They moved in no order. Manuel Otero, the interpreter, rode with Captain Ben, and just in front of them the Mexican lieutenant and one or two of his chums; Nordine and Colrick brought up the rear, the latter leading the pack-animals, which he had tied together in a string. The captain, while he was drawing from the interpreter the details of the robbery, kept his ears open to catch the conversation of the lieutenant and his two companions. It appeared from what the interpreter said that a party of ten traders had been murdered; but he dwelt particularly on the theft of the money. When the captain bluntly said that such a rich and successful body of traders must have been smugglers, the soldier smiled knowingly and remarked:

"Our pay is very little from the government, and we should fare but badly if we did not pick up something from friends along the border. If we could recover this American money it would be so much clear gain to us."

This information, and much more that was similar, was not without its significance to the captain, and would have brought the interpreter a slap from the sword of his lieutenant, had that officer known of his indiscretion. In the meantime, the plottings of the officer and his two companions had not escaped the captain. These worthies had decided between them to put him and his two men out of the way, if no money were found upon the dead Apaches.

"They are in Indian dress, and will count as Indians," they said.

The plan was to accuse them of being concerned in the robbery, disguised as Indians, and to tell them that they must submit to be taken back to Mexico as prisoners for trial; then to shoot them down as soon as they were bound, and to leave their bodies with those of the Apaches. All this was so coolly designed that Captain Denton could hardly believe his ears as he looked upon the smiling faces that were turned back to him from time to time.

When the arroyo was reached the captain told Manuel Otero to ask the lieutenant to halt for a moment. He told the officer, through the interpreter, that he had reason to believe that there were still other Apaches in the neighborhood, and that therefore it would be well to proceed cautiously up the arroyo, and to put the greater number of his men ahead of the pack-animals. The lieutenant smilingly assented, but at the same

time his face wore a perplexed look, as though he were trying to fathom any trick that might be in the captain's mind. However, upon entering the arroyo, he took the lead with eight of his men, and Manuel and another soldier were left to ride beside the captain and Nordine. The soldier in charge of the pack-animals of the detachment remained in the rear with Colrick. Although he pretended to comply with Captain Denton's advice, it was evident that the lieutenant intended to keep the three Americans pretty well under guard. He genially asked the captain if the order of march was satisfactory to him; to this Captain Denton replied:
"Perfectly so."

While the men were being shifted to their places, the captain found an opportunity to whisper to Nordine: "When I shoot the man next me and give the Apache war-whoop, follow suit with your man, and then go for the rocks and make for the ravine where we had our horses concealed."

Nordine replied by a slight nod. In a few minutes the captain told Manuel that, as he was thirsty, he would go back to the pack-animals for a canteen of water. The unsuspecting soldier said that he, too, was thirsty. Thus, in getting the canteen, the captain was enabled to give Colrick the same order he had passed to Nordine.

Then Captain Denton assumed a careless air and began to joke with Manuel concerning the profit in watching smugglers, and said he had a notion to join the army and go into the business on the American side. The soldier thought him more than half in earnest and assured him that no little money would fall into his hands.

VI
AN AMBUSCADE—THE MEXICANS IN
A HORNET'S NEST

Nordine and Colrick, though ignorant of the treacherous plot of the Mexicans, were far from being at ease. They had more fear of the loss of the wealth they carried than of their lives, and both determined to obey the captain's orders to the letter. And when the captain, with a meaning look, carelessly drew his finger across his throat, they needed no more to assure them of the fate in store for them, and as they passed from the arroyo of the mesa to the cañon of the mountains and drew near to the scene of their battle with the Apaches, each managed to loosen his revolver in its scabbard.

Presently they rounded a bend in the cañon. Captain Ben saw that the lieutenant and his men were nearing the spot where the dead Indians and ponies lay; glancing at Nordine and Colrick, he noted that they were both close to their men. Then he turned to Manuel, whose attention he called to an object on a high rock on the north side of the cañon, and asked him if it were not the head of an "Indiano." Manuel looked, as also did Nordine's guard, when he heard the word "Indiano." An instant later, while both were still gazing up at the rock, two revolvers cracked almost simultaneously, and Manuel and his Mexican comrade fell to the ground with bullets through their hearts. At the same moment Colrick fired upon his man, breaking his right arm, but not bringing him down. All three raised the Apache war-cry, and, to their astonishment, it was echoed by more than a score of wild voices up the cañon, accompanied by the sharp crack of as many rifles. The yells of the Mexican soldiers could also be heard mingling with the reports of their muskets.

As the Mexican wounded by Colrick was trying to pass the captain and Nordine, they brought him down with their revolvers, and then, with the Apache war-cry, stampeded his horse and pack-animals up the cañon, to add to the confusion of the soldiers, into whose midst the riderless horses had already charged.

"Keep up the yell!" cried Captain Denton. "It will encourage the Apaches, and prevent the Mexicans from falling back on us."

The firing up the cañon was almost incessant, and, with the yells of the combatants the place was a very pandemonium. Wafted by a gentle western breeze, the smoke of the battle filled and almost darkened the cañon.

"Now is our time, boys, to slip away and get out of this patch of country!" shouted Captain Denton. "Cut loose down the cañon, Colrick, but don't go faster than a trot, and hang on to the pack-animals. There is not such hurry that we need leave them behind."

In a moment, all had rounded the bend and were out of sight, even though a puff of wind had cleared the cañon of smoke.

When our party reached the level of the mesa, they left the arroyo.

"We must keep close in against the mountains," said Captain Ben, "because the Apaches have a lookout up there somewhere on the rock, and they are sweeping every part of the mesa. They never set a trap to fall into it themselves; besides, they very naturally fear that the squad of Mexicans they are fighting are merely scouts sent out by a larger force that is after them. If we keep close in along the base of the range, we shall get away without being seen by their lookouts."

"Was that a lookout you pointed out to Manuel, Cap?" asked Nordine.

"No, it was nothing but a bit of rock. Poor Manuel! Poor devil! It was like murder to place my pistol against his side and blow his simple heart out. But all the chances were against us then, and it had to be done. If the Apaches had only opened fire an instant sooner, I might have seen my way to letting him live."

"Mighty little good it would have done the feller; he would have been dropped the next minute by the Injuns. I don't feel sorry about my rascal. He wore a murderous mug," said Nordine.

"Hark!" cried Colrick, who had fallen to the rear with his string of animals on getting out of the arroyo. "Hark, they are still banging up there on the mountain."

"Yes, but the firing is less rapid now," said the captain. "They are beginning to get down to business. The Mexicans have enough horses and packs to build a good fort, but the Apaches will wipe them out—they have the advantage of the rocks on both sides of the cañon."

"I'll bet thar's a lot of 'em behind our old breastworks," said Nordine.

"Those Apaches were coming for us, too," said the captain, "and they would have got us if the Mexicans had not happened along. When they saw us leave the mesa and enter the arroyo they prepared their ambuscade."

"Wonder what they thought when they seed us three Indians with the greasers?" queried Nordine.

"They knew the caps and clothing we have on, and thought we were Mexicans who had been concerned in killing their friends, but after hearing us utter the Apache war-cry, and seeing us slaughter the greasers, they undoubtedly believe that we were the ghosts of their braves helping them, and no one will ever be able to make them think differently."

"See what a cloud of smoke there is up there," cried Colrick. "They are still bangin' away."

"Two hours hence," said the captain, "not a Mexican will be left alive."

"Good riddance!" replied Nordine, heartily.

The captain then told his companions of the plot laid by the Mexicans. He pointed out that they were at liberty to keep the money that they had captured, since it had been taken from unknown Mexican smugglers killed by the Apaches. At this the delight of Nordine and Colrick knew no bounds; never before in his life had either possessed, at one time, the fifth part of such a sum as he now had belted on his body.

They were drawing near, for the third time, to the ford at the northern extremity of the mesa. The captain was still far from at ease, however, while Nordine and Colrick were guessing as to how they were finally to get out of this country, when they perceived, rising at full gallop over the edge of a sand hillock, the blue coats and broad hats of a detachment of United States cavalry.

Very little remains to be told. How the same manoeuvers were gone through as with the Mexicans, and how, on drawing near, Captain Ben recognized in the captain of the troop an old friend of his scouting days. How they revisited the cañon, where nothing was left to tell the tale of the battle but dead bodies. Under the escort of the cavalry they finally crossed the creek.

Once on the other side, they fell upon a well-worn trail and pushed northward as rapidly as possible. At their first night's camping they changed their Indian dress for their old clothes, and, in a few days, without further mishap of any kind, they arrived safe and sound in Lordsburgh, on the Southern Pacific railroad.

Not before two or three days were Nordine and Colrick able to realize that they were secure in the possession of the money. They were thereby cured of all desire for further adventure in the wilds. It was Captain Ben Denton's opinion that they had earned a right to peace and quiet for the remainder of their days, and as soon as they had disposed of their "spoils of war," they pushed on to California. Once there, Captain Ben purchased two fine adjoining ranches, one for each.

As for the captain, he deposited his money in a San Francisco bank, and after a few weeks of rest, struck out for Montana, and once more roamed and prospected over his old scouting trails and battle-grounds. He was in the thick of the "Indian trouble" at Pine Ridge and Wounded Knee, and did good service as a scout and bearer of despatches. But among the Indians there he was more at home than he could claim to be with those of the Sierra Madre.

Cosmopolitan, June 19, 1895

EDITOR'S NOTES

"A Silver Man" was republished with textual modifications by C. Grant Loomis in "The Tall Tales of Dan De Quille," pp. 37–41.

De Quille may have partly tipped his hand in *The Big Bonanza* passage where he described the stones as being of an "irony nature." The first two parts of "The Traveling Stones of Pahranagat" were republished with textual modifications by Loomis in "Tall Tales," pp. 31–33. The same credulous reaction that he received to the first two parts from readers as far away as Europe was evoked by the third part as well. In his *Tribune* column of July 31, 1892, De Quille reported that the *London Tit-Bits* had quoted his March 6 article about the traveling stones of Nevada and then proceeded to give an account of stones in the Falkland Islands that also seemed to have locomotive powers. De Quille thus recorded another success of his hoax and at the same time set his trap for more unwary readers.

"Solar Armor" was republished with textual modifications by Loomis in "Tall Tales," pp. 33–37.

"The Troubles of John Smith" was later revised by De Quille and republished in the *Carson Free Lance* of February 8, 1886.

De Quille republished a slightly modified version of "The Boss Snorer" under the new title "A Pair of Snorers" in the *New York Times*. No date appears on the clipping in the William Wright Papers file of the Bancroft Library, but it almost certainly was published in the late 1880s or early 1890s.

"Tom Collette's Bath" was earlier published in a less polished form in the December 2, 1877, issue of the *Territorial Enterprise*.

"The Typical Prospector" was found as an undated clipping in the Bancroft Library's William Wright Papers file.

An earlier and shorter version of "The Old California Prospector," entitled "The 'Old Prospector,'" appeared in the *Salt Lake City Daily Tribune* on December 27, 1885. The old California prospector's prejudice against Chinese reflects a general feeling throughout the West. Western fear and resentment of "cheap Chinese labor" were instrumental in the passage by Congress in 1882 of the Chinese Exclusion Act, America's first restrictive immigration bill. De Quille here seems to record this prejudice objectively. He was personally much more sympathetic to the Chinese until the 1890s, when he turned against them.

The prospector's old friend, named Dandy, must have been an inside joke on De Quille's name. He was usually called Dan, but some friends called him Dandy Quille.

De Quille's account of Fair in "A Superintendent Who Was Fatherly and 'Smooth'" is supported by Oscar Lewis, who tells the same anecdote in *Silver Kings*, pp. 160–161. Lewis further describes Fair as being both tight-fisted and crafty and as having consequently earned the nickname of Slippery Jim.

The trip reported in "The Wealth of Washoe" was written up in a very different way in the *Cedar Falls Gazette* of May 17, 1861. The essentials of the trip through the mine were retained in the revision but many different human interest details were introduced. One of the most interesting and important is De Quille's sharp disagreement with J. Ross Browne's account of the Washoe district in the latter's "Peep at Washoe" series running in *Harper's* magazine. De Quille's two versions of the same incident are instructive for the light they shed on the ways he could retell the same experience for different audiences. His habit of recycling his work obviously got off to a very early start. "The Wealth of Washoe" was reprinted in 1981 by Dave Basso in *Silver Walled Palace*.

"Old Johnny Ranchero" was revised and enlarged by De Quille in the *San Francisco Post* of September 4, 1886. There it was entitled "The Under World" and its main character was named Bullock.

"The Wolf and the Wild Hogs" was republished by Lawrence I. Berkove in "Dan De Quille's Narratives of Ohio: Four Sketches," in the *Northwest Ohio Quarterly* (Winter 1989).

"Trailing a Lost Child" exists in at least two versions: the original appearance in the June 17, 1892, issue of the *Salt Lake City Daily Tribune*, and the revised version printed here that was found in an undated clipping in the Bancroft Library's William Wright Papers file. The revised version is generally better written, with the following exception, some useful information that occurred in the second paragraph of the *Tribune* account and that was dropped from the revision:

> When a child is lost in a wild region, search must be instituted at once. The distance to which even the smallest toddler will often wander is astonishing. Very often, too, children will become wild after being lost for a few hours and instead of showing themselves or answering when they hear voices calling will crawl into a thicket or some other hiding place and be as close and quiet as would a hunted animal. In the early days in Ohio a sixteen-year-old boy who had been lost in the woods for a day and a night suddenly made his appearance in front of his father's house, leaped a pair of bars and ran on like a wild animal. When pursued and caught by a man on horseback he for a

time fought with teeth and nails like a young wolf. He had been frightened out of his wits, temporarily, by the blowing of horns and the firing of guns, for in the early days when a child was lost in the vast primitive forests of the West a great racket was kept up during the night search in order to frighten away wolves and other dangerous animals.

For a fuller account of the historical and biographical background of "Trailing a Lost Child," see Lawrence I. Berkove's edition of the incident in *Palimpsest* (Fall 1988).

There is no mention in Storey County, Nevada, records of a Jasper Perry ever having lived there or having died in 1885. An unidentified clipping of an apparently earlier version of "A Dietetic Don Quixote" strongly suggests that it is fictitious.

"Tongue-Oil Timothy Dead" is the last revision of a popular story originally known as "Butter-mouth Bill" which first appeared in the November 8, 1874, issue of the *Territorial Enterprise*. The main parts of both versions are essentially identical except for the names, but "Tongue-Oil Timothy Dead" has a different beginning and ending. The story's various references to a Bengal tiger, the "beast of the jungle," etc., all allude to "bucking the tiger"—i.e., gambling.

De Quille was fond of using German words and references in his writing. In "A Female World-Ranger," *Welt-bereiser* may be translated as "world visitor" and *Welt-gänger* as "world traveler." The meanings are almost identical, but *Welt-gänger* might be slightly deeper. *Weltbürgerlich* means "cosmopolitan": acting in a manner befitting a citizen of the world. *Unter dem Pantoffel kommen* is an idiom meaning "to come under the [a woman's] slipper," i.e., to be bossed around by a woman. All these terms are used ironically.

Earlier and less well developed versions of "Rev. Olympus Jump" were published in the August 26, 1877, issue of the *Territorial Enterprise* and the September 8, 1877, issue of the *Argonaut*.

For a fuller account of the historical and biographical background of "Lorenzo Dow's Miracle," see Lawrence I. Berkove's edition of it in the *Northwest Ohio Quarterly* (Spring 1988).

De Quille anticipated "Death Valley" with extended descriptive comments on the region in his January 29, 1888, "Random Quille Drops" column in the *Salt Lake City Daily Tribune*. He returned to the subject at length in an August 30, 1891, *Tribune* column entitled "The Valley of Death" in which he repeated much of the information found in "Death Valley" with fewer dramatic touches. Some idea of how quickly and widely feature stories could spread through exchanges—and an author's reputation with them—may be inferred from the case of "Death Valley." On February 11, 1888, only thirteen days after it was first published in the *San Francisco Examiner*, it was reprinted in the *New York Daily Graphic* and credited to "Dan De Quille in *Chicago Herald*"! The text was unchanged but it had a modified headline: "The Valley of Death/A Desolate Region Called Thirstland Where Men Become Mummified."

An earlier and shorter version of "A Goblin Frog" appeared in the January 30, 1876, issue of the *Territorial Enterprise*.

The full text of De Quille's August 5, 1870, remarks on Twain's story was republished by C. Grant Loomis in "Dan De Quille's Mark Twain," pp. 343–344. Loomis does not link it to "Elam Storm"; he might not have been familiar with the story. He considers De Quille's remarks to have been meant as a jest or as an expression of longing for the absent Mark Twain. Some notes by De Quille indicate that the story was republished by the Lorborn Company of Baltimore before April 22, 1887.

"The Fighting Horse of the Stanislaus" may have been published again under the name of "Old Pizen" in the *New York Despatch* of July or August 1874. In an August 1874 letter to his sister, De Quille mentions seeing it there "the other day" with others of his stories and sketches. In an unpublished manuscript in the Bancroft, De Quille later softened the story's stark impact by adding a new conclusion in which Joggles is tamed by his wife's show of spirit.

Among the many mispronunciations of Mrs. Smiley in "Marier's Room" are "Bernicia" for Benicia (California) and Mount "Davinson" for Mount Davidson, which overlooks Virginia City.

An earlier and shorter version of "Bendix Biargo and His Three Sisters" appeared as "Bob Kemble's Sisters" in the *Nevada Monthly* 1: 4 (June 1880): 214–219. Although the main character's name in this version is "Bendix Biargo," the *Sacramento Bee*'s title reads "Bendix *Briaro* and His Three Sisters" (emphasis added). The title has been corrected for this anthology. Deleted from the original subheads for this story is one announcing "Written for the Christmas Bee by Dan De Quille." Despite that claim, De Quille reported in a letter to his sister Lou Benjamin on August 31, 1885, that he had just written a story for the *New York Weekly*. "It is entitled 'Bendix Biargo' and is in five chapters. The N. Y. Weekly is a story paper. Generally you are obliged to read about six months in it to get to a single marriage; now in my story I have a marriage in every chapter, which I think is a big improvement upon the stories that most of the young ladies are writing."

A possible point of contact with De Quille's own life might have been the occasions when his daughters came to live with him for periods of time and his Virginia City friends expressed an interest in meeting them.

Another point of contact is the story's reference to Mt. Vernon, Ohio, as the home of Bendix's spinster sister, Martha. De Quille was born in Knox County, Ohio, just a few miles from Mt. Vernon. The reference to the Fall Creek miners being dressed in "purple and fine linen" is ironic. It is an allusion to Proverbs 31:22, which describes the clothing of "a woman of valor." Another ironic allusion applies to Mrs. Clancey, who publishes the description of Bendix's sister to "Gath" and "Askelon." In 2 Samuel 1:20, when David learns of the deaths of Saul and Jonathan, he adjures his fellow Israelites "Tell it not in Gath; publish it not in the streets of Askelon" because Gath and Askelon were enemy strongholds.

Although a Bendix Beargo is listed as a "miner Ophir claim" in the 1862 and 1863 directories of Virginia City, no further mention of him has been found.

The numerous references in "The Seven Nimrods of the Sierras" to the Bible, mythology, and legend reflect De Quille's impressive knowledge of ancient sources. See his *Dives and Lazarus* for the best indication of how much he knew about them.

The original title of the story is "The Eagle's Nest." Because the story describes a nest of eagles, the apostrophe has been changed in this anthology to the plural possessive position. Duncan Emrich reprinted this story in his *Comstock Bonanza* (1950).

Cosmopolitan magazine paid De Quille $100 for "An Indian Story of the Sierra Madre." Frederic Remington was the illustrator.

RESEARCH REVIEW AND
SELECTED BIBLIOGRAPHY

Until very recently, most of the scholarship on De Quille has been indirect; he was mentioned as a minor actor in a work on somebody else or on the Comstock, and the same few facts and clichés were rearranged and built on. There is at present no full biography of him despite the eminence he enjoyed on the Comstock for being its daily chronicler, its historian, and one of its major authors. The most complete biographical studies of him are to be found in Oscar Lewis's specialized introduction to his edition of *The Big Bonanza* (1947) and in my introduction to *Dives and Lazarus* (1988). My introduction to the present volume reflects new information and insights about De Quille's literary career that have emerged in the last two years, modifies some statements I made in the earlier book, and adds details to a few generalizations. These biographical ventures can only be an interim solution to the need for a good De Quille biography. But before that can be written, first more of his works must be edited and published, and then more scholarly studies of his life and works will be needed. Both of these activities (as evidenced by this anthology) are underway. De Quille is clearly a more significant figure than anyone realized even five years ago.

The main sources of new information on De Quille will probably be the several collections of De Quille material available in libraries and the microfilm files of the periodicals in which he published. The two largest archives of De Quilleana are the Bancroft Library of the University of California–Berkeley and the State Historical Society of Iowa at Iowa City.

The Bancroft holdings are mostly in the William Wright Papers file. It contains the boxes of clippings of his own work, manuscripts, letters, scrapbooks, notebooks, and miscellanea that De Quille himself collected over the years and brought to his daughter's house in West Liberty, Iowa, when he retired there. This, therefore, is very important material but much of it is not in good condition; many of the clippings are yellow and brittle and they often are not filed in any logical order.

Additional De Quille information can be located in the Bancroft's C. Grant Loomis file. Loomis, one of the earliest serious De Quille scholars, painstakingly read through back issues of the *Territorial Enterprise* and *Golden Era* and made valuable notes about the contents of those periodicals, especially De Quille's contributions to them.

The Mark Twain Project office also has much important De Quille material. Some of it is a by-product of Twain research, and some of it consists of copies of material shared with the Mark Twain Project by the State Historical Society of Iowa.

The Morris Family Collection of Dan De Quille that is located at the State Historical Society of Iowa is a recent donation by three surviving great-grandchildren of De Quille. It consists of archival paper photo-duplicates of many letters, several scrapbooks, samples of clippings De Quille collected on topics that interested him, and some negatives of photographs.

The Nevada Historical Society at Reno has few De Quille documents but a good deal of information that bears on him. It has analyzed and organized its holdings, including rare and scarce publications, with the result that it is a valuable place in which to conduct De Quille research.

The California Historical Society at San Francisco has some interesting holdings, but most of its manuscript De Quille material has been published in James J. Rawls's edition of *Dan De Quille of the Big Bonanza* (1980).

Many of the periodicals in which De Quille published are mentioned in the introduction. He undoubtedly wrote for other newspapers and journals in the Nevada-California area, and for other periodicals elsewhere in the United States. If contributions to these periodicals can be determined and dated, then microfilm files will have to be examined. The Library of Congress has extensive holdings of back issues of periodicals and will circulate them—several reels at a time. The University of California–Berkeley, the University of Nevada–Reno, the California State Library at Sacramento, and the Nevada Historical Society at Reno all have important holdings of back issues or microfilms of western periodicals.

PRIMARY SOURCES

De Quille, Dan. "Artemus Ward in Nevada." *Californian* 4: 3 (August 1893): 403–406.

———. *The Big Bonanza.* 1876. Ed. Oscar Lewis. New York: Crowell, 1947.

———. "The Gnomes of the Dead Rivers." Ed. Lawrence I. Berkove. *Dan De Quille Journal* 2 (forthcoming).

———. "A Christmas Story: Under the Ice." Ed. Lawrence I. Berkove. *Palimpsest* 69: 4 (Winter 1988): 186–190.

———. *Dan De Quille of the Big Bonanza.* Ed. James J. Rawls. San Francisco: Book Club of California, 1980.

———. "Dan De Quille's Narratives of Ohio: Four Sketches." Ed.

Lawrence I. Berkove. *Northwest Ohio Quarterly* 61: 1 (Winter 1989): 3–12.

——. *Dives and Lazarus*. Ed. Lawrence I. Berkove. Ann Arbor: Ardis, 1988.

——. *A History of the Comstock Silver Lode & Mines*. Virginia [City, Nev.]: F. Boegle, 1889.

——. "Jim Gillis: The Thoreau of the Sierras." Ed. Lawrence I. Berkove. *Mark Twain Circular* 2: 3–4 (March–April 1988): 1–2.

——. "Little Lucy's Papa." Ed. Dave Basso. Sparks, Nev.: Falcon Hill, 1987.

——. "Lorenzo Dow's Miracle." Ed. Lawrence I. Berkove. *Northwest Ohio Quarterly* 60: 2 (Spring 1988): 47–56.

——. "Pahnenit, Prince of the Land of Lakes." Ed. Lawrence I. Berkove. *Nevada Historical Society Quarterly* 31: 2 (Summer 1988): 79–118.

——. "'The Red Wing.'" *Dan De Quille Journal* 1 (April 1989): 17–32.

——. "Reporting with Mark Twain." *California Illustrated* (July 1893): 170–178.

——. "Salad Days of Mark Twain." *The Life and Times of the Virginia City Territorial Enterprise*. Ed. Oscar Lewis. Pp. 37–53. Ashland, Ore.: Lewis Osborne, 1971. Reprint. Ed. Lawrence I. Berkove. *Quarterly News-Letter* 46: 2 (Spring 1981): 31–47.

——. *Silver Walled Palace*. Ed. Dave Basso. Sparks, Nev.: Falcon Hill, 1981.

——. "The Story of the *Enterprise*." *The Life and Times of the Virginia City Territorial Enterprise*. Ed. Oscar Lewis. Pp. 5–10. Ashland, Ore.: Lewis Osborne, 1971.

——. "Trailing a Lost Child." Ed. Lawrence I. Berkove. *Palimpsest* 69: 3 (Fall 1988): 120–131.

——. "Two Studies in Washoe Political Satire" ["State Mineralogist" and "The Feller What Ain't Runnin' For No Office"]. *Dan De Quille Journal* 1 (April 1989): 7–16.

——. *Washoe Rambles*. Ed. Richard E. Lingenfelter. Los Angeles: Westernlore, 1963.

——. "The Wonderful 'Liver Spring' of the High Sierras." Reprint. "A Search for Solitude." *Comstock Quarterly* 1: 1 (Spring 1989): 9–12.

SECONDARY SOURCES: BOOKS

Angel, Myron. *History of Nevada*. Oakland, Calif.: Thompson and West, 1881.

Blair, Walter. *Mark Twain & Huck Finn*. Berkeley: University of California Press, 1962.

Branch, Edgar M. *The Literary Apprenticeship of Mark Twain*. New York: Russell and Russell, 1966.

Cummins, Ella Sterling. *The Story of the Files*. 1893. San Leandro, Calif.: Yosemite Collections, 1982.

Drury, Wells. *An Editor on the Comstock*. 1936. Reprint. Reno: University of Nevada Press, 1984.

Emrich, Duncan. *Comstock Bonanza*. New York: Vanguard, 1950.

Fatout, Paul. *Mark Twain in Virginia City*. Bloomington: Indiana University Press, 1964.

Fitch, Thomas. *Western Carpetbagger*. Ed. Eric N. Moody. Reno: University of Nevada Press, 1978.

Goodman, Joe. *Heroes, Badmen and Honest Miners*. Ed. Phillip I. Earl. Reno: Great Basin Press, 1977.

Goodwin, C. C. *As I Remember Them*. Salt Lake City: n.p., 1913.

Lewis, Oscar, ed. *The Life and Times of the Virginia City Territorial Enterprise*. Ashland, Ore.: Lewis Osborne, 1971.

Lewis, Oscar. *Silver Kings*. 1947. Reprint. Reno: University of Nevada Press, 1986.

Lyman, George. *The Saga of the Comstock Lode*. 1934. Reprint. New York: Ballantine, 1971.

Mack, Effie Mona. *Mark Twain in Nevada*. New York: Scribner's, 1947.

Smith, H. Grant. "The History of the Comstock Lode: 1850–1920." *University of Nevada Bulletin* 37: 3 (July 1943).

Smith, Henry Nash. *Mark Twain of the* Enterprise. Berkeley: University of California Press, 1957.

Weisenburger, Francis P. *Idol of the West: The Fabulous Career of Rollin Mallory Daggett*. Syracuse: Syracuse University Press, 1965.

SECONDARY SOURCES: ARTICLES

Basso, Dave. "A Classic Western Writer." *Dan De Quille Journal* 1 (April 1989): 3–5.

Berkove, Lawrence I. "Dan De Quille [William Wright]." *Encyclopedia of American Humorists*. Ed. Steven H. Gale. Pp. 119–121. New York: Garland, 1988.

———. "Dan De Quille and 'Old Times on the Mississippi.'" *Mark Twain Journal* 24: 2 (Fall 1986) [Winter 1988]: 28–35.

———. "Dan De Quille Follows the Tracks of 'The Carson Fossil-Footprints.'" *Mark Twain Circular* 2: 7–8 (July–August 1988): 1–3.

———. "Free Silver and Jews: The Change in Dan De Quille." *American Jewish Archives* 41: 1 (Spring/Summer 1989): 43–51.

———. Introduction. *Dives and Lazarus*. By Dan De Quille. Pp. 13–48. Ann Arbor: Ardis, 1988.

———. Introduction. "Pahnenit, Prince of the Land of Lakes." By Dan De Quille. *Nevada Historical Society Quarterly* 31: 2 (Summer 1988): 79–86.

———. "The Literary Journalism of Dan De Quille." *Nevada Historical Society Quarterly* 28: 4 (Winter 1985): 249–261.

Boeser, Linda. "Two Comstock Journalists: Samuel L. Clemens and William L. Wright." *Missouri Historical Review* 59 (July 1965): 428–438.

Lee, Judith Yaross. "(Pseudo-) Scientific Humor." *American Literature and Science*. Ed. Robert J. Scholnick. Chapel Hill: University of North Carolina Press, forthcoming.

Lewis, Oscar. Introduction. *The Big Bonanza*. By Dan De Quille. Pp. vii–xxv. New York: Crowell, 1947.

Lillard, Richard G. "Dan De Quille, Comstock Reporter and Humorist." *Pacific Historical Review* 13 (1944): 251–259.

Lingenfelter, Richard E. Introduction. *Washoe Rambles*. By Dan De Quille. Pp. 7–12. Los Angeles: Westernlore, 1963.

Loomis, C. Grant. "Dan De Quille's Mark Twain." *Pacific Historical Review* 15 (September 1946): 336–347.

———. "The Tall Tales of Dan De Quille." *California Folklore Quarterly* 5 (January 1946): 26–71.

Mack, Effie Mona. "Dan De Quille (William Wright): 1829–1898. [Part I].' *Nevada Magazine* 2: 3 (September 1946): 6–9, 33–34; Part II. 2: 4 (October 1946): 6–9, 33; Part III. 2: 5 (November 1946): 6–11, 35.

Rawls, James J. Introduction. *Dan De Quille of the Big Bonanza*. By Dan De Quille. Pp. 1–17, 122–123. San Francisco: Book Club of California, 1980.